PERSPECTIVES
ON
POLITICAL
ETHICS

PERSPECTIVES ON

POLITICAL ETHICS

AN ECUMENICAL ENQUIRY

Edited by Koson Srisang

WCC PUBLICATIONS
1211 Geneva 20, Switzerland

GEORGETOWN UNIVERSITY PRESS
Washington, D.C., 20057, USA

Published for the Commission on the Churches' Participation in Development of the World Council of Churches by WCC Publications, Geneva, in collaboration with Georgetown University Press, Washington, DC 20057, USA
ISBN No. 2-8254-0751-8 (WCC)
ISBN No. 0-87840-407-4 (GUP)

Library of Congress Cataloging in Publication Data
Main entry under title:

Perspectives on political ethics.

1. Political ethics—Addresses, essays, lectures.
I. Srisang, Koson. II. World Council of Churches.
JF1525.E8P47 1983   172 .   83-5691
ISBN 0-87840-407-4 (Georgetown University Press)

Contents

Foreword   *Philip A. Potter*   vii

Introduction   *Koson Srisang*   ix

Notes on regional contributions   xv

Continuing an old discussion in a new context   *Konrad Raiser*   1

Ecumenical perspectives on political ethics: report of the Cyprus consultation   14

Political ethics in Africa   *Aaron Tolen*   45

Reconstruction of political ethics in an Asian perspective
Anwar Barkat   50

Some aspects of political morality in the Caribbean   *Neville Linton*   70

Political ethics in the European context: the ethics of peace
Wolfgang Huber   86

Political ethics in Europe   94

Morality, politics and violence: a Latin American interpretation
Orlando Fals Borda   105

Aspects of political ethics in the Middle East   *Gabriel Habib*   113

Towards an ecumenical ethics: a marginal American view
Alan Geyer 127

Political ethics in Vanuatu   *Fred Timakata* 155

APPENDICES

1. Towards a method in political ethics   *Roger Hutchinson and
   Gibson Winter* 163

2. Report of the Advisory Committee on "The Search for a Just,
   Participatory and Sustainable Society", 1979 174

3. Contributors 194

Foreword

The issue of political ethics is not a new item on the agenda of the World Council of Churches. In fact a deep concern for Christian witness in politics was part of the Council's inheritance. Ever since the World Council was established, the study of the theological bases for Christian involvement in social and political issues, and of the forms such involvement should take, has been an important element in its total programme.

During the last few years, however, there has been a more sustained effort to work towards an ecumenical political ethic. This followed the debate at the 1979 Central Committee meeting on the Programme to Combat Racism and the discussion of the report of the advisory committee for the "Search for a Just, Participatory and Sustainable Society".

From an ecumenical perspective the issue of political ethics has to do with the options which Christian people and the churches must take in their political witness, and with the biblical and theological foundations of such options.

At least three questions pose themselves with particular urgency. First, can Christians and churches go beyond issuing general statements to making specific political judgments? If it is agreed that they can, then on what bases may this be done? Second, how do we adequately deal with the qualitatively new situation brought about by modern science and the technological revolution? Technological developments tend to suppress the freedom of people, and the blessings of science are tragically mixed. How do we share in the benefits they bring without succumbing to their tyranny? And third, how do we evaluate the awakening of people and the organization of people's movements, their determination to struggle against the forces of death and their search for a fuller, richer life? Is the revolutionary option, for a while an inspiration for many, still possible and viable? If it is not, what other options are there?

The awakening of people challenges the churches in terms of their mission and witness. The emergence of the ecumenically related network of people's movements has had serious consequences. It is precisely here, where the churches are challenged to act in solidarity with the poor, that they find themselves at once renewed and divided. Both the churches and the action groups need practical guidelines.

We must of course deal with the crisis situations as best as we can. We must stress the significance of symbolic action, but also recognize its limits. We must at the same time pay attention to long-term goals and strategies, and to the "normal" situation where life is lived and decisions made and things happen. Our experience so far bears out that it is not always fruitful to think in terms of grand macro schemes. The indication from the study so far, as this volume bears out, is that the national contexts provide the proper focus around which the local and global problems can be usefully discussed.

This volume, *Perspectives on Political Ethics*, is the report of an initial attempt to deal with these and similar questions. Needless to say, much more work needs to be done. But at least some key questions have been identified and some directions for future work suggested. Particularly important is the richness of the regional papers included here, which may well serve as the basis for the continuing ecumenical dialogue on political ethics.

PHILIP POTTER
General Secretary
World Council of Churches

Introduction

> I look to the mountains:
> where will my help come from?
> My help will come from the Lord,
> who made heaven and earth.
> (Psalm 121:1-2)

The cry is at once one of despair and hope. Oppressed and desperate, people cry to heaven for help and deliverance; and their hope lies in none other than the Lord of heaven and earth.

Basically it is a cry for spiritual empowerment to combat the threats of death on the one hand and to recover the power of life on the other. It is indeed the deep yearning of human spirituality, when suffering people become aware of their plight and their power at the same time. It comes out of the struggle for survival, freedom, justice and peace. And God cares. He has promised: "Behold, I will create a new heaven and a new earth... The sound of weeping and crying will be heard no more" (Isa. 65:17-20).

Is the cry heard? How do we discern God's response to it? And how do we appropriate that response in our own work and programmes? These are some of the agonizing questions which many people are asking themselves, including those of us in the ecumenical movement.

An ecumenical contribution

One of the basic functions of the World Council of Churches is "to express the common concern of the churches in the service of human need, the breaking down of barriers between people, and the promotion of one human family in justice and peace". Based on the experience in trying to fulfill this mandate, the WCC has come to realize that

> The churches live in the midst of injustice, oppression, waste, poverty and deprivation. Very often these evils appear in organized forms or are the products of social systems. Very often too Christians and Christian communities have become involved in them. But today the peoples of the world cry for deliverance. They long for justice and freedom. They desire that the world's resources be shared more justly and freely. They want to care for the earth and its resources for life "abundant" so that it will sustain them and the generations yet to be born.

> Christians join in this cry for deliverance. We share in the search for a just, participatory and sustainable society. We are in this struggle because we believe that God hears this cry and promises deliverance.

> We believe that God's Kingdom comes in Jesus Christ and the signs of its coming are: preaching good news to the poor, proclaiming release to the captives, recovering of sight by the blind, setting at liberty those who are oppressed, and proclaiming the acceptable year of the Lord (Luke 4:18-19). We are in the struggle because of Christ's call to discipleship, to manifest Christian love through action and involvement (Central Committee Minutes, Geneva 1976, p. 96).

During the period following the 1976 Central Committee, the WCC Unit on Justice and Service undertook, among other things, programmes on transnational corporations, human rights, militarism and disarmament, and the search for a just, participatory and sustainable society (JPSS). Separate volumes have been or are being published, sharing the insights and experiences of these programmes, The present volume is a modest contribution on the initial results of the JPSS follow-up, with the focus on political ethics. It is offered as an interim progress report of a very important ecumenical dialogue which should continue.

Focus on political ethics
Since the Nairobi Assembly, the churches in the ecumenical movement have in many places asked themselves whether they take the existing power structures too much for granted. Consequently, fundamental questions of an

ecumenical political ethic have surfaced clearly, opening up a new dimension of ecumenical inquiry. It was no accident, therefore, that the 1979 Central Committee, after a difficult debate on the report of the JPSS Advisory Committee (see Appendix 2), decided to continue the search with focus on political ethics. As a matter of fact, that was the first recommendation of the Advisory Committee report itself.

A focus on political ethics, according to the Advisory Committee report, should aim at "an examination of structures of power, participation and political organization on local, national and international levels". This reflection should give particular attention to the relationship of church and state in various situations, i.e., in societies of pluralistic, socialist, authoritarian and theocratic orientation. Guided by a staff working group under the joint leadership of Dr Konrad Raiser and Dr Julio de Santa Ana, the study in its initial phase was conducted as a survey of positions held and issues faced by WCC member churches in the various regions. Meanwhile, specific attempts were made to draw out the relevant insights of major international conferences sponsored by the WCC — on "Faith, Science and the Future", 1979; "Your Kingdom Come", 1980; "Racism and the Challenges for the Churches", 1980; and the international conference to conclude the study on "The Community of Women and Men in the Church", 1981. The regional survey and the accumulated insights provided the input for a small working consultation held in Cyprus, in October 1981, leading to a report offering some "ecumenical perspectives on political ethics", which was received as an interim progress report by the 1982 Central Committee.

What have we learned?

Firstly, the process of reflection helped to clarify that the search for an ecumenical political ethic moves through several areas of enquiry where different and even conflicting affirmations encounter one another. This points to the urgent need for ecumenical dialogue. The areas include the interpretation of the world political situation, the understanding of the biblical tradition in the context of the recovery of people's cultural and religious heritage, the critical analysis and evaluation of various approaches to political ethics, and the formulation of guidelines and forms of Christian political witness, with special emphasis on ecumenical action in solidarity with poor and oppressed people.

Secondly, the study underlined that a comprehensive analysis of power and justice is fundamental to an adequate study of political ethics. The study has also shown that a people-oriented perspective is of the utmost importance. And finally, the study has opened up an interesting discussion about ecumenical methodology which will have to be pursued further as the study continues.

The present volume *Perspectives on Political Ethics* makes available selected papers prepared for the Cyprus consultation. It represents the ecumenical insights gained thus far. As already mentioned, it is offered as a progress report. We hope it will be of use to friends interested in the whole issue, and that it will be of special value for the discussion of the subject in the Vancouver Assembly context. We also hope that the volume will encourage further work in this very important area, especially within the ecumenical movement.

Dr Konrad Raiser's introductory paper "Continuing an old discussion in a new context", helps situate the Cyprus consultation in both the historical and contemporary context, and spells out the key issues to be faced.

The report of the consultation itself is presented in full: "Ecumenical perspectives on political ethics". Although it summarizes the actual discussion which took place at Cyprus, it is presented more as notes on the conversation than as a consensus statement.

Then follow selected papers which together reflect, at least in part, the regional positions on political ethics. Not all the regional contributions presented at Cyprus are included here. For reasons of space and balance, only one paper is selected from a region. It is clear that both the contents and the approaches in these regional papers vary a good deal. Yet a number of common themes run through most of them: justice and power, people's participation, the role of religion and culture, the imminent threats to survival and the yearning for peace and development, the paramount importance of the national context.

"Toward a method in political ethics" by Professors Roger Hutchinson and Gibson Winter is included as an appendix, because it illustrates the importance of the methodological question. They were asked to reflect on the whole process of the Cyprus consultation, using their own method. Appended also is the 1979 Report of the Advisory Committee on the Search for a Just, Participatory and Sustainable Society, a controversial but very substantial contribution. Apart from a careful delineation of the three key terms (justice, participation and sustainability), this report places particular emphasis on a theological interpretation of the people's struggle against unjust powers in the perspective of the messianic Kingdom.

An invitation

The reader is invited to join this dialogue in search of a clearer and more effective ecumenical political ethic. Bound as we are by our common humanity under God, rooted in our respective cultures and moved by our common search for justice and peace, we cannot avoid the vocation of caring. Perhaps today more than ever before, this ethic of mutual caring, at all levels of human association, is the key to all things, including political ethics.

KOSON SRISANG

Notes on regional contributions

For reasons of space and balance, not all regional contributions are included in this book. These notes are meant to help the reader get a more complete picture of the consultation process, and to acknowledge the other regional contributions. Where the sole contribution from the region is already included, mention is omitted from these notes.

Africa: In addition to Dr Tolen's paper, there were three other contributions: by Bishop Dr Henry Okullu of Kenya (published by CCIA in *Political Trends in Africa*, 1982); by Prof. John S. Pobee of Ghana; and the report of the Africa consultation on "Political Ethics in the African Context", Nairobi, May 1981.

Asia: Dr Barkat's paper, included here, is an abridged version. The other Asian input was Dr C. S. Song's "The Tears of Lady Meng: a Parable of People's Political Theology", later published in the WCC *Risk* book series in 1981.

Europe: Included are the report of the European consultation in Geneva, February 1981, and an integrated summary by Dr Huber of two substantial papers. The first of these is "Politics in Europe: Challenges to the Churches", by Prof. Wolfgang Schweitzer of the Federal Republic of Germany. The second is "Political Ethics in the Context of JPSS: the Point of View of an Orthodox Member of a Socialist Society", by Prof. Nikolai Zabolotski of the USSR.

North America: In addition to Dr Geyer's paper, Professors Roger Hutchinson (Canada) and Gibson Winter (USA) submitted "Political Ethics and the MacKenzie Valley Pipeline Inquiry". Their method, a major part of their paper, was reformulated to reflect on the whole Cyprus consultation; it is included here as an appendix.

The Pacific: Besides the contribution from the Deputy Prime Minister Fred Timakata of Vanuatu, Prof. James Veitch of New Zealand had contributed a paper entitled "Wrestling with Principalities and Powers: the Church and Politics".

Continuing an old discussion in a new context

KONRAD RAISER

The legacy

There is a particular urgency and a specific context to our reflection on political ethics. But there is also a continuity of ecumenical concern in this area. It is important that we remind ourselves of this legacy, if only to discover that most of our questions have been asked before.

I shall limit this review to a brief examination of the four main stages in the discussion so far. They are linked to four crucial events in the life of the ecumenical movement: the Oxford conference in 1937, the Amsterdam Assembly in 1948, the Geneva conference in 1966, and the period since the Uppsala Assembly in 1968.

The *Oxford conference on "Church, Community and State"* was the culmination of the first phase of ecumenical social thinking which started soon after the turn of the century. It was marked by several factors of historical significance: the experience of the depression years and the disillusionment with capitalism; the disappointment over the powerlessness of the League of Nations in relation to international conflicts and the efforts towards disarmament; the rise of totalitarianism in the form of fascism and communism; the effects of technological developments on the structure of society and the role of the state; and finally the increasing secularization of the Western world. Added to these features and reflecting the historical experiences there was a new and critical theological awareness of the relationship between church and society: a biblically inspired sense of Christian social and political realism.

It is no surprise that the Oxford conference, in spite of the preceding meeting of the International Missionary Council (IMC) at Jerusalem in 1928, reflected almost exclusively the concerns, hopes and anxieties of the churches in Europe and North America. Even though there was a clear awareness that the inherited Christian culture which had provided the moral and ethical framework for the Western world was breaking down, the great majority of the participants could not conceive of a just and peaceful community otherwise than on the basis of Christian values. Thus, secularism and totalitarianism, as well as messianic nationalism, were seen as pseudoreligious, demonic forces challenging the church to be truly the church.

Central to the thinking at Oxford was a new Christian understanding of the state and the responsible use of power. Oxford arrived at a sober and balanced view of the state as a historical reality serving the common good but, because of the increasing concentration of power and its monopoly of the means of coercion, potentially becoming the instrument of evil. "Since we believe in the holy God as the source of justice, we do not consider the state as the ultimate source of law but rather as its guarantor. It is not the lord but the servant of justice" (Report, p.23).

The state cannot be allowed to embrace and control the entire life of the nation or of society. In fact, Oxford recognized a set of orders, a structure of society, like family, law, nation, etc. which are universally valid and protect the freedom and personhood of the individual over against the power of the state.

But all states are themselves bound by an international ethos manifested in the emerging system of international law and the recognition of basic human rights. The conference developed a number of principles expressing its understanding of an international political order: the renunciation of absolute, national sovereignty; equal rights for all, including especially the right of religious liberty; equality of economic opportunities; responsible use of natural resources; peaceful settlement of conflicts in order to facilitate necessary change. The churches, through manifesting their ecumenicity, could make a significant contribution to the development of this international ethos.

Building on the basis of Oxford but responding equally to the new situation after World War II the *Amsterdam Assembly* is important particularly with reference to the emergence of the concept of the "responsible society" which served as the basic framework for ecumenical social thought for almost two decades. The concept has become significant on three distinct levels. First, it presents a methodological approach to the issues of social ethics which mediates between the traditional positions of an ethics of ends and an ethics of means, between a natural law stance and a biblical-Christological approach. It was the attempt to translate into specific ethical formulations the notion of "middle axiom" already introduced at Oxford. Secondly, the concept of the responsible society reflects the changes which have taken place in social and economic life and which have rendered the choice between laissez-faire capitalism and communism unacceptable. Both these are seen as challenging the basis for the affirmation of responsible freedom and the concern for a just distribution of wealth. Thirdly, the responsible society represents an attempt to come to terms with the new form of power and the concentration of power by insisting on an order which guarantees the distribution of power and the control of state power by the people, including the possibility of legitimately and peacefully introducing basic changes. The responsible society was an attempt to keep in balance the demands of freedom and justice within the framework of democratic order, based on the recognition of essential human rights.

This concept, which was developed further at following Assemblies, in particular at Evanston 1954, has proved to be an important point of synthesis and crystallization of ecumenical social and political thinking. But increasingly its roots in the tradition of Western liberal democracy were being challenged. The first challenge came from Asia. In particular in India the experience of economic and social development after independence led to a new appreciation of the role of the state and to the search for a "third way" in terms of democratic socialism. In other newly independent countries also the task of nation-building and rapid social and economic change led to questions about the basic assumptions of the concept of the responsible society with its bias for constitutional, democratic change. The main challenge came in the 1960s from Latin America, calling in question the theological, economic and political assumptions underlying the concept of the responsible society.

The *Geneva conference on Church and Society in 1966* has become the symbol of this challenge. The conference tried to respond to a twofold task: it tried to come to terms both with the technological and the social-political revolution of our time. The two responses of the conference remained essentially unreconciled; they cut across regional differentiations. On the one hand there was the attempt to maintain the position of the responsible society by stressing its dynamic elements, by recognizing the demand for international social justice and developing further the criteria for a society promoting social welfare for all. On the other hand there was the rejection of any reformist approach in terms of modernization, calling for fundamental and revolutionary changes in the social and political structures, for a redistribution of political power aiming at liberation and genuine participation by the people. Apart from the consultation on "rapid social change" at Salonika 1959, this was the first time since Oxford that the issues of the state and power, of law and participation in political life, were fully discussed again in the ecumenical movement. However, here as well as in the other areas under consideration the Geneva conference did not arrive at definitive conclusions in the sense of replacing the time-honoured concept of the responsible society by a new perspective. Rather, it served as catalyst by bringing together the main elements of ecumenical discussion on social and political ethics since Oxford and by providing the basis for a wide variety of action-reflection progammes which have been a feature of the years since then.

There is no need to present the specific lines along which the discussion has developed especially *since the Uppsala Assembly*. But taking the Geneva conference as a conclusion as well as a new departure, it is interesting to examine both the continuity and discontinuity with the earlier phases. In many areas we observe a return to issues which had been at the centre of attention in earlier periods but had subsequently been left somewhat aside. This is true especially with regard to the question of human rights. While the earlier discussion had focused largely on religious liberty as the point of entry into the human rights concern, the new discussion is characterized by its emphasis on the social and economic rights of people as a manifestation of the demand for international social justice. The passionate debate about war and peace, about nuclear armament and the conditions of world peace, which was carried on in the years following the Amsterdam Assembly, has come back on the agenda. The question of violence and the legitimacy of rebellion or revolution, which had been discussed at Oxford and in the following years, is back again — with the same unresolved basic issues. The problem of church and state, absent for a long time, has been taken up again after the Assembly at Nairobi with no clear follow-up as yet.

The continuity is perhaps even more apparent if we take the issues of racism, science and technology, or the search for an international social and economic order. But here also the discontinuity comes to the fore very clearly. First in terms of methodology: there is a clear change from study to action, translating the consolidated consensus into specific initiatives for change. For ecumenical social thought this has meant that research and reflection have become intimately related to areas of active involvement with an increasing degree of specialization and fragmentization. In most areas the earlier theological and ethical basis of agreement had been taken for granted. But more and more there is a need for renegotiation of precisely these basic affirmations.

The second change is a shift from the universal to a contextual approach, from a concern about structures to an emphasis on people and participation in ongoing struggles. There has been progressive disillusionment with a development approach based on interdependence and efforts at changing international structures and systems; but there is a similar loss of faith in global strategies and ideologies of revolutionary change. However this very concentration on the struggles of people brings again to the surface the need for a more concrete understanding of the Christian vision of society, the need to move from prophetic criticism to the development of criteria for assessing options, means and levels of action.

A further change which can be observed is related to the three central elements embraced by the concept of the responsible society: freedom, justice and order. While in the earlier phases the primary emphasis was placed on the concerns for freedom and order, the central notion since the Uppsala Assembly has become justice in its economic, social and progressively also its political dimensions, and the concern for freedom is now being expressed in terms of "human dignity". This shift of emphasis has brought to light, however, that justice is still a controversial concept in the ecumenical discussion, in spite of its widespread use. There is no ecumenical consensus so far on the basic criteria of a just society, as there has been an earlier consensus on what constitutes a free society. Much attention has been given to structures of injustice but less has been done to spell out in positive terms the vision of a just society and to relate it to the Christian hope for the kingdom of God and his justice.

Another obvious change concerns the cultural context which conditions ecumenical social thought. The earlier apologetic or missionary attempts of defending the values of a "Christian culture" as the only basis for freedom and justice in a responsible society have given way to a new appreciation of religious and cultural pluralisms and the need for a genuine dialogue of culture. This leads to a critical review of the basic assumptions underlying ecumenical social thought which still reflect a particular cultural world.

A last change might be indicated which is related to the first two: there is a clear move away from expert analysis of problems to initiating processes of education, learning and conscientization.

It is interesting to note that the Oxford conference has a special section on education; but only under the impulse of Paulo Freire's "pedagogy of the oppressed" has the relationship between education and liberation, learning and empowerment appeared on the social agenda of the ecumenical movement. Related to it is the recognition of the extent to which the means of public information are being used to perpetuate the current distribution of power. Given the complexity of the present international debate about social, economic, military, technological and political issues, there is a growing need to provide "counter-information" and thus to enable people to participate intelligently.

The new context

The preceding remarks have already prepared the way for a closer examination of the context in which this new debate about political ethics is placed. By the time of the Nairobi Assembly in 1975 the international exposure through the UN of several global issues like environment, population, food, habitat, a new international economic order, coupled with the experiences in a number of WCC programmes on racism, human rights, science and technology, had led to the conviction that the various problems are closely inter-related and call for a comprehensive approach. This need surfaced clearly when in 1974 the Central Committee of the WCC received two presentations on "Threats to Survival" and on "Economic Threats to Peace" together with the call to search for a "just and sustainable society" coming from the Bucharest conference of the WCC on "Science and Technology for Human Development" held earlier that same year. This was the background against which the Nairobi Assembly discussed issues concerning "Structures of Injustice and Struggles for Liberation" (Section V) and "Human Development: Ambiguities of Power, Technology and Quality of Life" (Section VI).

In its recommendations for future programmes of the WCC, the Assembly identified "the struggle for true humanity" as one of three overall programme guidelines. The Assembly recommended that "all programmes should be conceived and implemented in a way that expressed the basic Christian imperative to participate in the struggle for human dignity and social justice and, at the same time, maintains the integrity of action and engagement by the churches as rooted in the biblical faith" (Nairobi report, p.299). The identification by the 1976 Central Committee of the "Search for a Just, Participatory and Sustainable Society" as a major programme emphasis of the Council in the years to come was a further development of this new approach.

The question obviously arose: What is meant by a programme emphasis, and how can it become effective and serve as a concentrating focus for a variety of individual programmes directed towards distinct constituencies and following different methodologies? Among the programmes directly related to this emphasis on a just, participatory and sustainable society were the following: studies on the New International Economic Order and on ecumenical sharing of resources; action/reflection programmes on militarism and the arms race, on human rights and on new life-styles; finally the process leading up to the international conference on "Faith, Science and the Future" in 1979.

Two difficulties became clear very soon: the effort of spelling out the programme emphasis was perceived by many as an internal, bureaucratic concern of the WCC with little or no relationship to the struggles of people in their situation. On the other hand, the attempt not to remain on the level of general affirmations and to become specific created the impression that this was in the end another programme alongside others and potentially competing with them, or at least not inclusive enough. Thus, an early proposal developed in 1976, suggesting three foci around which the various issues could be organized more clearly and in an inter-related fashion, did not survive for long. These foci were: (1) the search for a New International Economic Order; (2) the changing role of the nation state in an interdependent world; and (3) the contribution of faith, science and technology to the struggle for a just, participatory and sustainable society.

There was yet another difficulty, which had some parallel in the early discussion about the "responsible society". How were the three elements of justice, participation and sustainability to be related to one another? Was there not an unavoidable tension between the demand for justice, in terms of equal distribution on the one hand, and each of the two other demands? Particularly the notion of participation, which introduced a clear political dimension into the debate and challenged the hidden or overt technocratic assumptions about the relationship between justice and sustainability, created problems. However, as the debate continued, the conviction grew that the time had come to explore more directly the political implications of the ecumenical concern for social justice; that justice was not only a matter of distribution or of equal opportunity but of basic rights of people, also in long-range perspective. Thus, participation and sustainability were perceived to be necessary elements of a contemporary understanding of justice. This led to the conclusion that the basic framework had to be worked out more fully before engaging in an effort of relating and coordinating a wide range of programmatic activities.

In 1977 the Central Committee of the WCC appointed an advisory committee on "The Search for a Just, Participatory and Sustainable Society". The Committee held two meetings and profited from imput and reactions coming from regional groups and sub-units of the WCC. It might be worth lifting a few points from the final report of the Committee.

There is first the decision not to try "to elaborate and present a blueprint or a Christian programme of an ideal society which would be just, participatory and sustainable". Rather, the advisory committee placed its search in the context of the present historical reality of the struggles of people for justice, participation and sustainability.

This led to the question: "How can the churches arrive at a common understanding of historical reality and become significantly involved in this struggle through their lives and action, their witness and service?" The response of the advisory committee pointed to the promise of the messianic kingdom of God which provides a purpose and a goal to the present struggles. "Christian faith understands the present struggles and contradictions as a part and as a manifestation of a dynamic of history pressing for eschatological fulfilment, thus defending history against both pretension and discouragement."

It was this attempt at theological interpretation which caused the controversial discussion at the meeting of the Central Committee in January 1979. The old debate about the relationship between the kingdom of God and history which had been carried on around the Oxford conference came back with much the same tensions and contradictions. Meanwhile, the Melbourne conference on "Mission and Evangelism" in 1980 has provided an occasion to take the issues further and has formulated a basis which could also be useful for our present efforts. I am thinking in particular of the two section reports on "The Kingdom of God and Human Struggles" and "Christ — Crucified and Risen — Challenges Human Power".

The report of the advisory committee gave particular attention to "issues in the struggle", areas where Christians do not as yet agree with one another. "The struggle requires a constant review of immediate and long-term objectives.... The JPSS programme emphasis is an invitation for open debate of these issues, so that a common sense of purpose can develop. There is need to spell out concretely the basic convictions which sustain Christians in the struggle." These sentences are probably the clearest expression of the task as defined by the advisory committee.

As we look at this section of the report we see that almost all of the issues mentioned, i.e. people as the subject of the struggle, the validity of the models of a "secular" state and a pluralist society, the understanding of power, structures of participation, etc. relate directly or indirectly to the question of an ecumenical political ethic. This is a confirmation of the initial assumption that the traditional ecumenical debate about economic and social justice had to be broadened to include the dimension of political justice. The tentative formulation of the issues in the report of the advisory committee which was intended as the basis for further ecumenical debate reveals something else as well: that the ecumenical discussion following the international agenda as formulated in the UN context has largely neglected a critical examination of the political realm, of the changing nature of power in society, of effective structures and modes of political action. Much work has been done on economic, military, technological issues, but much less on the political conditions for effecting change. In this context it is important to note that the International Advisory Group on Economic Matters established by CCPD has come to the conclusion that a new "paradigm" is needed for economic analysis and action, recognizing the fundamental ethical choices involved in political economy. From a very different starting point the international conference on "Faith, Science and the Future" has come to similar conclusions regarding the use of science and technology in modern life.

In considering ways to continue its reflection the advisory committee, therefore, arrived at the conclusion that the broad perspective of the initial programme emphasis should be narrowed down and that priority attention should be given to a continued process of study and reflection on "political ethics", i.e. "an examination of structures of power, participation and political organization on local, national and international levels. This reflection should spell out the ethical insights gained in recent ecumenical programmes, giving particular attention to the relationship between church and state in various situations. It should attempt an assessment of existing sociopolitical frameworks in which Christians live today, i.e. societies of pluralistic, socialist, authoritarian, theocratic orientation." It also added proposals for priorities in the areas of support, solidarity action, and education.

While not accepting the theological rationale offered by the advisory committee, the Central Committee in 1979 recommended further work along the lines suggested, encouraged the preparation and circulation of a popular statement on the JPSS emphasis, and anticipated as a result of these efforts "the clearest possible consideration of the clusters of issues in the Assembly context".

Where to go from here?
In many ways, this is a new departure in ecumenical reflection. "Political ethics" is not even a generally accepted term. This is confirmed by the regional contributions to the debate. The usage varies from political morality to political theology, placing political ethics somewhere in this spectrum. There is little, if any, precedent in ecumenical discussion for a focus on political ethics. The early discussion at Oxford and Amsterdam took place in a context and on the basis of assumptions which have radically changed since then. I have pointed to some of the changes as they are reflected in the ongoing ecumenical debate. Even those basic terms and concepts like the state, the nation, the legal order, etc., cannot be taken as evident starting points any more. The experience of more recent debates and actions in the areas of development and racism has changed the basic perception of political reality

and of the nature of power both nationally and internationally. There is a wealth of insights and experiences but no common language with which to apply them more consistently and bring them into conscious interaction with the tradition of our faith and of the Christian church through the centuries.

It therefore seems to me that we first of all need to clarify in our own mind what we mean by "political ethics". The brief which has come from the advisory committee and which I have quoted again has been critically examined in some of the regional contributions — and I think with some reason. At least it needs clarification and spelling out. Now, it is interesting that the proposal to initiate a process of study and reflection on political ethics received broad approval not only in the Central Committee, but equally in the churches in very diverse situations — and probably for very different reasons. Let me try to indicate what I perceive to be some of the expectations with which this effort is being followed in the churches.

Expectations depend on one's perspective or vantage-point. Thus, there is a clear expectation among some of the majority churches, particularly in Europe, that this discussion would address itself in the first instance to the question of the basis and the limits of the churches' action in the political field. It is the hope for ethical guidance in the very complex and controversial field of church-state relations far beyond the legal issues involved. Then, there is the large group of Christians who, as lay people, are actively involved in politics in one way or another, and who are confronted by basic questions regarding the values sustaining political life, the norms and criteria of good government, the limits of the political realm in view of the tendency towards a total politicization of social life. They search for ethical guidance and are sometimes frustrated by the lack of response and understanding within the churches, either because of a basic avoidance of the political field or out of a "prophetic" self-understanding which leaves ethical problems to the politicians.

Both positions are not new; they are echoed widely in the earlier discussions and reflect the situation of those — mainly in Western countries — who are in or close to positions of power and responsibility, who are confronted with the task of making political choices and faced by ethical dilemmas. Whatever political ethic has been developed in the Christian tradition — and to a large extent also in the ecumenical movement — has addressed itself to the situation of the "powerful". The decisive change which has occurred is the shift of perspective to those without immediate power, to the people, the victims or those affected by decisions without the possibility of influencing them directly. It is obvious that the issues of political ethics raised from the perspective of the people are very different, irrespective of whether they are raised in the context of a constitutional-democratic framework or in an autocratic setting. Much of the confusion and the emotionalism in ecumenical debates related to issues of political ethics arises from the fact that the fundamental difference between these two perspectives has not been recognized or that exclusive validity has been claimed for either one of them. The two perspectives obviously are in conflict with each other. The conflict reflects the basic political character of the tension between rich and poor, black and white, powerful and powerless, even within the churches and the fellowship of the ecumenical movement. Thus it becomes a burning issue of ecumenical political ethics to find ways of facing this conflict within the Christian community.

From the perspective of the subjects or victims of political power in the broadest sense, the crucial question, and thus the expectation regarding our effort, is to find criteria and ways of effectively controlling power, of affirming the participation of the people on all levels of political life, or simply of providing goals, options and mutual support in an unequal and seemingly hopeless struggle. How to respond as a Christian community without power to the brutal exercise of unjust power? What guidance can be given for such situations? Obviously, there is not only one option, one strategy of action. How is the choice to be made, and how is one to act against resignation and hopelessness?

This very preliminary attempt to identify the different perspectives and expectations which influence the understanding of what political ethics is to be about leads to one important conclusion: there is probably no such thing as one set of propositions for a political ethic which would be universally valid. The issues to be addressed vary from one context to the other and even within the same context, and thus the responses are different.

Obviously, the acknowledgment of a wide diversity of interpretations is neither new nor as such very helpful. The ecumenical task only begins here, in the sense of finding ways of engaging in an open dialogue where the different partners challenge and correct each other, where we begin to look at our own situation through the eyes and with the awareness of experiences in other situations. This requires authenticity and integrity and the readiness to acknowledge conflict.

This in turn requires the effort to struggle for elements of a common language and for a basic frame of reference. It is important to underline this need, which implies that we have to bring the language and the basic affirmations of our Christian faith into the dialogue. Political, ethical and theological positions and choices condition each other mutually. It is true, there is in this field, as in others like mission and unity, a certain body of consolidated convictions which have emerged from decades of ecumenical dialogue. We are not starting from scratch and, in spite of continued or renewed opposition and criticism directed against this "tradition" of ecumenical social and political thought, we should not hesitate to place ourselves squarely within this context. There are questions which can be taken as having been answered definitely.

However, it is my impression that this basic frame of reference in the area of political ethics is more fragile and less explicit than for example in the area of racism, development, etc.

It is my personal conviction that the very early proposal of J.H. Oldham to work out "middle axiom" or intermediate criteria still has validity today and that, in fact, we have followed this direction in many other areas of ethical concern. Thus, the definition of development in terms of social justice, self-reliance, people's participation and economic growth is in fact something like a middle axiom. And yet, as the example shows, the task of unfolding and explaining such a frame of reference never ends and it may undergo basic changes.

I see an even more urgent need to work on a basic frame of reference in the area of political ethics. The term "people", to take one example, which has received a central significance in the present Asian discussion, does not necessarily carry the same meaning in different contexts. "Participation" obviously refers to different realities in Kenya and in the USA. We have gone through this difficult process of clarifying the meaning of terms with regard to militarism and militarization, or concerning violence. This may seem to be a very elementary task and a far cry from an ecumenical political ethic. However, there is sufficient evidence to suggest that the chances of ultimately engaging in common political action are spoiled already at this point: the inability to understand each other. In addition, it is one of the difficulties of the present debates that central terms like "peace" or "justice" are being coopted, and emptied of their basic meaning, leaving people in uncertainty.

Let me point to one further complication in our task: obviously there is a basic difference between the political realities on the level of an individual country and internationally. The Oxford conference and subsequent Assemblies and consultations have clearly distinguished between these perspectives and assigned them to different sections. On the national level, for example, any discussion of political ethics has to address itself to the role of law in controlling power, but also to the possible perversions of law as an instrument of oppression. While there is a body of international law, it clearly is of a different quality. The problem arises in connection with the discussion of human rights. There is a difference between civil rights as part of the constitutional provisions of any one state, and the basic human rights as listed in the Universal Declaration of Human Rights. The political and ethical issues regarding security, distribution of resources, etc. are different on the national and the international level.

However, all these examples also reveal the extent to which the relationship between states influences the internal political realities in any one of them. The most obvious example is national security and military alliances. Another area is the transnationality of business, science, etc. This must lead us to consider again the issues of national sovereignty and the changing role of the nation state. The period of nation-building and consolidating political independence in Asia, Africa, the Caribbean and the Pacific has led to the discovery of the interlocking character of international power-elites who use national sovereignty for their own benefits.

Our concern with political ethics is part of the ongoing search for a just, participatory and sustainable society. That search is broader than the question of political ethics. Our concentration on this aspect is due to the feeling that it is most in need of further development.

Report of the Cyprus consultation

Preface

In 1976, the Central Committee of the WCC adopted four major programme emphases for its work following the Fifth Assembly at Nairobi in
1975:
1) the expression and communication of our faith in the triune God;
2) the search for a just, participatory and sustainable society (JPSS);
3) the unity of the church and its relation to the unity of humankind; and
4) education and renewal in search of true community.

In order to provide guidance on the second emphasis, the 1977 Central
Committee appointed the JPSS advisory committee which submitted its
report to the 1979 Central Committee (Jamaica). It elicited a mixed response
and gave rise to difficult debate. Receiving the report, the Central Committee
instructed Unit II and other sub-units concerned "to pursue the JPSS concern in cooperation and in their respective programmes in the coming years;
their foci should be the study on political ethics, and the support of people's
movements". The results of this pursuit were to "be brought together, as
preparations proceed for the next Assembly, to facilitate the clearest possible
consideration on the clusters of issues in the Assembly context" (*Minutes*,
1979 Central Committee Meeting, p.18).

It was only a year later that the JPSS follow-up, with the focus on *political
ethics*, modestly began to pick up. A small staff working group under the
shared leadership of the Unit II staff moderator and the director of the Commission on the Churches' Participation in Development (CCPD) has guided
the work. Its secretariat was located in CCPD.

As an initial working definition, political ethics was understood as having
to do with "an evaluation of the understanding and the exercise of power, in
faithfulness to the gospel for the sake of social justice, human dignity and

authentic community". Based on this minimal definition, a process of regional reflection and dialogue was set in motion, with the aim of surveying and assessing how Christians and churches in the various continents deal with the issue of political ethics in their respective situations. Meanwhile, relevant insights were solicited from major WCC conferences on "Faith, Science and the Future", "Your Kingdom Come", "The Churches and Racism", and "The Community of Women and Men in the Church". In addition, cumulative wisdom was sought from the experience of many other commissions such as CCIA and CCPD.

The results from the above processes formed the input for a small consultation which met in Cyprus, 18-25 October 1981. The intention was more to explore the issue and work out future agenda than to produce a conclusive document.

Regrettably, in spite of our efforts to listen to all the major voices, the actual dialogue at the consultation lacked an adequate contribution from the Orthodox and the socialist experiences. On the other hand, pronounced perspectives based on actual if particular experiences strongly emerged and are reflected in this report.* The twenty-nine participants, plus ten staff, represented a fair geographical, confessional, sex and age cross-section.

Focusing on political ethics has proved worthwhile. It has served as a common concern on which a true dialogue has started, evoking keen interest across the various lines of contention.

During the consultation, after introducing the subject, two days were devoted to plenary discussions of *four* issues suggested by the annotated agenda: power and justice, identity and participation, sustainability, and ecumenical political ethics. Then the participants divided into three groups, choosing to focus on *three* issues: ecumenical political ethics, justice and power, and people's participation in politics. It was felt that the sustainability issue is a general aspect of all ethical action and behaviour, and as such it seemed appropriate to leave it out of a brief treatment of political ethics.

This report summarizes the actual discussion which took place at Cyprus; it is presented more as notes on the conversation than as a consensus statement. It begins, in part I, with the four initial assumptions for the discussion, a summary of Dr Konrad Raiser's introduction to the consultation. Parts II, III and IV come out of the results of the three group discussions. Part V reconstructs some of the major methodologies operative in the whole pro-

---

* Perhaps the most clearly pronounced experience which was shared at the consultation is from Asia, where the notion of "people" has emerged as a new central symbol.

cess. And finally, Part VI puts together the various recommendations which the consultation has made to the WCC.

It is hoped that this initial report will contribute to the continuing search for a just, participatory and sustainable society in general and to the discussion of political ethics in particular.

I. BASIC ASSUMPTIONS

All over the world humankind faces a double and interlocking crisis: the crisis of justice and the crisis of order. At all levels of human existence, peace and survival are threatened, justice denied and dignity violated. In this situation, the poor and the oppressed people suffer most. Christian churches, together with communities of other living faiths, are also exposed to these threats and are challenged by them in their life and witness.

Hence the urgent need in many churches and within the ecumenical movement to search for a new articulation of a Christian political ethic. Recent experiences in the context of ecumenical programmes, especially on development, racism and militarism, have led the WCC to initiate a process to explore and identify elements for a Christian political ethic in an ecumenical perspective. This report is an account of the first phase in a debate which will have to continue.

A number of initial assumptions have guided the discussion and they need to be stated clearly at the beginning.

The *first* of these refers to a "minimal definition" of political ethics as put forward in the annotated agenda for the consultation: "An ecumenical political ethic has to do with the evaluation of the understanding and exercise of power, in faithfulness to the gospel, for the sake of social justice, human dignity and authentic community."

Though this definition was not discussed as such, it served as an implicit point of reference to indicate a shift of ethical consciousness to a new emphasis on "justice, participation and peace/shalom" as guiding political criteria. This shift, however, does not invalidate the concerns for "order, stability and security". It simply implies that they need now to be seen from the perspective of justice and participation.

The discussion did not lead to a revised "definition" and it is clear that more work needs to be done to articulate the issue of a political ethic in relation to the field of political economy and to the concern for the sustainability of life under the conditions of modern science and technology.

The *second* initial assumption relates to the fact that the churches have diverse experiences in dealing with political questions, due to different historical, cultural and political circumstances. Any attempt to articulate a political ethic is marked by the actualities of a particular situation. At the same time, all situations are influenced by worldwide political forces and events which impose their own dynamic and call for a common understanding and response.

In addition, Christians interpret political realities in their particular as well as their universal significance on the basis of a common confession, their shared faith in Jesus Christ and their shared hope for the kingdom of God, all of which implies a common calling for political witness in the world. However, this also points to the fundamental ecumenical challenge: How are we to reconcile with this confession the diverse claims we make in the area of political action, apparently on the basis of the same confession? The conflicting character of the different truth-claims inherent in the many contextual articulations of a Christian political ethic constitutes an ecumenical task and must lead to a dialogical process of mutual questioning, listening and learning.

The *third* initial assumption is equally important. Christians are not alone in reflecting on a viable political ethic in the present human situation. Their search must remain open to dialogue with people of other religious and ideological convictions. It would be presumptuous for Christians to offer a blueprint for an ideal political order. The attempt to articulate elements of a Christian political ethic in ecumenical perspectives is meant in the first instance to serve Christians and churches in their own life and witness. The "political" life-style of the churches internally is an essential element of their witness in society.

The *fourth* assumption acknowledges that an ecumenical political ethic can only be an "ethic of responsible discipleship". This implies methodologically that it will constantly have to relate faithfulness and convictions to the probable consequences of actions guided by these convictions. It will also have to acknowledge the inter-relatedness of political goals and the means available for their implementation.

II. ECUMENICAL POLITICAL ETHICS

The debate at the consultation suggested that the search for an ecumenical political ethic moves through several areas of inquiry where different, and potentially conflicting affirmations encounter one another and where ecumenical dialogue is urgently required. These areas include the interpretation of the world political situation, the understanding of the biblical tradition, the approaches to political ethics, and the forms of Christian political witness.

1. Discerning the signs of the times

An ecumenical political ethic has to come to terms with the task of discerning the signs of the times, i.e. interpreting the significance of political events at all levels from a Christian perspective, as these affect Christians and churches in their different situations. The ecumenical Christian community responds to the political situation with a special sensitivity to the sufferings of people everywhere. In practice, however, Christians respond in different and sometimes contradictory ways to world political events, reflecting different contexts, experiences, interests, fears and hopes. The ecumenical movement has contributed to a sharpening of critical awareness of world political issues among the churches and has drawn them into the difficult task of discerning the signs of the times through mutual exposure and accountability. This is an essential element in any effort at articulating an ecumenical political ethic.

The participants at the consultation came from very different parts of the world. In reviewing recent political developments on the world level a common perception began to emerge, focusing on a number of issues which have critical significance.

a) Militarization

The militarization of human societies has reached a level where the very survival of humankind is threatened; and yet, the arms race continues. Military expenditures worldwide have exceeded a total of 500 billion US dollars per year. Since World War II more than 130 wars have been fought, all in regions of the third world. The likelihood that atomic weapons will first be used in conflicts in the southern hemisphere is growing.

The process of developing military technology has generated a momentum which increasingly determines political decisions and contributes to accelerating militarization and politics. There are signs of a return to an analysis of world politics in cold war terms, placing excessive emphasis on military power and security.

In this situation it is imperative to reaffirm the authentic value of political life in all societies and to search for new forms of political cooperation and resolution of conflict in non-military terms. In the industrialized countries, there is an urgent need to find effective ways of working for disarmament, especially in the area of nuclear weapons, for demilitarization and for stopping the expansion of the arms trade among nations. Peace movements in some nations and indications of a growing awareness among the people are two of the few signs of hope that have emerged. In the developing countries, people struggle against the effects of militarization manifested by the spread of national security systems and the establishment of military dictatorships which distort social and economic development and suppress the rights of people.

b) Awakening of people

It is a remarkable sign of our time that in many situations hitherto silent and oppressed people have begun to wake up and to grasp the realities of their political condition. They speak out against oppression and, with their own voice, express their authentic hopes and aspirations for a new political future. Some have begun to organize themselves in order to determine their own political destiny.

Many such movements must face the brutal forces unleashed by oppressive structures. However, once the suffering people have seized a new hope, a political dynamic is generated which cannot be entirely suppressed. The voices of the people form a new and important element in interpreting the present political processes at national and international levels.

c) Political processes and international economic structures

The present international monetary system came into being at the end of World War II in order to preserve economic stability in the Western world. Today this system has become a major obstacle in the way of human development, especially in the Southern hemisphere. Its maintenance absorbs vast political energies. It progressively eliminates the autonomy of political life by making political processes and decisions exclusively dependent upon economic logic and calculus.

Under the present pattern of international political economy, industrialized countries are facing growing and chronic unemployment, inflation, environmental problems, unsustainability of systems of public welfare and resulting internal political pressures. The same world economic process reduces political life in the developing countries to an endless struggle for economic survival.

As a consequence of this situation, it is being realized by a growing number of politicians and economists that a new understanding of the world economy has to be developed and that political life has to be liberated from economic determinism by reordering the relationship between economic means and political goals.

d) Struggle for self-determination in the interdependent world

Most nations and peoples of the world suffer from growing global tensions and conflicts. Many countries are in fact locked in systems of hostile military alliances. The structure of the East-West conflict has been transferred from the Northern hemisphere and imposed on countries in the South as well, even though the futility of such conflict is recognized, since the security of both sides is increasingly being threatened. More and more countries are trying to affirm their independence from the two leading super-powers and to work towards instruments which offer security and peace for all. For more than twenty years a vision of non-alignment has persisted especially among developing countries. It has inspired their struggle for self-determination even though the vision is yet to be fully appropriated, providing a new alternative.

e) Growing role of political religion

One of the signs of the times particularly important for the Christian community is the emergence of political systems which fuse together religious authority and political power. In such systems, political power becomes absolutized and people's rights to determine their own political future are set aside. Religious and political minorities are thus seriously threatened. This poses a challenge to any political ethic, Christian or otherwise, which perceives a dialectic relation between religion and politics and thus recognizes the validity of a critical religious witness in the political field.

2. Reconstruction of the common Christian confession

A new exploration of a Christian political ethic in an ecumenical perspective is confronted with the double fact that any Christian ethic is rooted in the common biblical tradition and that this same tradition is understood and used in different and sometimes conflicting ways. The ecumenical movement has been guided by the affirmation of the Lordship of Christ over all realms of life. But what are the concrete political implications of this confession? Time and again, initiatives taken and statements made by ecumenical bodies have been challenged on the ground that they are not in accord with the witness of the scriptures. The credibility of the common witness of the churches is at stake in this debate.

During the discussion at the consultation the need for a clear biblical frame of reference was recognized. This is all the more important since some churches and Christian traditions have not developed a conscious, systematic approach to the problems of a social and political ethic, out of respect for the freedom of conscience of the individual believer. For the common biblical tradition remains the only unambiguous reference point. A determined ecumenical effort has to be made, therefore, to root the leading ideas and concepts of a contemporary ecumenical political ethic in the biblical witness. To what extent can biblical symbols help us in the interpretation of political reality? The following paragraphs are a summary of the suggestions and insights which emerged in the course of the consultation. It should be underlined that this is only the beginning of a discussion which will have to continue.

a) Emphasis on a holistic understanding of the biblical witness

In the past, Christian approaches to political ethics have often been based on one particular aspect of the biblical tradition, e.g. the Pauline thinking, especially his advice in Romans 13. Repeatedly it was affirmed during the consultation that the biblical witness has to be holistically interpreted and understood. This holistic approach rejects absolutizing particular aspects, accepts and makes creative use of contextual differences, and most importantly focuses on the Bible's testimony to Jesus Christ and God's messianic kingdom. Furthermore, it calls for a conscious effort to keep together creation and fall, the understanding of the human person created in the image of God and marred by human sinfulness, salvation through conversion and forgiveness of sins and the beginning of new creation transforming the old order of things, the cross and the incarnation of Christ, his resurrection and the gift of the Spirit and — not least — the Old and the New Testaments.

This emphasis on wholeness, which has been present in the ecumenical movement since its beginning, does not deny the existence of tensions between the various elements in the biblical witness; however, it tries to avoid any separation, e.g. of two kingdoms, and the establishment of any antithetical opposition between the diverse elements.

b) History and eschatology

The emphasis on wholeness becomes particularly important with regard to the relationship between human history and the eschatological promise and hope. This was one of the special difficulties encountered in the efforts of the earlier advisory group on a "Just, Participatory and Sustainable Society" whose work had preceded the present discussion on political ethics. The consultation did not enter into this difficult theological debate in any detail. However, there was general support for the affirmation made that as Christians we are part of two realities, the historical reality of political events and the eschatological reality of messianic promise and hope.

The concrete, particular historical reality and the universal eschatological reality must be kept together; any separation should be avoided. Yet these two realities are not identical; all human action in history remains relative and is subject to critical judgment in the light of God's action in fulfilling his eschatological promise. As one participant said: "We live on Saturday, between the Friday of the crucifixion and the Sunday of the resurrection. The real question is how can we walk tall and upright without having yet seen the final fulfilment of the resurrection from the dead?" The hiddenness of the eschatological reality under the contradictions of historical reality is a crucial point for any discussion about a Christian political ethic.

c) Two key symbols

During the Cyprus discussion, two central biblical symbols emerged as particularly relevant. The first of these is the Old Testament symbol of the *covenant community*. Here, the right relationship between God and his people is the focus for the biblical understanding of justice, righteousness and peace/shalom.

Justice here is a relational concept and the central criterion for the exercise and control of power. Justice is realized in the protection of the poor, the widows, the orphans, the strangers as part of the community of the covenant. Justice does not aim at simple equality or equity in the distribution of goods, but at the establishment of peace/shalom between God and his people, between members of the community and even between human beings and God's creation. The rediscovery of the notion of the "people of God" as an image of the church in recent ecumenical discussions about ecclesiology has important implications for a Christian political ethic. But beyond its ecclesiological validity the symbol of the people, the community of the covenant, opens important perspectives for interpreting political realities. It offers an alternative to the traditional organic understanding of state and society, including the relationship between church and state, or church and society as symbolized in the Pauline image of the body. It places the central emphasis on the participatory, cooperative, or — as it was put during the consultation — the "federalist" nature of the political community. The consultation was convinced that this approach should be further developed.

The second symbol is related to the first, but it has its own distinct identity and integrity: it is the New Testament notion of the *messianic kingdom,* the messianic community of the new covenant in Jesus Christ. This New Testament symbol builds on the covenant tradition. But it projects a community without power of domination, the fulfilment of the promise that God will live among his people, that the people will reign with the Messiah. Its historical manifestation is the community gathered under the cross of the suffering Messiah, the community of those moved by love, placing their hope in the transforming power of the cross. It is an eschatological symbol: it cannot be converted into a political ideology to be realized historically. Its importance is that it provides a critical perspective for interpreting political history and a vision of hope beyond historical hopes. Thus it can become a powerful force within the historical realm of political contradictions.

Recent ecumenical discussions within the World Council of Churches (e.g. in the context of the Melbourne conference on "Your Kingdom Come" in 1980, as well as within certain regional and national contexts, e.g. Minjung theology in Korea) have underlined the significance and value of this symbol for the effort of reconstructing the biblical basis for a contemporary Christian political ethic.

3. Approaches to political ethics
a) In search of a political ethic
As noted earlier, nations and communities are facing the crisis of justice and the crisis of order. This in a new way and with a new sense of urgency. Many interlocking factors are behind this double crisis. *Firstly,* the new alliance and concentration of power, based on the control of modern science and technology and the will to profit and domination, have not only blocked justice but also seriously threatened peace and survival.

Secondly, the emergence of socialism has presented a threat to some and a promise to others. For still others, socialism has lost its charms. Nevertheless it has brought about fundamental changes which have to be taken into account in rethinking a political ethic.

Thirdly, in spite or perhaps because of the two challenges mentioned above, poor and oppressed people have begun to assert themselves, struggling to participate in the creation of a new and viable social order. *Fourthly,* there is also the challenge of renascent religions making ideological and political claims, along with new coalitions of religious and political power.

Finally, in the midst of all these, Christians and churches in their particular historical and cultural contexts find themselves struggling to be faithful to their religious confession on the one hand and to be contextually authentic on the other. This is especially important when it comes to their participation in politics. All these point to an urgent need to rearticulate an ecumenical political ethic.

b) The influence of the churches in public and political life
A variety of approaches to the issues of a Christian political ethic emerged in the consultation processes. Descriptively one can distinguish between a church-centred, a politics-centred, and a people-centred approach. The three represent different but not mutually exclusive emphases.

The first approach, a legacy of the earlier phases of the ecumenical discussion, can be called *church-centred,* with a strong emphasis on the churches' influence in public and political life. Based on the commandment of love for our neighbour, this approach recognizes political authorities as ordained by

God to establish and preserve a just order of society under his rule. This usually means for Christians loyal and responsible participation in the work of governments. The nature of that participation depends on the type of state. When active participation is impossible, the responsibility of Christians may have to be expressed, in extreme cases, in resistance to a particular government, often at great cost to themselves because of their obedience to God rather than the rulers of this world.

c) The value and the legitimacy of politics

The second approach was represented at the consultation particularly by participants coming from churches in Europe and North America; it would probably also apply to Australia and New Zealand. This approach, in comparison with earlier ecumenical positions, is more clearly *politics-centred* and much less preoccupied with the institutional issues of church-state relationships. It focuses on two dominant concerns, i.e. the value of politics in the total context of society, and the legitimacy of political structures and decisions.

In the face of the growing disintegration of the political process it has become imperative to re-examine the goals of politics and the functions of the state at national and international levels.

Politics as a process of people's participation needs to be emphasized over against economic, military and other criteria.

This will be possible only if the political process is once again clearly related to ultimate social goals which, from a Christian perspective, are represented by the values of justice and peace in their inseparable relationship; human dignity embracing freedom and equality and the protection of life; human rights, including the satisfaction of basic human needs, the right to free association, self-determination and dissent.

Political ethics following this approach has further to do with the legitimacy of political structures and decisions. The churches have always affirmed that political powers ultimately stand within the sovereignty of God and are accountable to his law. This conviction was elaborated further with the help of the tradition of natural law. More recently, legitimation in the Western democratic tradition was based on the notion of due process and proper procedure. However, there is growing evidence that procedural legitimation, independent of the recognition of common values, can be used to defend almost any policy. The loss of validity of these forms of legitimation leads to a general loss of trust among the people in the political process and in those carrying a political mandate.

In this context a Christian political ethic must give renewed attention to the protective as well as creative function of law. In national situations the growing complexity of the life of society radically challenges the credibility of laws. Legislation will have to be developed further in order to incorporate new political values and goals. Internationally there is a clear need for the development of a "new international legal order" continuing the tradition of international law.

A final point which is important from this perspective concerns the relationship between religion/faith and politics. It was felt that the distinction between religion and politics, as it has been developed in many parts of the world, including the Western tradition, should be maintained and defended over against tendencies towards a new sacralization of politics. The principle of religious liberty was considered a crucial criterion for an ecumenical political ethic since it provides the basis for a critical, prophetic stance and, where called for, opposition and resistance to the political powers. It is clear, however, that distinction does not mean total separation. The Christian community cannot abdicate its political responsibility.

d) Political aspirations of the people

The third general approach to political ethics is based on a perception of political reality which focuses on the aspirations of the *people*. The term "people" as a new category was introduced consciously into the discussion in order to point to a new political reality: the awakening of the people who have hitherto only been the silent objects or victims of political power. The term "people", particularly when translated into some languages, is not free from ambiguity. It should not be surprising, however, that the appropriate term is not readily available to identify a political reality which was largely absent even from earlier ecumenical approaches to political ethics.

Various attempts were made to unfold the meaning of the term "people" or to communicate the experience which is crystallized around this term. There is agreement that "the people" are not simply all citizens of a given political community. Some employ a certain form of class analysis: the term then refers to the common people, to workers, peasants, to the exploited classes. Others start from a more political analysis: here the term "people" refers to the ruled vs the rulers, to the oppressed vs the oppressors, to the powerless vs those who are in control of political power. Sometimes the "people" are considered identical with the "deprived, oppressed and poor" in society.

Over against these more negative formulations it was strongly stated during the consultation that the importance of the term is related to its positive function of affirming the cultural, political and religious identity of the people as subjects of their own history over against imposed social and political patterns. The cultural-political dimension of the term is thus considered more important than its social-economic meaning. The purpose of a *people-centred* political ethic, therefore, is to affirm the importance of the people, of those who are often considered as non-people and who feel like strangers in their own land. It has to do with the reconstruction of the people's history and the articulation of a new political destiny.

From this perspective, the paramount feature of political reality, particularly in the developing countries, is that the process of nation-building has not led to a just society and legitimate forms of government; rather, political power is widely being exercised without any effective participation of and control by the people. The classical models of legitimation, inherited from the colonial powers, have broken down or no longer function. Instead of striving to restore the imported framework of political process, people begin to rediscover their own forms of political life rooted in their own culture, reinterpreted and reappropriated by the people themselves.

A Christian political ethic in this situation draws its inspiration from the hope that the messianic kingdom represents the ultimate destiny of the struggle of the people and, at the same time, remains the criterion of human responsibility. It seeks to articulate a new vision of political life among the people and to practise new forms of political community. It does not simply work for a "transfer of power" or the "empowerment of the people", but rather for the transformation of political power under the image of the cross of Jesus Christ, the suffering Messiah.

This approach to political ethics is sometimes articulated from within extreme national situations where political power has lost all legitimacy and has turned into extreme oppression. In such situations, the Christian community, following this line, must renounce all political calculation and, for the sake of its own integrity as well as the integrity of the political life of the people, make its political witness through resistance to the powers that be.

4. Political witness of the churches in ecumenical solidarity

While recognizing the differences of contexts, of perceptions of political realities, and of approaches to political ethics among the participants, the consultation felt that the possibilities of common political witness by the churches should be seriously explored and that the lines of active ecumenical solidarity should be strengthened. Rather than developing a blueprint for an ideal political order or defining "middle axioms" for an ecumenical political ethic, the consultation considered witness and solidarity as the areas needing priority attention in the further process. The following observations are offered as a contribution to this search for a "living political ethic".

a) The political involvement of the churches

Wherever they are, the churches are part of the given political reality, be it by conscious political involvement in many different ways or without acknowledging their role. All churches, therefore, must examine the integrity and faithfulness of their political witness and involvement, in the light of the common confession, through mutual critical dialogue and encouragement. They also need to broaden their perceptions of political realities and their political analyses. They can learn from their respective experiences of political witness and actively support each other in their political actions through the exchange of ecumenical delegations, by providing each other with authentic information, by making representations on behalf of other churches to their governments, etc. Various forms of ecumenical solidarity have been developed within and between the churches, like public intercession on behalf of detained persons and oppressed people, open prayer meetings with the families of victims of political oppression, acts of worship, and symbolic actions expressing solidarity with people in their struggle.

b) The political dimension of the gospel

Because the churches are part of the political reality, they cannot escape their accountability in the exercise of their own role within that reality. The gospel has an inescapable political dimension which manifests itself most clearly where it is proclaimed under conditions of extreme oppression. There, the gospel inspires and sustains the oppressed; the Bible can even become a subversive book in the eyes of the oppressor. This is due to the clear bias in the biblical witness in favour of the oppressed, the poor, those under domination and without power. The mutual encounter of churches in the ecumenical movement helps them to grow in faithfulness to the biblical witness, to discover possibilities for common prophetic witness and service, and to renew the forms and styles of life of their own communities in accordance with the biblical imperative.

c) Suffering with the people as political witness

As followers of Jesus Christ, the suffering servant, the churches in the ecumenical community are called upon to share in the pain of the world. The incarnation of God in Christ found its fulfilment on the cross, which is the symbol of the power of love against the love of power; ecumenical solidarity can take the form of an "incarnational" participation in the suffering of the people as they seek to transform their political predicament. The suffering of the people constitutes in itself a witness against the illegitimacy of power, crying out not only for its rectification but for a fundamental transformation.

There are special situations where martyrdom is again becoming a form of Christian witness with political implications.

d) Encouraging Christians in their political vocation
As citizens and as followers of Jesus Christ, Christians are called to a political vocation, i.e. active participation in politics. Many have accepted this vocation in various capacities, depending on their national situations. The churches should acknowledge them more fully and provide them with appropriate support and criticism. For example, churches and the ecumenical movement can help clarify the ethical criteria for political participation and responsibility.

e) Focal points of political action by the churches
The following points might serve as additional ethical indications in determining the forms and focal areas of political action by the churches:
— the churches should be prepared to assist and support the victims of political decisions and to intervene, where possible, with governmental authorities on their behalf;
— in situations where the human rights of people are systematically and continuously being violated, the political action of the churches should go beyond assistance and efforts to rescue the victims; it must address the root causes and structural origins of such violations of human rights;
— under all circumstances, and whatever the given relationship to the political structures may be, all churches are called upon to bear witness to the truth. Beginning with the transformation of their own life and structures, the churches are called to be "the salt of the earth" as well as the "light of the world";
— the integrity and dignity of politics should be respected, maintained and, where undermined, restored. At the same time, persons in political office have to be reminded of their proper tasks and responsibilities.

Conclusion
In the foregoing sections of this report profound differences of perspective, approach and context have been clearly acknowledged. At the same time, it was affirmed that the churches share in an emerging global political reality, a common confession of faith, common ethical convictions and commitments, and in the search for a new political vision. The various contextual approaches to the issues of a Christian political ethic are not limited in their validity to the respective contexts alone. They have wider implications for the practice of the political vocation of the people of God in other situations, for

broadening the bases of common understanding and for mutual accountability. In this connection a special plea was made for strengthening, with the help of the ecumenical fellowship, the interlinkage between the churches and Christian communities living in similar situations in Africa, Asia, Latin America, and other regions of the southern hemisphere.

III. THE ISSUES OF JUSTICE AND POWER

1. Contexts

The various inputs prepared for the Cyprus consultation on political ethics made it clear that religion and politics are always intertwined. However a church defines its relationship to the state, it has implications for the way power is exercised and legitimized. This was accepted as a truism. Therefore the consultation focused on particular contexts which revealed aspects of the nature of power and how it works.

In many contexts people are powerless because the dominating power of the state is too centralized, and thus repressive, controlled by transnational capital. Access to the exercise of power is limited to the ruling elite — like business people, politicians, military, police and intellectuals, etc. "People's power" in such situations comes primarily from the organized efforts of the people to confront this system of domination. Allies in the struggle of the people for justice and participation are on the side of people's power. There was general agreement that the role of the churches ought to be supportive of the people in their attempt to overcome their powerlessness. Often, however, churches are part of the power structure and not sympathetic to the goal of recovering the history, culture and spirituality of the people.

In other contexts there is a feeling that state power can reflect most of the interests of the population in spite of the lack of electoral parliamentary democracy. In such cases the churches can affirm the role of the state in meeting human needs and critically cooperate with the state in the pursuit of peace and justice.

At the Fifth Assembly of the WCC (Nairobi 1975), it was stated that power "is to be conceived as the capability to orient and to implement decisions. This capability can be of economic, political, ideological and/or military nature, being all these components in a dynamic inter-relation among themselves" (*Breaking Barriers*, p.129). Since the Nairobi Assembly the churches have deepened their perception about problems related to power. On the one hand, the interlinkages among different kinds of powers have become more clear; in our present world, dominating power is often a constellation of financial, technological, military powers combined with international alliances. Such constellations of power exist among groups or countries which sometimes have different ideologies. Generally these alliances aim to keep and to extend control of the situation. On the other hand, there are manifestations of people's power which express the aspiration of popular sectors in society to overcome injustice in structures of domination and dependence.

People's power becomes decisive when it grows to the point of a consolidated people's organization based on awareness of the unjust situation, clarity of goals and commitment to structured corporate action. In this process unity among the people is very important. Unity of people demands the building and joining up of social forces. At some point, changes in quantity also become qualitative changes. Through the pooling of forces, powerlessness can become meaningful political power. In order to achieve this it is necessary to remain open to dialogue, and to exercise a good deal of flexibility. It is not through theological dogmatism that people's power can be built up.

People's power is a necessary instrument for the achievement of justice. People who suffer injustice long for equity and respect for human rights. It is the persistence of people's movements in this kind of struggle which has contributed to the change in public feeling about apartheid, imbalances in the distribution of wealth, the violation of human rights, etc. The vision of a just society has nurtured and sustained people in their persistent effort to change structures and institutions.

People's movements for social justice are called to exemplify in their own life, organization and action the values which they profess: participation, justice and human dignity. However, people's movements are not always organized in a participatory way. Political ethics calls for coherence between ends and means. If this does not exist, it is difficult to avoid opportunistic behaviour.

History proves that parliamentary regimes come about because people are ready to struggle for them. However, stories were also told of the lack of participation and justice in spite of structures of parliamentary democracy and the widespread assumption that people have access to power. It was noted that such societies have experienced a deepening crisis, with unemployment rates growing and social differentiation increasing. The signs of the times call for a reaffirmation of the commitment to view each situation from the standpoint of the victims and to give a high priority to the empowerment of people's movements.

A participatory society at the end of the twentieth century calls for improvement of democratic forms of social organization. The quest for democracy is at the heart of the political struggles of our times, when we are becoming aware of the shortfall of both liberal and centralized democracies. Growing uneasiness among people is revealing the inability of existing structures and institutions to provide space for people's participation. The concentration of power in our time is such that new forms for the sharing and the control of power are needed. The search for these forms must be a major point in future reflection on ecumenical political ethics.

2. Issues

Some of the issues which emerged from the discussion are:

a) Confrontation and violence

When peoples' movements are organized and engaged in the struggle for justice, they often experience repression by established powers. They discover that normal channels of democratic participation are blocked. Then for the sake of justice, confrontation (in its manifold forms) is the only way forward. Confrontation does not always imply violence; however, in many situations there is a temptation to oppose military power with the same kind of power in a grossly unequal struggle.

Violence is no doubt a major issue in political ethics. The whole dilemma of non-violence versus violence has remained an unsolved problem for the churches. It is obvious, however, that for Christians priority must be given to non-violence, recognizing that there are times when people may need to turn to revolutionary violence. In the final analysis, the problem is not violence vs non-violence, but how to confront illegitimate powers which create injustice.

In the history of human struggle, there are situations where non-violence can become an expression of power in the search for justice. It is not possible to deal in abstract terms with these questions: the context within which the decision on non-violence or violence must be made is of vital importance. For example, it must be recognized that some prevailing expressions of the doctrine of national security mean a growth in state repression promoting further violent responses.

Because of the suffering, the pain, and the human waste which result from violent confrontations it is essential to recognize the role of negotiations and other techniques in the process of fostering justice and resisting injustices. Space for de-escalation of violence must be allowed. Nonetheless, within the ambiguities of politics, many people find it difficult to dismiss the option of violence.

The issue of violence and non-violence is not new to the WCC (see "Violence, Non-violence and the Struggle for Social Justice", *The*

Ecumenical Review, WCC, Geneva, October 1973). But it is also clear that this issue must be given renewed attention.

b) Latent strength

The common people, especially the poor and the oppressed, long for wellbeing, justice and peace. It is in search of these goals that their power, usually latent, is manifested.

Facing injustice or indignity, or otherwise inspired, this latent strength is unleashed. Its expression ranges from silent protest to taking up arms for revolutionary changes. For sure the dominant powers do not want this power unleashed; if necessary they will do anything to repress it. The issue is further complicated by the nagging question as to how it may be ensured that the people themselves will not become tyrannical once they gain control of power. It needs to be pointed out that this kind of question has been too often asked to perpetuate unjust situations.

c) Economics and politics

Prevailing economic systems — with their emphasis on growth, social stability, capital intensive technology, inputs and order at all levels — have created the national security systems which in turn give priority to economic performance instead of seeking wellbeing for all. National security is valued by international economic systems. Regimes big and small are caught in the situation where economic considerations dominate politics. This has negative effects on political life because the will to economic and military power becomes the guiding principle. There is thus a necessity for economics once again to become political economy, with primary emphasis on the overall direction of society. Basic changes in human values are a prerequisite for such a transformation.

d) Legitimacy and power

Is power legitimate when it is established on the basis of force? Is power legitimate when it has the consent of the people? Can power be legitimate when it does not provide more justice to the deprived? Do elections give a sound basis for the legitimization of power, especially when they are manipulated, or only a minority can take part in them?

Legitimacy is often taken for granted. But it is often necessary to challenge the concept of legitimacy. The source of legitimacy is the people, not the governments or the anonymous power which operates through transnational corporations, or even ideologies. It is necessary to indicate that governments can lose legitimacy in the people's eyes, and that it is valid to have a concept of delegitimization of authority, so as to create alternative power. Since there are illegitimate powers, it is important to promote and formulate criteria for legitimacy — such as justice, participation, the respect and promotion of basic human rights and human dignity.

e) Disunity in the struggle
Where churches have attempted to support the oppressed, sometimes groups being supported have split and made competing demands. Such cases highlight the need for competence in analyzing the situation and for ethical criteria. They imply that very difficult choices must be made. Sometimes outside support precipitates split among people.

f) Domination by international power systems
The pervasiveness of the dominant international systems means that both the direction and pace of development of national power of the weaker states are determined by the international agenda. Other routes are often restricted, and self-reliance is not a ready option.

3. Spirituality
Throughout history people have manifested their spiritual strength, resisting injustice and paying a very high price in the struggle for change and participation. This spiritual strength has been expressed in songs, poems, stories, etc. Clearly, spiritual power cannot be ignored in any consideration of political ethics. It is precisely here that religious communities, Christian churches in particular, can make a contribution.

What is the source of this spiritual power? For Christians, the Bible in the guidance of the Holy Spirit is clearly the most important. Yet, different social and personal backgrounds can lead to different ways of relating to the biblical message. Christian symbols can also play a political role in people's struggles. For example, the cross symbolizes God in Christ bringing salvation, and liberation from sin, to all people, reconciling them to God and among persons and communities. Politically speaking, for some people the cross symbolizes the unavoidable defeat, even death, which is inherent in all power struggles. However, defeat and death can be faced because the cross was followed by the resurrection of the crucified Christ. That is, Christian symbols can help people to keep their commitment, and not give up. Moreover, the cross is the symbol of *freedom* to face defeat and death, the source of ethical courage in political action.

Others place more stress on the spiritual significance of the awakening of peoples. The stories of persons who have experienced a conversion from being nobody to somebody, from being an isolated victim to a sister or a brother in a people's movement, tell a religious story. Through such living stories, it should be possible to do theology in our day.

Although such stories cannot be questioned, there is a need to reflect further on them. Is it a life-giving story? Is the dynamism of *kenosis* — one's own life given to others — manifested through political action? Are their actions compatible with the individual and social rights necessary for a self-reliant, sustainable human life? Is their enthusiasm linked to appropriate strategies for social change?

Spiritualities are experienced, nurtured, tested and invigorated in communities. As with their relation to people's movements, the churches sometimes facilitate and sometimes frustrate the search for a spirituality in political action. We are convinced that the Spirit of God is awakening peoples who have been oppressed. This Spirit reinforces and challenges, gives peace and kindles moral outrage. If it is the Spirit of God, it will transform the power of domination into a relational, co-creative power directed towards justice, participation and shalom.

IV. PEOPLE'S PARTICIPATION IN POLITICS

1. The issue of people's participation

The search for friendship, community (koinonia) and shalom has always been an integral and inspiring force in human history. The concern for people's participation, which has in recent years gained recognition in ecumenical and international agenda, is but a modern version of this same search. It is timely that this theme regains its rightful place. For the concentration of wealth and power in the hands of the few, the more demonic side of the lack of people's participation has made most people poor and powerless. They have been deprived, marginalized, excluded, oppressed and alienated. They have been rendered objects, without voice and power in the decisions which affect their very lives. This lack of effective and meaningful participation of the people is both the manifestation and the root cause of the injustice which prevails today.

Like poverty and affluence, the lack of people's participation and the monopoly of wealth and power are the two faces of an unjust social order. This injustice takes different forms in different countries, regions and ideological blocs. But its effect is the same; it creates apathy, loss of cultural identity, and threats to peace and survival.

The poor and oppressed people have not always taken this unjust situation lying down. In fact, they have stood up and struggled. Their vision, at its best, is no less than fundamental social tranformation, moving towards a just society. But this struggle is indeed difficult and costly. For apart from apathy, ignorance and fear among their own ranks, poor people are faced with technologically sophisticated weaponry and extremely well-financed and well-organized systems of suppression on the part of the exploiter. Besides, various imported and self-perpetuating lies have been told to legitimize the unjust situation.

In the light of this situation, the ecumenical movement must ask: What are the spiritual resources in the Christian faith and in other religious traditions that would enable humanity to break out of its present structural captivity? What are the foundations on which a just, participatory and sustainable order can be built?

One of the most important elements of the ecumenical answer to these questions centres around the concept of people's participation. But what do we really mean by people's participation? What constitutes authentic participation? Do any and all forms of mass involvement constitute people's participation? What are the conditions and requirements for authentic participation? Participation in what and for whom? And finally, what about participation within the churches? What is the role of the churches in promoting authentic people's participation? What biblical and theological wisdom do we have? These are some of the questions we posed at the Cyprus consultation. Obviously, a full discussion was not possible, and the process needs to continue.

2. People's participation in politics

The particular concern at the Cyprus consultation was from the perspective of political ethics. Our focus was therefore on people's participation in political decisions.

What do we mean by people's participation in general? People's participation cannot simply mean their participating in the programmes or activities initiated, or worse, imposed by dominant classes in the nations or by imperialist powers. Rather, authentic participation has to do with people becoming the makers and shapers of their own history. Therefore, people's participation aims at people's power to act in order to liberate themselves from all forms of bondage and oppression on the one hand and to create a new community of justice and dignity, self-reliance and identity, freedom and compassion, friendship and celebration on the other. This, of course, presupposes that people's basic needs of food, clothing, shelter, health care, education and employment are adequately met.

And what do we mean by people's participation in political decisions? We mean people's participation in the exercise of power to create a just society. It implies the guaranteed right and power to initiate, create, choose and exercise legitimate control over the issues pertaining to the life and wellbeing of society. It requires involvement in the political process from decision-making to action. It seeks to improve the human condition, to respect people's cultural roots, to stimulate indigenous creativity and the wisdom of the people, to uphold the right to one's identity and creative self-fulfilment, the right to dissent and the opportunity to share in the life of the community.

In short, political participation is a way of empowering people to become viable members of a community. To participate is to belong and to have a stake in the community while working for the common good, leading to justice and peace. We advocate participation not only in terms of an inalienable right but also in terms of a climate and structure in which people are able to feel the duty to participate. Authentic participation is koinonia, where the people not only share what is to be had but joyfully celebrate life in its fullness together.

At the same time, in discussing people's participation in politics, we need to recognize the reality that in power politics where the rulers have claimed the right to act "for" the people, there is little or no room for the people to participate. Here the notion of people's power and participatory politics as new and alternative political space, especially at the grassroots and national level, is worthy of consideration. Ultimately faithful to the crucified Christ, Christians are free to identify completely with poor and oppressed people; completely identified with the people, Christians transcend all political regimes.

3. The churches and people's participation

Why should the churches take seriously the issue of peoples participation?

Jesus went around visiting all the towns and villages. He taught in the synagogues, preached the Good News about the kingdom, and healed people with every kind of disease and sickness. As he saw the people, his heart was filled with compassion for them, because they were worried and helpless, like sheep without a shepherd (Matt. 9:35-36).

As disciples of Jesus, Christians and the churches must be "filled with compassion for the people". The love of God as we see it in the compassion of Jesus Christ moves us to commit ourselves to support and participate in people's struggle. This means that we must commit ourselves to help the people recover and develop their own genius and power. That is, we need to take seriously such issues as those of land, appropriate technology, people's power and people's organization, development of local leadership, and wider networks of solidarity and support. All this for the sake of combating the threats of death posed by the various forms of the monopoly of wealth and power on the one hand, and recovering the power of life promised by God on the other.

We recognize different contexts of the churches' presence in the world; those contexts partly determine the agenda for action by the churches. This is part of their mission, being sensitive to and learning from the respective contexts.

We also recognize that the churches respond to their respective contexts in terms of their different traditions. As they have become related to one another they have begun to challenge and learn from each other to become more relevant to their social contexts.

In the light of the problem of participation discussed above, the churches need a critical self-examination of their own life and work, relationships and structures, so as to discourage the tendency towards elitism of leadership. They should seek to practise authentic participation so that their witness will become more credible and effective. For example, the complementarity of roles and functions of the clergy and the laity should be heightened; participation of women, youth, the disabled and other marginalized people should be promoted. There is need to re-examine the life-style of both the clergy and the congregations.

The churches need to be more faithful to their mission to the world, sharing the sufferings and aspirations of the people, even where the people may play no active role in the life of the churches. The witness of the churches should be relevant to the total life of society.

The churches must transcend their confessional and national boundaries and be in dialogue with people of other religions and ideologies for mutual challenge, sharing and learning.

Finally, the churches need to support the people's struggle for justice, human dignity and social transformation. The experiences and insights of many churches of the poor in recent years have been a challenge and an inspiration, not only to other churches but to the wider society as well.

Given the above understanding, the challenge facing us today is: how do we move in order to structure and guarantee people's participation at all levels of our life and work? In various ways, the programmes of the World Council of Churches are meant to respond to this challenge.

4. Methods and strategies of participation

Based on the discussions which took place during the Cyprus consultation, the following points were noted as ways in which people express themselves in search of authentic participation:

a) joining various existing organizations or structures, such as trade unions, peasant committees, action groups, political parties, etc;

b) protest and mass mobilization: in the face of unbearable injustice and exclusion, people are moved to protest and to search for alternatives; demonstrations, strikes, walk-outs and various forms of people's protests are examples;

c) quest for truth, for example, exposure of the illusion that participation exists when in fact it does not exist, exposure of failures and lies of those in control, publication and various pronouncements on certain pressing issues of unjust acts or situations;

d) creating space for participation, such as easing the burden of people so as to free them to produce and to contribute to society (child care facilities, adult or informal education, etc.);

e) involvement in revolutionary movements in order to overthrow the unjust regime is a form of political participation at a very high level and at a very high cost;

f) participation in the various forms of communal celebrations, with the eucharist as one of the highest religious symbols of participation.

The consultation also considered strategies to promote people's participation. The following points were among the most noteworthy:

a) Motivation for action and participation is most effective when the people themselves, their interests and aspirations, are at the centre of attention. This includes cultural and spiritual values as well as economic gains and political participation.

b) Awareness-building and communication through concrete involvement, authentic information (as opposed to misinformation and deceit), employment of people's language and folk symbols, people's telling their own stories, and the recognition of their wisdom.

c) Participatory leadership is of the people, for the people and by those who identify with the people. Potential leadership exists among the people, and needs to be developed. Authentic leadership promotes people's power, and motivates and inspires them to become shapers of their own history. True leadership is participatory, ready to be replaced.

d) Empowering the people through the recovery of their cultural roots, their wisdom and their identity.

e) Wider network of support and solidarity is of crucial importance for people's struggle for participation.

f) At the deepest level, people's participation is rooted in the religious vision. The cross and the resurrection of Jesus Christ have evidently been one of the most powerful inspirations of people's movements for participation.

V. METHODOLOGICAL CONSIDERATIONS

As already apparent from the preceding sections, a number of methodological approaches were operative at the Cyprus consultation. In fact, the various contributions to the consultations embody different methods, implicitly or otherwise. Through the discussion, however, it became clear that the shift towards a people-centred approach has clear methodological implications. Questions were raised as to the adequacy of the action-reflection method which has prevailed in the ecumenical movement in the last decade or so.

The JPSS advisory committee already indicated the need for a new and more adequate methodology, which, they said, "should take the following elements seriously:

a) the historical, cultural and religious heritage of the people;

b) the contemporary power structures of human society;

c) the commitment of faith to search in hope for the messianic kingdom where justice and fullness of humanity (life) will be realized".

These elements were affirmed at Cyprus. As the ecumenical movement continues to participate in the search for a just society, the question of methodology also needs careful follow-up in the future. Notably, these methods have a lot in common in spite of the fact that they have emerged in response to particular contexts.

1. *An ethic of responsibility.* Articulated by some European participants, this method discerns the following essential points:

a) Political ethics is fundamentally an ethic of responsibility. The question here is how to bring together convictions within the framework of conditions in which political actions are to be taken and with the foreseeable consequences of those actions.

b) The method of political ethics has itself to be participatory. It is not enough to construct political ethics without the participation of the people who are themselves deeply involved in politics, in political experiences and in political struggles for participation and justice. Only when its method is participatory can political ethics be at the same time a matter of conceptualization and of orientation towards concrete actions.

c) Political ethics is one example for a dialogical procedure in ethics. This requires stepping over given social, cultural and religious barriers. It is a basic element of political ethics to bring the "genius of other historical, cultural and religious traditons into the discussion".

d) An ecumenical political ethic should be reflected in the life of the churches themselves. In fact it is through the reordering of their own economy, structure and involvement in mission and witness that the churches can win credibility for the political ethic they advocate.

2. *Participatory action research method.* Articulated at the consultation by a Latin American participant, this method has been developed by a critical school of social scientists associated with some specialized agencies of the United Nations. Commonly referred to as PAR (Participatory Action Research), this method focuses on the context of and active involvement in the struggle.

The key to this method is a call for theology to overcome its isolation, not only from political and social sciences, but also from people's life and the way that people understand it. This method, therefore, is a combination of context, life, values and non-negotiable assumptions. More specifically, it responds especially to the needs of the people, taking into account their aspirations and capacities for knowing and acting. It seeks to promote self-reliant development from below and relative independence from outside.

This method rejects any absolute value in scientific knowledge, positing that such value varies according to the interests of the classes involved in the shaping and accumulation of knowledge. Positively, it considers popular science or popular wisdom at the base of society to be crucial to people's empowerment in their struggle.

3. *Paradigm of reading a text.* Articulated by some North American participants, this method focuses on the interpretation of symbols. What, this method asks, in the totality of human dwelling, is taken as the subject matter for interpretation? It posits that the text for political ethics is the people's story or social biography. The people's story is a praxis, an historical-political struggle for liberation from suffering and oppression. "People" is therefore a central symbol in the work of political ethics.

Three moments of interpretation or reading are the essence of this method:

a) *Guessing or discerning:* This refers to the fundamental sense or meaning of the central symbol, the people. For example, in the Cyprus consultation, the liberation of the people is the paradigmatic sense of the story.

b) *Explanation:* As a people recovers selfhood, it assumes responsibility for its story, for reshaping its future in its own terms. The explanatory moment means the tracing of the patterns of oppression, points of leverage in the system of oppression, and strategies for extending the people's participation in shaping its own future. Various analytic models may be useful in tracing the sequence of oppression and liberation, but no model or style of analysis can lay claim to finality. In this sense, social scientific, ethical and theological styles are all embedded in ideological projections which distort as well as illumine possibilities of justice, peace and participation. Here, the wisdom of the people provides the one sure resource for creative ethical work. For the people are the bearers of the possibility of overcoming oppression in the name of justice and peace.

c) *Comprehension:* This refers to the moment when those doing political ethics are consciously grasped or appropriated into the world of the people, sharing their plight and participating in their struggle for justice and liberation. The crucial question for political ethics here would be how the religious community and its institutions can contribute to the political responsibility of the people in shaping its future. Lending a supportive hand as well as providing a critical and prophetic voice within the struggle of the people are two primary ways of action.

4. *People's story.* Articulated by some Asian participants, this method is based on the insights gained from the struggles of Asian people. Four closely related elements are central to this method:

a) *Search for the messianic kingdom:* Faced with abject poverty and systemic oppression, and inspired by the "new heaven and the new earth", the people are engaged in the struggle for a just society.

This struggle is at once political and religious; yet the two dimensions are not identical. The religious refers to the deepest dimension of being human, as persons and in community. It refers to the human experiencing of the sacred. As such, it is an authentic spirituality, a full consciousness and expression of the divine dimension of human experience. The political, from this perspective, refers to the realization of the religious vision in human history, involving the exercise of power in order to combat the forces of death and to create conditions and structures for human fulfilment.

b) *Reinterpreting and recovery of heritage:* In search of their identity, poor and oppressed people reinterpret and recover their historical roots, their cultural and religious heritage, their collective memory and their folk wisdom, at the national as well as the local level. These sources of identity are embedded in significant historical epochs, foundation myths, folk-tales or folk-lore, and the arts and literature — in short, in the legacy of symbols which provide the living ethos for the people. In reinterpreting and recovering this heritage, the people are empowered, their identity established, and their destiny clarified. All this happens when people remember and retell the legacy of their sacred history, sharing it with the new generations and with other peoples.

c) *Articulating the present reality:* Speaking their own language, the people reassert their humanity by telling the actualities of their suffering and oppression as well as of their hopes and dreams. Here people say "no" to the demonic forces, and "yes" to the power of life, not without ambivalence. Story-telling in this perspective at once embodies the articulation of the reality, social and political analysis, projection of strategies for action, and dreaming of a just world. This articulation, furthermore, is an integral part of people's doing their political ethics.

These two dimensions, the recovery of the roots and the articulating of the suffering, provide the people with an excellent political education.

d) *Sharing the cup of suffering and joy:* The three dimensions above are in fact part and parcel of people's sharing their suffering and joy. Yet, the act of solidarity, expressed in common action and celebration, constitutes the final link in the circle of people's story-telling method. Together these four dimensions are but a mode of people's search for a just, participatory and sustainable society.

* * *

It should be reiterated that the above methods, incompletely articulated as they are, were examples only. Other methods, perhaps as many as the number of participants, were also operative at the consultation. It seems clear that as the dialogue on political ethics continues, efforts are needed to ensure that these various methods are more fully articulated, recognizing both their diversity and particularity. More important, attempts should be made to spell out their common elements which may serve as a common frame of reference for our future work.

VI. RECOMMENDATIONS

A. Ecumenical political ethics

1. We recommend that the dialogue on the issue of political ethics be continued. The following areas should be further explored:

a) forms of political participation going beyond representative democracy;

b) violence and non-violence in the struggle for social justice;

c) an ecumenical exchange on different understandings of the term "people";
d) the use of the biblical tradition in making ethical choices;
e) the integrity of the Christian commitment in response to the plurality of political positions;
f) a deeper study on the issues of freedom, equality, participation, justice/ equity, human rights/righteousness, and peace/shalom as integral parts of political ethics;
g) an exploration of the political potential of the ecumenical community, going beyond power politics, in realizing a just, participatory and sustainable society.

B. Justice and power

2. We have experienced that churches do not share the same methodology in analyzing political problems. Therefore, we recommend that the WCC through its appropriate sub-units clarify and articulate how churches do political analysis with special attention to story-telling, concrete historical approaches, the adequacy and comprehensiveness of various approaches, and the sources and tools of the churches' analyses.

3. We recommend that the WCC study the problem of the legitimacy of power.

4. We strongly recommend that the WCC facilitate churches' consideration of appropriate support of people's coalitions which aim at the satisfaction of people's deeply felt needs (e. g. coalitions for peace activities, land rights, human rights, participation, etc.).

5. Taking into consideration the work already done by the WCC through its study on violence and non-violence as well as the Programme to Combat Racism reflections on the issue of violence, we recommend that in the JPSS/political ethics follow-up the WCC undertake further study on violence and social change, giving special attention to the current worldwide context of the national security state model.

C. People's participation in politics

6. Since people's participation requires a new and deeper theological perspective, the ongoing effort of the various sub-units of WCC in this regard should be pursued, aiming at a fuller articulation, particularly in connection with the issue of political ethics. In pursuing this theological articulation, the following aspects should be emphasized:
a) recognition of the over-riding importance of the total context;
b) dialogue in depth and action with people of other faiths and ideologies;

c) actual experiences of parties, movements and communities committed to the practice of people's participation;

d) participation within the churches or participatory ecclesiology.

7. In order to promote fuller understanding and more effective practice of people's participation in political decision-making, the following aspects should be pursued:

a) special attention and support to people who are excluded, powerless and voiceless in the decision-making which affects their lives;

b) education, documentation and leadership training from people's effective participation in politics;

c) re-examination of the role of the "laity" within the church and the ecumenical movement, taking into account the previous work done by the WCC.

Political ethics in Africa

AARON TOLEN

Is power exercised in Africa without any guiding principle? Is force the only criterion for political action? What are the objectives of the exercise of power? Why have Africans come to demand the end of colonial rule? What is the moving utopia behind the African political debate? These are some of the questions anybody who wants to understand the political scene of Africa today must deal with.

I want to discuss the subject by dealing with the traditional typology, the reactions to colonial domination, the parameters of nation-building, the issue of state's development vs people's development, and the way ahead.

Centralism and anarchy: the traditional typology

As my focus is on black Africa, I want to limit myself to the traditional typology we have. It can cover the difference between the savannah and the forest.

People living in the savannah have centralized social structures with centres of power clearly identified and located in the hands of a chief, who is very often a political, religious and economic ruler. The organization of the community at large as well as the organization of the family is based on strong centralization of power, which calls for absolute respect and discipline. What the chief and the important people feel is good for the community is accepted as such. The rulers' interests are supposed to be identical with the community's interests.

The Sudanese tribes do enjoy this type of social organization. Some have seen the reasons for such organization in the need to face some problems like the use of water and land and the need for discipline in the use of natural resources. To these reasons one must add the intrusion of Islamic principles from the eighteenth century.

In the forest, with plenty of land and water and the possibility to live in small communities, the social organization has been anarchical. The power is in the hands of heads of very small groups and families. The chief, who is also the warrior, is a political leader. The priest, and all those who participate in helping the community to relate to God, have religious power. The land is the property of families.

In this context, the Bantu and semi-Bantu do enjoy a more open society than the Sudanese. A certain consensus is needed for all decisions. To use Western typology, the chief in the Bantu tribe needs the approval and the support of others to exercise power. He is to some extent a democratic leader, while the Sudanese is an autocratic leader.

These differences explain why it has been possible to build up strong empires in the savannah, and why it has been difficult to maintain power in big communities in the forest. But one must always keep in mind this dichotomy when trying to understand some of the problems facing African states with both forest and savannah.

The reaction to colonial domination

Western countries brought with them a set of political concepts which have tried to replace by force or by seduction African traditional concepts. The way colonial power was exercised was nearer to the Sudanese power model. It was autocratic, centralized and global. The colonial master had the monopoly of deciding what should be done in all fields of life. His way of life was the civilized one, and ours obscurantist or savage; his religion was enlightenment, ours was sorcery; his power was liberal, ours was tyranny. In that situation, some tried to assimilate the African element in their civilization, others affirmed that it was impossible to accommodate both conceptions in one community. The result was either apartheid, or the creation of second-class citizens.

But the contradiction between what was done in the colonies and what was happening at home brought about a division among the colonial masters themselves. How can a democratic country use autocratic power? Democracy as the government of the people by the people, and the advocacy for human rights, human dignity and cultural dignity, made the Africans aware of their plight as a dominated and an alienated people. The general movement for freedom and the exposure to socialist ideas has given rise to a new momentum.

When the Africans ask for independence, it is to promote a government of the people and by the people through elections, to recognize the human dignity of African people and to affirm their cultural identity. The 1960s are not seen as years during which we were recognized as nations, but they were also the years when masses of people expected an improvement in their daily life. They were looking for the fostering of their dignity, the promotion of their human rights and liberties and the development of their cultures.

We have had flags, national anthems, seats at international gatherings, national governments and assemblies. We have had the creation of a new elite promoting a certain economic growth. But what have we done with the ideals which have moved our masses in the 1950s? To what extent have we promoted social justice, human rights and cultural dignity?

From the tribe to the nation

With our independence won from colonial powers, Africans were faced with the choice of government. Again, we have to choose between centralization and democracy. The debate around multi-partism and the one-party system is a reflection of our historical tension. It is a modern way of trying to find a compromise between the savannah and the forest, autocracy and democracy.

But the problem is more complicated because we are not just concerned with solving our problems on a limited space and for a limited population. We have to organize ourselves so as to be in a position to discourage any attempt at reconquest, and to assure enough of cohesion and consensus so as to transcend tribal divisions, and to build a nation. At the end, what we have is a conflict between unity and centralism on the one hand and pluralism and human rights on the other. In the search for unity, many governments eliminate all democratic mechanisms and they institute instead tyrannic rules called "African democracy". The open dialogue embodied in the "palaver" becomes a monologue in a one-party system, led and dominated by one person. And everybody is expected to consider that as a good government. The opposite is presented as anarchy and subversion.

At the regional level, the choice between nationalism and pan-Africanism will give another possibility for confrontation. Before independance, the majority of Africans were not happy with the division of our people within artificial boundaries. They refer to it as "balkanization" and they reject it. After independence, many have become so concerned about their position within their nation that they are not willing to search for African unity. Kwame Nkrumah, and after him Julius Nyerere, are among the very few who have maintained that Africa must unite if Africa wants to be autonomous and self-reliant.

Unfortunately, the Organization for African Unity insists more on the respect for borders inherited from the colonial era. It thus tends to be a "heads of state union", primarily concerned with its members' interests and not with people's problems.

State development vs people's development

The concentration of power in the hands of one person, the identification of that person with the state, the organization of all activities for the profit of "the state" — all this under the pretext of the need for unity, stability, peace and development — that is Africa today.

There is no people's participation in decision-making. Even elections are emptied of their content as people are only called upon to give approval to a list drawn up by those who govern. All over Africa, a small élite monopolizes power and all that power provides. Peasants are exploited, and the vast rural sector is used for the profit of the minority living in urban areas. In the cities you have good schools, good health institutions, running water, electricity, social insurance, better houses, etc. Social justice is denied elsewhere.

At the same time, because the majority are excluded from the profit of development, those who are in power make themselves more and more dependent on foreign powers. Self-reliance, one of our main objectives, has become a dream. The masses are not allowed to decide on what they want to do for their development. Leaders must depend on outside forces because they do not have the confidence of the masses. We are going back to the past.

Where do we go from here?

Some African leaders are becoming aware of the danger. In Senegal, the former President L.S. Senghor recently completed the first phase of a historical experiment. He moved from the one party system to a "controlled multipartism", with three political parties. Then, at the beginning of 1981, he decided to resign from his position and to allow a smooth change in leadership.

Senghor has tried to prove that multi-partism and change in leadership are not necessarily against national unity and stability. There is more participation; there is a greater openness in the political life. Let's hope that these will promote social justice and a better stewardship of national resources.

In Ivory Coast, President Houphouet-Boigny has another approach. He is still convinced that multi-partism poses a danger for the fragile national unity. But he is aware of the need for more participation from the masses, particularly youth.

In 1980 he decided that the party will no more nominate candidates for election, but as many people as wanted could run for the same seat. It is up to the people, the masses, to decide.

For the first time in years, there has been a great change in the nature of leadership, and young people have come strongly into the business of politics. The objective was to prove that the one-party system can be and is the best way to educate the masses politically and to consolidate national unity. The other basic motive behind the move was the commitment to people's participation in decision-making.

In these two experiences, one can discern a real African contribution to political science theory. On the one hand, democracy has to be organized to avoid anarchy and demagogy. It must be kept within the limits of possibility or feasibility. Something must be done to limit the number of political parties in a country. On the other hand, the one-party system is improved by the introduction of a certain kind of pluralism at the level of candidature. In socialist countries where the system has existed for years, as well as in many African countries, there is one party and that party alone has the right to nominate candidates for election. For each seat, the party appoints only one candidate. To some exent the choice is made once the party has nominated the candidates and the election becomes only a rite. People's participation is made ineffective as people have only to say yes to what has been decided by the elite.

In the Central African Republic, in March 1981, the country came back to total multi-partism, after the imperial period. Some time later on, a coup d'état brought the military back to power.

The problems in Africa today are the lack of people's participation, social injustices in all aspects of life, and the lack of concern for ecology.

Attempts on the part of foreign powers to recolonize Africa are encouraged by African selfishness. They can succeed only if Africans are not united and allowed to participate in political life. Unfortunately, Africa is today a peopleless continent. That is, for many governments, it is possible to conduct national affairs as if the people did not exist.

Reconstruction of political ethics in an Asian perspective

ANWAR M. BARKAT

Introduction

It is difficult for any one person from Asia to present a comprehensive and detailed analysis of Asian experience in any field of human endeavour, especially in history, culture and civilization. Asia is so vast, and has such pluralities of ideas, cultures, religions, histories and civilizations.

Contemporary Asia's experience with history was the subject of K.M. Pannikkar's classic *Asia and Western Dominance* which exposed the relationship between modern Asia and the structures of domination, control, and imposed hegemonies of imperial and colonial powers. Some of the new vitalities and powerful creative impulses all over Asia, from China to India, Korea to Pakistan, awakened and demanding their own heritage, cannot be understood apart from the experiences of manipulation and control exercised by the European and American powers in Asia, especially from the beginning of the eighteenth century. Asian politics and history have been shaped by this experience of European domination which makes it difficult today to distinguish between a genuinely Asian discourse in politics and the dominating Western tradition in politics. The predominance of Western philosophical, political and cultural ethos, along with the institutions and structures of politics based on that ethos, led to an eclipse of the Asian traditions and political experiences. Such a pervasive domination of one homogeneous cultural perspective based upon its assumed superiority often led to the outright rejection of Asian civilizational and cultural perspectives. It also means serious neglect, if not total rejection, of structures of local initiative and self-perception. Asian culture and politics were not considered worthy to be taught as academic disciplines in the Asian educational institutions, thus divorcing the Asian people from their own experience in politics.

There are at least two major issues to be taken into account for a proper understanding of Asian political reality. One is the transplantation to Asia of

Western institutional models and political structures. These may have been based on important ideas of human dignity, equality before law, human rights as natural rights, limited government, right to dissent, and other major concepts related to democracy as understood in the Western tradition, but no serious intellectual effort was made to find whether similar ideas and concepts may have been practised in the cultures and societies of Asia with a definite Asian philosophical rationale. It was generally assumed without proper examination of the evidence that these ideas were uniquely Western and did not exist in other cultures. Thus Asian theory and practice of government became politics of imitation of the Western political experience.

The other major issue is the transference of the Western scientific and technological perspective, especially the scientific method with its positivistic philosophical perspective, which had emphasized the divorce between ethics and politics, science and religion, power and morality, thus removing any constraint upon the exercise of power. Politics divorced from its ethical roots became an instrument of domination and control rather than justice and human development. It is important for our reflections on political ethics to look at this divorce between politics and ethics to show its alienness to Asian political realities.

Western political thought up to the end of the eighteenth century had been concerned with a few basic and fundamental questions: What are the *ends* of state and government? What is the best form of government? What are some of the ethical constraints on power and how is power to be limited?

It was generally assumed that government and politics had ethical goals. There were references to "first principles" in politics, economics and law which were drawn from religion, speculative philosophy, history of Western political ideas, and historical evolution of Western civilization. Among the various sources of the principles, a prominent place was given to Christianity and the law of nature. Most of the Western political thinkers considered justice, welfare, order, security, even freedom and equality, as proper goals of government.

The rise of a positivistic perspective, with its emphasis upon scientific method as applied to social and humanistic sciences, had the serious consequence of excluding ethical concerns from politics because they could not be scientifically verified. No ethical and critical judgments could be established in politics. How could political practice be judged in such a situation? The answer was to look at the broad general agreements drawn from the Western political tradition, as the basis of politics and political judgment. These broad principles included emphases such as: government should be based on respect for the dignity of the human person and freedom of conscience, independence of judiciary, equality before law, no slaves, no torture; the principle of *habeas corpus* — the right of detained to be heard; freedom of the press, assembly, and dissent; government should serve the greatest happiness of the greatest number, at least within a given society.

But who was to determine what were the criteria of "happiness"? No criterion seemed to exist in terms of which actions of those in power could be considered "immoral", "unjust" and "evil". The rise of Nazism, fascism and totalitarianism had seriously undermined the so-called ethical neutrality of such a perspective. There were no ethical criteria of judgment in the face of serious denial of human rights, unlimited practice of racism, even outright "liquidation" as proper means of exercise of governmental power to achieve its stated ideological goals. It was difficult to prove the moral superiority of democracy over fascist dictatorship without reference to an ethical contract which had already been dismissed as a "myth", "dogma", and "ideology". It created an unprecedented crisis for Western political thought. It also set it apart from other traditions of political reflections, especially Asian traditions, which took the reality of moral and religious issues in politics seriously, and considered them central to politics.

Religion formed the central core of practically all societies of Asia. It was from religion and religiously oriented philosophical reflections that politics took its moral contours. Therefore, any discussion of the Asian dimensions of political ethics will rest upon our ability to place the religious traditions of Asia in their proper historical perspective. It is at this point that Christian reflections on political ethics will meet other religious traditions and ideologies whose aim of creating communities of shared moral and political goals may not be opposed to an authentic search for a just, participatory and sustainable society.

Religion as a relevant political factor in political ethics

Most authoritative commentators in the Western and Eastern intellectual tradition agree that religion has been a factor of great importance in the development of political ideas and institutions. Despite the secularization process of the last four centuries, belief in God has continued to play a significant role in political ideas, motivations, and institutions up to the present. This is demonstrated by the rise of religious states, like Pakistan and Israel, and the vigorous religious resistance to the contemporary phenomenon of secularism, materialism and totalitarianism. Hardly any Western writer on politics fails to recognize the importance of the Judeo-Christian tradition in the development of political thought in the West.

This contribution is of special importance in relation to the rise of capitalism and democracy. Some even regard this religious heritage as leading to the rise of colonialism and imperialism which have been considered as extensions of secularized versions of the Christian civilization. Even Karl Marx, no particular lover of religions, acknowledged that "democracy is based on the principle of the sovereign worth of the individual, which in turn, is based on the dream of Christianity that man has an immortal soul".

Politics in its classical understanding has indeed been understood as a search for a moral community in which people as free citizens could participate to enlarge their social and political life. People stripped of the moral protection of the community become victims of the monopolistic claims to formal authority of the nation states with coercive powers to appropriate the role of specifying the goals of community life and the common good. This lies at the heart of the rise of modern totalitarianism: national security states, and military dictatorships which are ready to use their police and military power to deny the people the right to set up goals for their own communities. People stripped of the power to set communal goals become impotent in politics and their ability to participate in the political processes becomes merely ritualistic and formalistic. In place of the politics of justice and participation based on dialogue on the shared goals, it becomes rather a politics of bargaining and power, subject to manipulation, propaganda, and intimidation. The reconstruction of political ethics would therefore require the restoration of politics to its moral goals and contents, as a prerequisite for a just, participatory, and sustainable society. Reconstruction of political ethics requires reinstating these moral considerations into politics. Raghavan Iyer has rightly said:

> Politics is inseparable from life — from human concerns, moral considerations, religious and secular beliefs, modes of living, inherited myths, dreams, nightmares; from preconceptions and presuppositions about fundamental issues, transcendent themes and values; and from distinction between right and wrong, good and evil, pleasure and pain, freedom and tyranny, egotism and altruism. Ultimate questions, even if unanswerable, are never irrelevant to the politics of free men.[1]

What is required, therefore, is a rethinking of the very foundations of conventional politics. The contours of politics need to be redrawn, if the task of redirection and transformation of politics from its obsession with power and its instrumentalities towards the politics of people, and the creation of a moral community of shared goals in a global context is to become a reality.

The ultimate goal of politics as the creation of a moral community of shared goals based on justice for all and the possibilities of participation of

---

[1] *Parapolitics: Toward the City of Man,* New York, Oxford University Press, 1979, pp.10ff.

the widest possible number of people could not be forced into any one single, preconceived, modality. Politics of participation would be a clear departure from the politics of stability, power and self-preservation. Ultimately it would be a politics of human fulfilment.

It is clear that such a gigantic task cannot be performed on the basis of any one tradition, one culture, or one civilization. It would require cooperation and dialogue among the various religious and cultural traditions of the world. Its major focus would be the creation of an ethical-political framework within which human government could be organized.

This cannot be an exclusive concern of Christians, but a shared concern of all religious faiths and ideologies. All faiths have the common task of saving people from the forces of dehumanization, domination and oppression. All religious traditions are engaged in a struggle to recover their past, and show its relevance to the overwhelming human concerns of economic and social justice. The ecumenical community of Christians can make this struggle a shared quest.

The imperial-colonial tradition in Asian politics

With the exception of Japan and Thailand, and to some extent China, every Asian nation was under colonial domination. The colonial powers established political, economic, cultural, and educational patterns of governance which continue to influence and shape the content of the political realities of Asia. It is against the background of this colonial experience that the Asian nations are struggling to create a meaningful future for their people.

The cultural and political penetration of the West into the social and cultural fabric of Asia was so pervasive that it is difficult at times to discover genuinely Asian political categories of social discourse in terms of which contemporary Asian realities can be understood. It is because of this that the struggle for national independence in Asia was a struggle for the "discovery" of Asia in terms of its own historical selfhood which had been totally submerged under colonialism.

The European imperial powers in Asia not only imposed their own cultural and political ethos, they also fragmented Asia by cutting off age-old cultural and civilizational contacts among the various Asian nations. Asians could now communicate with each other only through the brokerage of the European nations. It not only imposed isolation among Asian nations but also between the peoples of Europe and Asia except in terms of imperial relationships. Therefore, Asians generally remained ignorant about more humane developments in European cultures. The new ideas of social and economic justice, political freedom and equality, political participation on the basis of representational norms, and the rise of new organizations consolidating the power of the poor and dispossessed, did not for long influence the political realities of Asia. The European industrial revolution, the economic and political revolutions, the humanitarian and social revolutions, which changed eighteenth and nineteenth century Europe, instead of bringing economic and political revolutions in Asia, only provided more sophisticated rationale for the exploitation of the Asian people. Asians had to discover some of these ideas in the European tradition through the Westernization of its own intellectual elites. Asian struggle for independence was truly a discovery and retrieval of suppressed Asian civilizational experience, and not simply an experience of establishing independent nation states in Asia. It was a major revolution in the "soul" of Asia to discover complex structures of habits, knowledge and belief which had been suppressed for centuries.

Most of the European political institutions which were transplanted into the soil of Asia were designed to control the people and resources of Asia for the benefit of the metropolitan countries. Their initial purpose was not to prepare people for self-government or for eventual independence.

Nevertheless, the colonial government stressed the importance of regularized laws under common administration, applicable to all within a given colonial territory. Although some of the legislative institutions were based in the metropolitan centres of colonial nations, yet there developed a concept of rule of law applicable to the colonized people. Later on this concept of legislative state, however imperfect, was to be introduced into practically all of the Asian nations directly under the European colonial powers.

It was to end the conditions of dependence and servitude that people all over Asia "stood up" and launched a struggle, through the means available to them, for the liberation of their societies. Despite different ideologies, different methodologies, and different cultural histories, all Asians were united in the struggle for independence. They were aware of the limitations of their own historical experience in creating and managing modern statehood, but they were also firm in their conviction that nothing worse could befall a people than to be under an alien or foreign domination, however benign and humanitarian it may be. The only rightful destiny for all people was to be able to determine freely their own political, cultural and economic institutions.

The struggle for independence in Asia was not simply a political and economic struggle. It was essentially conceived as a moral struggle based on the proposition that all people had the right to determine their own destiny and no people had the right to manipulate, exploit and use other people for their own ends. Power was not a morally and ethically neutral category. Its use and abuse have moral consequences. Power could be used to create social justice, economic development, participation of people, equality and happiness of the people. Power is an essential part of self-identity and cultural self-determination, therefore colonialism and imperialism were essentially evil, and no people could really be free when total power is concentrated in the hands of alien rulers.

Various efforts at reconstruction of political ethics in Asia

It is within the above almost universal imperial-colonial tradition in Asian politics that we shall try and analyze two different movements of political struggle in Asia.

1. Mao Tse-Tung: reconstruction of Chinese political ethics

Mao Tse-Tung's reconstruction of political thought for contemporary China has been a matter of considerable debate among scholars. The main point of the debate is the relationship of Chinese thought to Mao's Marxist thought. It has been a rather inconclusive debate since it has been difficult to assign relative weight to various components in Mao's political and philosophical thought. The matter rests with the agreement that Mao is both a Chinese and a Marxist thinker. His worldview and perception of reality remains Chinese and he uses Marxist categories to undergird the basically Chinese reality and experience.

Chinese culture and civilization are among the most pervasive and ancient Asian social and political realities. China has been a country and had a culture long before any other Asian societies. Chinese empires had risen and fallen without destroying the continuity of the Chinese state. China helped develop one of the most sophisticated bureaucratic states with well-defined principles for recruitment and selection, which lasted for close to two thousand years.

Part of Mao's historical and cultural background was drawn from one of the greatest systems of ethical and political thought, expounded by Confucius. He had based his teachings on the belief that tradition alone could provide society with intellectual tools with which to reconstruct a sound social and political order. Therefore Confucius did not regard himself as an innovator or a creator of a new political tradition, but rather as a transmitter of the great Chinese tradition. Historical reflections on Chinese experience in history were the central aspects of Confucian political thought.

One of the basic ideas in Confucian political thought was the concept of the ideal of "the Superior Man", *Chun Tzu*, "a son of a prince", a gentleman. The emphasis is upon merit and not on biological origins. A "superior man", a member of the ruling elites, could be judged by his conduct. If he did not act in a superior way, he could be regarded as an ordinary man.

The Confucian political ethics was based on the concept of *Jen*, benevolence. It could also be interpreted as "goodness", or "human-heartedness". *Jen* assumes basic harmony in human relations, mutual affection and respect for each other, beginning with the immediate to the far removed. All governmental relationships should be like those of our extended family. Harmony in a person leads to harmony in the family, village and government.

The best way of governance is through moral persuasion and not by coercion. Government by a superior man exercising benevolence and moral persuasion was superior to the government of laws and institutions. Intimidation and force were the lowest instruments of government. Confucius did not want to eliminate laws, punishments and weapons as governmental instruments, but the basic function of government was ethical education of the people, providing for their material wellbeing, and organizing them for internal and external defence.

Since "superior man" is important for the healthy polity, it was government's primary duty to find these men who could participate in rulership. The superior men would be attracted through the character of the ruler. These men had to go through rigorous training and would be selected through a stiff selection process. At the core of this selection was the merit system. Education was the instrument to increase one's merit. Although the system was open to all, it was more weighted towards people of means who were able to pay for their education and had the natural advantage of an educational environment which people of humbler means did not have. It bred elitism.

The Confucian political ethics can be summarized in these words: "A government of benevolence functioning through the suasive power of virtue, embodying cosmic harmony in the ritualization of relationships, and relying on the judgment of cultivated men, ideally needed no new codes to be vindicated and no other defences than the attachment to it that people naturally feel towards it, as members of the family towards family head."[2]

The later thinkers in China worked within the general Confucian political and ethical ideas. These main parameters provided guidelines in which future developments could take place through interpretation and reinterpretation, but any serious departure hardly ever succeeded.

For nearly two thousand years, conscious political reflections in China were done in Confucian terms, although the actual organization of the

---

[2]Frederich W. Motz, "Chinese Political Thought", in *IESS*, Vol. 2, p.399.

Chinese Empire leaned towards legalist practices. The main vocabulary of government, politics and ethics were drawn from Confucian tradition and even "those rare thinkers who consciously espoused non-Confucian ideas did so in Confucian terms".[3]

The concept of an ethical cosmos remained continually a part of the Chinese political tradition. Later writers, especially of the Neo-Confucian period, agreed on basic political principles: government as benevolent institution governed by men deeply concerned about the moral rightness of their action and about the welfare of the people. But they also reinterpreted the metaphor of the supreme ultimate in its hierarchy of cosmic forces, sustaining and ordering the myriad forms of life. They extended this metaphor to the supreme emperor, son of heaven, as exalted capstone of a hierarchy of political forces and social reality. This reinterpretation and an official misuse of an ethical metaphor, was often to be employed to enhance imperial authoritarianism.

Mao was aware of these Chinese traditions in politics, but he was also aware of the Marxist tradition which was beginning to make an impact upon several Asian societies living in the context of imperial and colonial domination, especially India, Indonesia and Indo-China. The young leaders of national liberation movements, young intellectuals, were coming to grips with Marxism as a transnational and transcultural ideology. But Marxism was nevertheless a Western import, with Western ideological assumptions, and arose out of the socio-economic conditions of capitalism and industrialization. Its rise could not be understood apart from its basic Western origin. Therefore, it could not be totally applied to Asian conditions, without a basic reinterpretation and adaptation. Mao accepted Marxism with these reservations, and tried to apply it to Chinese socio-political reality. In doing so, he made a considerable contribution not only to the development of Marxism, but also to the reconstruction of political thought for the modernization of contemporary China.

Mao contributed considerably to the development of political ethics for a new Chinese state. As an inheritor of the vast Confucian tradition and as the practitioner of Marxist-Leninist tradition, he had to decide what was relevant for China in its struggle for a truly just and participatory society. Of course, he was also concerned with the power, wealth and dignity of China among the modern nation-states of the world. He retained the Confucian concern for the moral and ethical cultivation of the individual but put it in the context of the service of the people. People for him were the source of all power. People were central to all political processes in human history. People had

---

[3] *Ibid.*, p.403.

always been part of the political thought of China, what Mao did was to make them central to change and revolution in history. There was some notion that people were a kind of self-constituting force rushing through history like a torrent breaking down barriers and creating a free and good society of the future. The people united create their own vision of a just society.

His understanding of revolution and social change in history drew both from Chinese resources and Marxist resources. He did not totally accept the Marxist notion of contradictions or class struggle. He recognized the centrality of the peasants. He used the concept of "proletarian spirit" as a cluster for moral qualities and these could be internalized even by non-proletarian groups, like intellectuals, semi-intellectuals and peasants. The emphasis on moral qualities of self-sacrifice, self-reliance, self-discipline, applied both to the leaders and the people. He emphasized the moral solidarity among the people and the leaders. The cultivation of this moral spirit was more important than material resources, either economic or military.

His main ethical ideas are expressed in two long essays, "On Contradictions" and "On Practice". He did not consider contradictions as essentially destructive or conflicts as necessarily bad. He distinguished between principal contradictions and secondary contradictions. He saw in contradiction and conflicts not only the motor for change and development; they were a part of the social reality. He said that meaningful contradictions even persist in socialist societies. Mao insisted upon the universality of contradiction and suggested that the best way to deal with them was to bring them to the surface so that they can be dealt with openly. He also made a distinction between contradictions among the people and contradictions between the people and the enemies of the people. The latter can only be dealt with through the "reformation" of the anti-people forces. The "five bad elements" such as landlords, rich peasants, counter-revolutionaries, bad elements and rightists, all have the possibility of joining the people through internal reformation.

His emphasis upon "permanent revolution" was important for keeping and mobilizing the revolutionary zeal of the masses and its leaders for the transformation of society. Human and moral forces require constant renewal which the notion of "permanent revolution" could keep alive. It could also help keep the focus on a broader vision of society and help eradicate constant temptation to self-interest and selfishness.

Another important aspect of Mao's thought was his emphasis upon the relationship between the masses and the leaders. He emphasized the principle of the central guidance by a revolutionary elite and at the same time he stressed the "mass line" in which "all correct leadership is necessarily from the masses, to the masses". Ordinary people can also be the source of new ideas on which correct policies can be made and people can judge and understand good policies.

Leadership in Mao's thought must listen to the people if it wishes to lead correctly and effectively. They must understand what is happening below. Without this "it would be impossible to achieve unity of understanding and unity of action, and impossible to achieve true centralism (democracy)".

What was the relationship between "theory" and "practice" in the building up of a just political order? Mao showed an aversion to mere book learning and abstract thinking. "Theory" and "practice" both are important for a correct perception of reality. It was this emphasis that helped him in the process of "sinification of Marxism" as applied to the concrete reality of China's peasant society. The truth of Marxism had to be combined with concrete practice. All these ideas have a great significance not only for China but also for other Asian societies where peasantry is the main segment of society. The centrality of the people as heart of the political reality and source of power has tremendous implication for Asian political ethics. The credit goes to Mao who based his political thought upon the centrality of the people.

2. Mahatama Gandhi: reconstruction of Indian political ethics.

Mahatama Gandhi's effort to reconstruct political ethics in the Indian context was undertaken with a full consciousness of the great Hindu historical traditions; the subjection of India to various humiliating occupations and invasions including Greek, Islamic and European; and the contemporary problems of building a nation. Gandhi was aware that ancient Indian religious and political traditions, especially embedded Hinduism and Buddhism, have played in Asia a role similar to the one Hellenistic culture played for the West. India, along with China, had established the dimensions of its social, political and philosophical thought independently of Greek and other civilizations. These ancient cultures and civilizations were part of the basic religious beliefs, symbols, myths and rituals in terms of which reality was comprehended by people both individually and collectively. The Indian religious writings like the *Upanisheds, Dharma Sutras* and the *Vedic* literature, spoke of political order as analogous to the cosmos and its creation. This relationship was emphasized to ensure the proper and harmonious function of the social and political order.

Vedic literature took monarchy as a form of government, but there was no emphasis on the divine right of kings. The king had no priestly functions; these were assigned to a separate caste. Monarchy was elective. The relationship between the king and the people was based upon kinship. Priests had a special place in the social structure. They were the interpreters of the scriptures, and they had a special place which was considered even superior to the king's. Priests helped justify the hierarchy of power in the social structure through the doctrine of Karma which became the foundation of the social structure. It has been rightly said in this context that:

> we are confronted with a society so effectively integrated by religion that political institutions need only play a minor role in regulating conflict. And indeed, through most of the Indian history, social coordination was accomplished through caste and village institutions.[4]

The primary duty of a king was the preservation of the *Dharma,* meaning the totality of rules and duties of the eternal and necessary moral law, truth and justice. *Dharma* included theology, ethics and law. Political authorities were subject to *Dharma* and were responsible to ensure compliance with *Dharma* even if there was provision of sanction and coercion (*Danda*). Political authority existed as the guarantor of peace, social order, and hierarchy of duties and privileges. But as the power of the ruler increased, he assumed the function of law-giving and showed increased independence from the moral code by placing himself above the law.

The great epic poem *Mahabharata,* and within it the *Bhagaved Gita,* consolidated the Hindu social structure and the role of the *Kshatrya,* the knight or the ruler, in political power.

The law of Manu of the *Arthasastra* writings is considered to be the most important political document in Indian cultural history. It is said to date back to 500 B.C. In Vedic literature, politics was termed as *Rajadharma* as well as *Arthasastra;* it included both economics and politics. *Arthasastra* is intended to guide the ruler and his ministers on such matters as public administration, economic regulations, foreign policy, civil law and techniques of warfare.

Kautilya, the minister of the first Mauryan Empire, is said to have compiled the code. There are three ends of human life: virtue, wealth and enjoyment. The most important is wealth, but virtue and enjoyment should not be ignored. The main objective of a ruler is to ensure the effective functioning of the state. Political expediency should be used in the exercise of power and unscrupulous tactics in the use of power should only be used against those who subvert the social order.

The author emphasizes the economic basis of power. He opposes the tendency towards decentralization which would weaken state power. The

---

[4]Charles Drekmeier, "Indian Political Thought", in *International Encyclopedia of Social Sciences,* 1968 Vol. 7, p. 171.

state is advised not to exercise total power over economic life, but leave room for community action. The king should have no other interest than the welfare of his people. He should seek the prosperity of all, which would in turn increase the power of the state.

The last major work of ancient Hindu thought, *Sukranitisara* (900 to 1300 A.D.) is a moral as well as a political treatise. Its emphasis is upon moral values and norms. There is no sharp distinction between ethics and politics in it.

All these reflections did not challenge the class and caste systems which were well established. No challenge existed against the domination of the *Brahmins* and the *Ksatriyas* over the total social and legal structures of the territorial state. The inegalitarian caste system, and its foundation in the doctrine of Karma was challenged by Buddhism, and later on by Islam, and by the Indian national movements. But it was the teaching of Buddha that provided philosophical and ethical challenge to the caste system with its emphasis upon the primacy of *Brahmins* and *Ksatriyas*. It redefined Dharma as a supreme principle of religousness and virtue and not simply of power and force. It emphasized internal discipline and control, making external force unnecessary. It helped to free political and social institutions from priestly control, thus providing for greater secularization of politics. Buddhism also provided a new definition of human and social structure, the nature of man and society, as a basis for social, religious and cultural reconstruction.

The Buddhist emphasis upon moderation, self-discipline, elimination of wasteful and conspicuous consumption, austerity and struggle in the path of truth, greatly influenced Gandhi's political thought. His search for social and political justice in the Indian society was partly based upon his retrieval of the Indian historical tradition. The quest for truth as the essence of human existence and the foundation of structures of justice remained the main religious and philosophical premises for his political work.

Following the Hindu and Buddhist traditions and the various writings, Gandhi led a whole generation of Indian political leaders not only to struggle against foreign domination and control, but also to engage in social and cultural revolution in which all the dispossesed, discriminated against and excluded of the Indian society, especially the untouchables (whom he called the Harijans—Children of God), women and landless peasants could be made an integral part of the Indian society. His basic struggle for social and economic justice in India was based partly on the recovery of the fundamental spiritual resources of Indian traditions and partly upon the Indianization of modern European political ideas and structures as they had influenced Indian social and political life.

In this regard, he was like Mao Tse Tung of China in more than one way. As Mao loved China, Gandhi intensely loved India and stood for its liberation in all aspects. He also sought close relationship between theory and practice. Both stood for the integrity of the means and the ends. Both called for integrity in leadership by living personally selfless lives. Both were trusted, and exercised well-accepted authority within the political leadership of their nation in the process of struggle. Yet there were also significant differences between them not only because of the differences in their personalities, education and social context, but also because of the nature of the forces they were contending against. While Mao was fighting against the national government, well supported by foreign powers, Gandhi was fighting against a long established tradition of foreign colonialism and imperialism. Gandhi's fight was primarily against foreign domination and for an independent India, while Mao was fighting against the domestic imperialism and dominating classes and for a political and cultural revolution to free China for a more participatory and egalitarian society based on the freeing of the peasantry. The difference in their choice of methodologies was due to the differences in their perception of the nature of the struggle and the nature of the enemy.

Mao taught his followers to "hate" the enemy, while Gandhi taught them to "love" the enemy. For Mao the struggle could be violent and intense, and for Gandhi, it was to remain peaceful and non-violent. Their differing strategies of social change continue to influence the choices of Asians as they struggle to create societies based on social justice, economic growth, and respect for individual and corporate human rights. Both remained idealists in their perceptions of the human situation, but Mao's idealism was rather tempered by the exercise and holding of political office in the New China. Gandhi did not accept any party or governmental office as he tried to create a social revolution from grassroots upward.

Gandhi has left an impressive legacy of social and political thought which still has a considerable relevance for Asian struggle for just societies.

Gandhi's political reflection obtained within the parameters of the Hindu religious and social thought. He understood the essential religiosity of Indian history and culture, and he called for a spiritual recovery of the Hindu heritage. He defined a really free person as one devoid of selfishness and independent of all attachments. Here was an alternative to the commercialism and the mindless consumerism, but how was this to become a part of the corporate Indian economic and political ethics in the context of the massive human suffering and deprivation? How can the ideals of austerity, asceticism and poverty become the source of social and political revolution in the context of massive poverty and rigid economic and cultural inequalities? These remain relevant questions for Asian political ethics as well as for Indian political thought.

Another mainspring of Gandhian political thought, also drawn from traditional Hinduism was the ideal of *ahimsa,* commonly translated as "non-violence". He based his strategy of social action and civil disobedience on the concept of *ahimsa* and the doctrine of non-violent resistance against evil. He combined *ahimsa* with the doctrine of *satyagraha,* the struggle for truth. In Gandhi's thought truth was the end, and *ahimsa* was the means. In the ancient Indian thought the idea of *satya,* or truth, was based on the conviction that it was possible for all people to progress through their experiments with relative truth, towards the absolute truth. The doctrine of *ahimsa* meant more than non-injury or non-coercion; it was a positive faith that non-violence could convert opponents into co-seekers, effectively resist injustice, remove untruth, and protect the weak against the strong. In the interconnection between *satya* and *ahimsa,* or truth and non-violence, the chasm between means and ends was bridged in Gandhian political thought.

The fundamental political problems were thus open to the possibilities of ethical solutions if truth and non-violence were accepted as twin moral absolutes which were interdependent. Violence and non-violence were not merely alternative means towards the same end, but they were morally different in quality and essence. The following statements are relevant in this regard:
1. It is enough to know the means. Means and ends are convertible terms.
2. We always have control over the means but not over the end.
3. Our progress towards the goal will be in direct proportion to the purity of our means.
4. Instead of saying that means are after all means, we should affirm that means are everything. As the means so the ends.

Gandhi was convinced that justice cannot be secured through unjust means, freedom through tyrannical actions, welfare of the people through enmity and coercion, and social justice through national security state.

Gandhi stood for decentralization and maximum participation of the people through the encouragement of khadi economics and local handicrafts. He would encourage not only participation of people but also stimulate local initiative in all spheres of the social and political life. He insisted upon the participation of the people in the management of their village life, through the *Panchayati Raj.* All his life Gandhi has insisted on real *Swaraj,* where freedom could really be freedom for the Indian villages. He said in 1946:

> I consider the growth of cities to be an evil thing, unfortunate for mankind and the world..., and certainly unfortunate for India. The British

have exploited India through its cities. The latter have exploited the villages. The blood of the villages is the cement with which the edifice of the cities is built. I want the blood that is today inflating the arteries of the cities to run once again in the blood vessels of the villages.

He saw the possibility of India developing as a republic of villages, independent and self-reliant in all aspects. He wrote in 1942:

My idea of village swaraj is that of a complete republic independent of its neighbours for its own vital wants and yet interdependent for many others in which dependence is a necessity... The government of the village will be conducted by the Panchayat of five persons annually elected by the adult villagers, male and female, possessing minimum prescribed qualifications... The Panchayats will be the legislative, judiciary and executive combined to operate for its year of office.

Gandhi believed that the village units could become the basis of Indian democracy. India could not be really free unless the peoples of the Indian villages could become effective participants.

One of the most enduring contributions of Mahatma Gandhi was his passion for social justice and equality for all the citizens. His struggle on behalf of the millions of the untouchables of India and against the religiously sanctioned caste system was among his more enduring contributions.

Asian experience with governance since independence

The Asian struggle for liberation and independence had been long and intense and one which had helped raise the consciousness among the people that once colonialism and imperialism folded up, it would mean a new age, a new era of freedom, liberty and security for all people. The period of national stuggle had created new solidarities and new equalities which cut across the traditional rigidities of Asian societies. It had united the people not on the basis of traditional village, tribe or religion, or even caste loyalties, but on the basis of their commonness as a people. There was a new discovery of being a people all over Asia because all sectors of society had joined in the struggle. A new level of equality and participation had been achieved in Asia, never witnessed before in its history. Surely each country and nation in Asia chose its own methodology of struggle, depending upon whom or what they were struggling against, yet what united them was not simply the notion of a common enemy, but the possibilities for a new future for a free people. The rural peasantry, urban dispossessed, traditional religious and political elites, the intellectual and business elites, all joined together because they saw the possibilities of being an independent and free people. They had perceived the possibilities of creating their national identities and legitimate systems of government in which there could be universal participation of the people in creating just societies. The leadership of the national liberation movements had witnessed the power of the people because national independence could never have been won without the participation of the people.

Another important factor shaping the consciousness of the people was the awareness of the vast changes that were taking place around them in which they were not mere objects but subjects. This consciousness of the reality of change and its implications for the future of their societies was the essence of modernization and development in Asia. The people were convinced that they were on the threshold of a new age at the time of independence from where they could launch a new economic, political, cultural, social and religious revolution which can change the shape of their future history.

This goal of free, independent, self-respecting, and self-reliant people remained a political and psychological agenda of the charismatic leadership of independent Asia. These leaders provided a new verbalization and symbols for sustaining the participation of the people and creating habits of freedom and independence so that their liberation could be sustained. But the fundamental question as to how to create just societies in Asia remained. How were its great historical past and its experience under colonialism to be employed for the creation of such a political set-up in which people would exercise real power? What part of colonial experience was meaningful for the struggles of the people for participation and justice? What elements in various religious and cultural traditions could help Asian nations in creating a truly human future for its people?

It is impossible to discuss the polity and experimentation of each Asian nation or region in order to show how the fundamental questions of justice and participation for all have been dealt with. It was generally assumed that most of the Asian nations had a common struggle to create a more humane future based on social justice and participation. The existing structures of economic and political life had often worked against the people because they were based on false assumptions that Asian people want order, stability and security, and not justice, participation, and *shalom*. On the pretext of dealing with the massive problem of poverty, dictatorial and military regimes in succeeding years imposed on people the "politics of poverty", characterized by the "politics of silence", which takes away the rights of the people for self-expression and self-direction. This politics of silence has been massively used in Asia for destroying the self-confidence and self-respect of the people, thus creating new habits of dependence which was the hallmark of colonialism.

Therefore the new question in Asia is how people can be freed from this new domestic colonialism. How can mass participation in determining their own future again become a pattern of politics? How can people's consciousness be enlarged to safeguard their own rights to be human and rediscover new possibilities of participation for creating societies based on social-political justice for all?

This requires a number of important initiatives in Asia. First priority should be given to increasing awareness, especially of rural peasants, landless and bonded labourers in Asian societies. Millions of people live in the rural areas of Asia. Most of the human rights concern so far has concentrated on the urbanized sector, emphasizing important but basically bourgeois freedoms. Their rights can best be achieved through the promotion of peasant political and economic organizations to increase their ability for self-protection and self-development; otherwise the vast majority of the peasantry would continue to be "colonies" of the cities. Power to the peasants should become an important element of just and participatory societies for Asia. M.M. Thomas emphasized this relationship between justice, participation and people's awakening of human rights, at the Penang Assembly of the Christian Conference of Asia:

> Human rights are not just civil rights (civil liberties) but political rights is the basic framework for people to participate in the struggle for social and economic rights (social justice) and to safeguard them when they are realized in any measure. There are a number of foolish leftists who consider dictatorship or authoritarianism of government to be an instrument of social justice, and thereby they have played into the hands of those who want to suppress people's awakening and movements. Freedom and bread are integral to each other. And it is more so in a traditional poor society when poverty is intertwined with fatalistic attitude of stagnant cultures. People's awakening and democratic struggle are essential to overcoming poverty.

Another important prerequisite for creating just and participating societies in Asia is the rediscovery of people's cultural and religious roots. The roots of creativity and innovation of the people lie in the cultural and historical experiences with power and its uses and abuses. The religious cultures of Asia are not esoteric or rigid. They are flexible and pragmatic, without being unethical. They are at the centre of the cultural and social histories of Asia. We need to discover the centrality of the people as the heart of the political process. This is not an exercise in the glorification of the cultural history of Asia, but a demand for the retrieval of the political experience of the people that can be used meaningfully for the reconstruction of a genuinely Asian political ethics based on the richness of its own historical past.

Prof. Masao Takenaka is never tired of reminding Asian intellectuals that:

> In order to enact justice we need the participation of people. In order to foster participation of people we need to revitalize the cultural expression of people. One of the first steps for the restoration of the selfhood of the people is to let people express themselves. As long as people are robbed of their own language and thinking they are enslaved by the ruler's power...
>
> The cultural reformation and renaissance now happening in Asia is a sign of the beginning of the process where people are speaking in their own language and clarifying their own aspiration and goals in their own terms.[5]

Conclusion

The reconstruction of political ethics in an Asian context requires that we take the total range of Asian experience in politics, ancient and contemporary, into consideration. Hinduism, Buddhism, Confucianism, Islam, and Christianity, have all contributed significant political ideas and experiences, but so has the contemporary experience with imperialism and colonialism. The nationalist struggles for independence and liberation drew inspiration from the ancient civilizational experience and from the contemporary experiences of Asian societies. It was this synthesis that provided a measure of cohesion and solidarity among the people during their struggle for liberation. So long as public policy was based upon a measure of this synthesis, it was able to engage people's enthusiasm and energies for their own development. As more emphasis was put upon imitative development on Western conceptions, it led to an alienation between the public policy-makers and the people. People became objects rather than subjects of their own development as they were divorced from the centre of their moral and spiritual tradition. The source of legitimacy for political power and authority was also lost, thus opening the way for manipulation and exploitation of the people. People lost control of the political processes. This created a serious threat to the life, liberty and happiness of the people because there did not exist any positive limitation upon the exercise of power.

The reconstruction of political ethics in Asia must rest upon rediscovery of the religious ethos of the various religious traditions of Asia. Politics in Asia

---

[5] Masao Takenaka, "A Reflection on Social Responsibility in the Asian Context", in *Escape from Domination,* Tokyo, International Affairs CCA, 1980, p.17.

cannot be a completely secular and autonomous sphere of experience. It must be rooted in the deepest form of religious experience. This has nothing to do with the restoration of the clerical or the priestly classes to the place of pre-eminence in the political order. It also does not mean turning religion into an ideology. Authentic religious ethos means discovery of that source of judgment which prevents politics from degenerating into an instrument of repression.

In the context of Asia, therefore, the task of the reconstruction of political ethics will have to be dialogical — a dialogue between various religions and ideologies, each operating from its unique centre and spirituality. The quest for justice, equality, change, order, stability, participation, and welfare of the people, is a common agenda for all people in Asia. People must stand at the centre of all this as a collective symbol.

Some aspects of political morality in the Caribbean

NEVILLE LINTON

Caribbean history and reality

The Caribbean is an unusual part of the third world in that the societies were formed by migration, voluntary and involuntary, from the old worlds of Africa, Asia and Europe. The Latin American mainland, which shares the experience of migration, still has substantial sectors of its populations coming from the Amerindian people who were there before the European incursions. But these can only be found in pockets as minorities in the Caribbean, although there are considerable mestizo populations in the northern islands.

The modern Caribbean was thus shaped wholly out of colonialism, racism and slavery, and therefore this affects the style of political ethics in the region in a fundamental way.

The geographic position of the Caribbean islands on the edge of the Western hemisphere made them the first prizes to be fought over by the European invaders. It also contributed to the wide variety of cultural influences in the region today. All the leading maritime powers had colonies there — Spain, Holland, France and Britain — as well as the late imperial maritime power, the USA.

Colonialism and slavery are, by nature, conditions of domination and exploitation and thus essentially undemocratic. The historic experience of the islands therefore did not favour the development of high standards of political morality. Indeed the movements of political democracy and the tradition of intellectual debate which were growing up in Europe and America during the eighteenth to nineteenth centuries had no parallel in the Caribbean region. There were no populations, native to the region, to develop and refine a historic domestic culture. Rather, there had to be movements of rebellion and the recourse to conflict to get rid of a conqueror. It was only in the twentieth century that progressive change came to the region. Those who exercised power began to introduce changes in the government, thus imparting a concept of peaceful change and of government based on some philosophical and ethical principles.

This latter phenomenon occurred in the British, Dutch and American colonies where, after World War II, the authorities made significant constitutional changes towards self-government. Such changes did not come until later in the French territories, although independence was precluded until very recently.

In the northern Caribbean there had been, of course, the striking early and unique case of the Haitian revolution, the precursor of all third world revolutions. That experiment, however, soon foundered under the pressures of external hostility and internal class and ethnic dissension. In a relatively short time Haiti degenerated into dictatorship, and that has continued. In the nineteenth century, civil strife in Haiti and the neighbouring independent Dominican Republic contributed to a political culture based on the crude use of power and established the principle of the rule of the leader — the caudillo.

The ruling group surrounding the caudillo could exploit the country and the people at will and they opened the society to the exploitation of foreign capital for their own profit. A mendicant and corrupt political culture developed in these countries, since the elites did not even have a tradition of *noblesse oblige* or of magnanimity, as is possible with a class of old indigenous elites. Nor were there any significant cases of "enlightened dictatorship". Moreover, the military emerged as an important political and social force. Indeed the power of the ruling group has been so strong that the pacification of the people has been quite effective, particularly in Haiti where the social and intellectual growth of the people was restricted. In the Dominican Republic, there remained open avenues for ideas from Europe and America and the struggle of democratic parties to survive led to open conflict in the sixties and to eventual democratic elections in the seventies.

In the south of the region, which until post-World War II was colonial, the political experience was not as harsh. In these essentially small societies there was some respect for due process and some defence of the rights of the individual even under colonialism. The fact that the societies did interact with the metropoles also meant that there was some flow of ideas. There was also an active role for political parties (save the Marxists who were often restricted if not banned), even if those parties did not operate on a basis of full adult suffrage until just before independence. Puerto Rico and the French Antilles were of course special cases of integration into one political system with the metropole, the former in the fifties and the latter in the sixties.

The English-speaking islands became independent, therefore, within the political tradition of the British Westminster system and more or less assumed the political ethics of that system, since there were no major competing concepts either from the African or Asian background. However, partly because of colonialism-bred elitism, and partly because of the residual influences of the non-European societies remaining buried in the pysche of the people, there was a tendency to look for a father-figure in political leadership, and thus "charismatic" leadership flourished. Also because of the small size of the societies a leader, once chosen, could remain in power for a long time. This type of practice modified the principles on which the Westminster system was based and opened the way even more to political patronage. A political party in the West Indies is often a broad communal institution and not just a political one.

These characteristics are also more or less true of the politics of the Netherlands Antilles, even though the formal political system is based on the European continental model. More importantly, those territories, like the French and American, did not have any strong independence movements. The main thrust towards independence and towards what might be called third world consciousness and awareness obtained primarily in the English-speaking territories. All the non-Latin territories achieved independence without any physical conflict. The process was smooth and virtually uneventful; as a result there was no crucible of struggle to strengthen the sense of nationalism and unity of the populace. This is a particular shortcoming for these New World societies where the sense of nationalism is not always very strong, where there is a colonial tendency to give superior value to things metropolitan rather than things local — due to the cultures not having jelled for long, nor having achieved any prominence. There is also a strong tradition of outward migration for economic reasons, since the economies in the post-war period, when the plantation system declined seriously, could not, as organized, support their populations. That much of the modern political ethic is thus opportunistic is not surprising, particularly in societies where poverty and lack of power for the majority have been the norm.

An interesting aspect of the Caribbean region is the lack of inter-state conflict after the period of maritime imperial competition. There is no history of wars between the territories save for the two neighbours of Haiti and the Dominican Republic. There are no large military establishments capable of overseas adventures save in contemporary Cuba, and the US holdings which carry major US bases. As a result, a tradition of peace has been the norm in inter-regional relationships, and there is a strong feeling that this is part of the accepted morality of inter-state relations in the Caribbean. Cuba's military establishment is not seen, so far, as a threat to this concept.

The political style, outside of the large, older independent island states to the north, has generally been moderate in the region, in part because of the harmony of inter-ethnic relationships amongst very mixed populations. It is a mark of the *independent* Caribbean that there is a high degree of ethnic tolerance. Political competition has rarely reached a stage of violence or of such ethnic exclusiveness as to cause major resentment.

Of course, being a region wholly created and dominated by the powers of Euro-America, the economics of the region reflect this dominance and so do much of the ethics. Since the economic circumstances of the region historically expressed extreme forms of exploitation and dominance of foreign ownership and of white supremacy, the immorality of the system was extreme, sycophancy was rampant and conceptions of cultural superiority/inferiority were deep-seated. The independence period has been used by the new states, in the post-war era, to offset these.

One institutional development towards the above has been the establishment of a regional integration movement by the English-speaking states — the Caribbean Community (Caricom). The Caricom idea assumes that self-reliance is a needed politico-economic goal. In this respect, a commitment to serious political-economic development is a way of testing the morality of regimes. In the region the older independent states, e. g. Haiti, the Dominican Republic or pre-Castro Cuba, were not dedicated to the development process in the true sense. Moreover they were also not involved in the pursuit of independent and creative foreign policies, but rather were appendages to the American hemispheric system and global policies. The post-war history of much of the Caribbean, save for a couple of exceptions, has not been filled with the extreme abuse and poverty which characterizes much of the third world. Therefore the state of political morality is not at the most corrupt levels.

For all of the Caribbean the history of the last twenty-five years has been a struggle for identity, for just development, for self-reliance, and true independence. These add up to a search for a wholesome political society.

Political ethics in the Caribbean context

Modern political life is dominated by the state system. It is through the vehicle of the state that we are in contact with political reality whether at the domestic or international level. Therefore, the nature of the state, that enterprise which the citizens share in common, is fundamental to the formation of the political ethic.

The ethical health of a society in the contemporary world predominantly depends upon the purposes of and the principles by which the state is run.

The post-war era has been characterized by the dominance of ideological conflict. Thus the approach to political ethics has been seen very much through ideological glasses; concepts of democracy, law and social organization, for instance, have been ideologically defined.

Since most of the third world emerged into political independence within this period, these states have essentially shaped their political values on the pattern of the dominant metropolis to the North rather than from their own cultures or environments. The current experiment in Iran, whatever one thinks of it, is one of the boldest and most serious attempts to break away from this pattern.

The Caribbean, due to its New World origins, is a particularly dependent part of the third world. It is, even more than most, a society by reflection and much of its political development, social institutions, customs and value structures were and are defined by the patterns of the North. In brief, throughout the region imperialism has left a tradition of competitive societies, organized economically on capitalist lines, operating governmentally, whatever their size, conventional and shopworn concepts of the "national interest", "raison d'état" and "sovereignty".

Since these states have had a longer experience of colonialism and dictatorship than of independence or democracy it is not surprising that, in reality, there is more concern for the rights of leaders or elites than for the rights of the masses, and that real power continues to be concentrated in the hands of a minority.

The historical background of these territories means that there has never been any serious examination of fundamental questions such as "What is the nature of the state?", "What are the purposes and functions of governments?", "Who is the state for and is it necessary?", "What form should the state take?", "What form should elections take?" All of these are matters of inherited and received opinion. The region lacks a sense of political philosophy and indeed, for the most part, lacks an established political class.

Thus the area, in its political style, is divided between those states to which democracy came as a post-colonial gift and those, longer established, which have had to struggle, successfully or otherwise, to achieve democracy e.g. Cuba, Haiti and the Dominican Republic. In the former, politics has been basically conservative, electoral and constitutionally stable.

The absence of a political class or the existence of only a very small one has serious implications for the maintenance of an acceptable political ethic. The presence of such a class implies a significant group of people who are both politically conscious and dedicated to serving the society. In the colonial societies there often was such a group, albeit small, which led the movement for independence. The group was usually high-principled and many had an idealistic view of politics and a genuine calling to serve. What has happened in the post-colonial period is that the struggle for power and for spoils has seen an emergence of the professional politician, agent of the political party and of particular interest groups rather than servant of the people, with his values rooted in the exploitative past.

The extent to which regional politicians have become vulnerable to corruption has drawn attention to the question of their remuneration. In the absence of a political class operating from principles of *noblesse oblige* and/or a comfortable economic base, we have more and more the politician who looks to his political salary for real income, or uses his political position for economic gain. There is therefore serious support for the view, novel in most of the Caribbean, that the remuneration of politicians should be as generous as possible so as to restrict the possibility of venality. This view had been held before only for judges; now interestingly enough it also includes the police. There has also been, again a novelty, a tendency to create legislation dealing with the integrity of politicians and senior public officers.

There is an acute need in these societies for tackling questions regarding the utility and morality of elections, the ethical rules for bureaucracy, police military and judiciary, and the ethical standards that should inform decision-making. Here it should be noted that the political class, properly conceived, is wider than the direct actors such as the politicians and bureaucrats, and involves those citizens who are aware of the state as a political vehicle and use it as such. The morality of this group therefore helps to set the morality of the political actors. It is an unfortunate fact that some sectors, like the educated or professional classes, are themselves corrupt and so cannot call the politicians to accountability. It is clear that engineers and scientists, for instance, often do not bear public witness about the reprehensible decisions which are often being taken in the society and which often lead to major environmental, energy or health problems later. Such environmental crimes are particularly evident in societies which are more economically sophisticated such as Puerto Rico.

A case in point in the region is oil-rich Trinidad where there is a serious debate raging about priorities in the spending of the national wealth, on whether prestige projects should be built in a context of both domestic and regional poverty and as to whether or not Trinidad wealth should be shared with its Caricom neighbours. Again there is great questioning of the probity of the judiciary in recent years in Suriname and Guyana, and a first-time confrontation with the issue as to what extent the judiciary should be free of executive influence. In Guyana and Grenada the question of the nature and necessity of elections is a pregnant one — in both cases there is an underlying and debatable issue: the concept of a necessary phase of dictatorship by a "progressive party" with a "revolutionary" function in history.

In relationship to political morality it is obvious that the factors of information and education are crucial. The information system of this area is patterned on Western lines but, for the most part, lacks the varied infrastructure which would make a Western-type media system tolerable. Thus we have a situation where the area is dominated by the information priorities and prejudices of the international Western media system. This has significant impact on social and cultural life-styles, quite apart from the economic and political effects. As to education, the underlying philosophy of our systems educates people to expect and tolerate privilege and inequality, to think of exploitation as normal and to accept the struggle for material advantage as the norm of social organization. Thus technology as it comes into the society lacks a guiding morality and is used more to increase exploitation rather than to improve the quality of life. There is no significant input which is non-Western, even though there are peoples of African and Asian descent and considerable sectors of the population follow Hinduism and Islam. This neglect of culture is an area of political immorality.

Fundamentally then, the turmoil, instability and loss of faith which we are seeing in the Caribbean is because the old systems are failing. That is not necessarily a tragedy as those systems were not based on the needs and values of the peoples of these lands. It is therefore a characteristic of a period of transition but that raises moral questions even more sharply as to the goal of transition.

What is needed now therefore is the first serious engagement with basic issues of political philosophy as a people seek to shape a future of their own making. This is a responsibility which all sectors of the politically aware class should share, not leaving things to politicians as is the tradition. There is some hope that this is possible as the knowledge explosion of the twentieth century has affected the Caribbean, and there is a widespread desire to attack the structural roots of backwardness and an evolution away from a naive acceptance of explanations of what happened in history.

But a new type of politician is needed in the region, one who is prepared to encourage participatory systems, one who cherishes the world of the arts and who cares about the environment and is ready to give prominence to these areas above material development. There is also need for political leadership which will break the pattern of undemocratic leadership and authoritarian party structures, which believes in the possibility of achieving liberation from poverty and can offer the people valid goals of really free societies. The concept of a free society and an understanding of it is still to be achieved in the Caribbean. Currently there is a dangerous tendency, because of the sufferings of the past, to reduce progress to material welfare and to accept unbalanced development. It is true that the improvement of living standards is a moral imperative, but one must always be alert to the fact that most development decisions have ethical implications which, in the long run, are of utmost importance. The pressures on new states are such that there is a particular need for a sense of moral direction in the difficult first phases of economic development. Effective systems of accountability are therefore needed.

These states should seek to go *against* the current of less and less attention to values such as the rule of reason, the blessing of courtesy, the importance of justice and the necessity for high standards in all types of endeavours. In the Caribbean questions of cultural continuity and identity are of the highest moral importance, as the region has been culturally subjugated for so long. The survival of the desire for national identity both in the French-ruled territories of Martinique, Guadeloupe and Guyana and in US-ruled Puerto Rico, and the rejection of the lure of an unequal integration, are remarkable examples of integrity.

Whereas, at the individual level, it is possible for the powerful to show generosity or domination to the weak, at the inter-state level exploitation of the weak by the strong is the norm. The current international system is thus by nature immoral. The exploitation of the third world by the powers, i.e. states and corporations, is assisted, at the domestic level, by politicians and elites who share the competitive ethic.

What is particularly sad in the Caribbean is that this domination is so comprehensive that it even affects the approach to major international issues. There is a lack of strong moral interest, in the society at large, in major global issues of liberation and human rights; and a tendency of the elites to line up on these matters, outside the question of racism, according to the standpoint of their metropolitan patrons of the right or the left. It is an unfortunate fact that only in states of a Marxist orientation are the masses seriously educated about the realities of the international system.

Throughout the region there is a depressingly similar pattern of loss of faith in the morality of politicians of the conventional political systems. Only in little Barbados would there be an exception to the above statement, since the public there continues to believe in the probity of the political leadership. Cuba's socialist experiment would also not be included in the above, as it is a non-conventional system. There the efforts towards a non-exploitative and participatory system are so novel that the issue of political morality would require a particular case study and a new yardstick of judgments.

It is generally expected that there will be corruption, and that there will be pay-offs for most deals involving the government. People are not surprised that politicians get rich in office, they even expect it — and are ready to tolerate this if the politician is efficient. In much of the region the world of public office is more and more seen as being associated with benefits for the holder — gains in money and status — rather than with service, both by the public and by the office-seeker. What this reflects is the growth of the approach to political office as a high status job rather than of individuals being drawn into the field through burning conviction.

It should be noted here that in most countries people are cynical about politicians but not about the political system. They still, for the most part, believe that the system can work, i.e. when there is a democracy and not a dictatorship. They continue to support the liberal-democratic ideals. There is no strong demand for a more participatory system: rather there is a desire for a fair working of the existing democratic order. The focus is on the immorality of the actors rather than of the system.

While this is the public view it is a questionable one. For there seems to be a link between underdevelopment and political corruption. Certainly at the level of the international system the link is clear — it is well established that the system works for the exploitation of the third world to the benefit of the developed world. In this respect the corruption of the decision-makers and power brokers of the industrialized world — both political and non-political — is a harsh reality.

Nothing demonstrates this more than the failure in getting any significant progress on the half-way house of the New International Economic Order. The unwillingness of the industrialized powers to undertake even marginal adjustment reflects a tradition where dependence has been internalized as the moral norm and interdependence is not understood.

At the domestic level it can be argued that much of the disorder in the third world, the poor record of the governments there and the moral failure of the politicians is the result of the international system of dependence. Thus corruption breeds corruption. For many a third world politician, and this is true of the Caribbean, resorts to political oppression when the government cannot cope with the demands of the society and of the times. But often the inability to cope is not just because of political or economic inefficiency but because of the harsh pressures of the international economic system.

Political and economic oppression in the Caribbean has led to the rise of oppositions so motivated by moral concerns that they are ready to take extreme political action. This came to a head in Cuba and the subsequent Castro regime has been seen as a regime with a liberating political morality, and as a standard-bearer for a people's democracy. Revolutionary action is therefore even being seen as a purifying process and is not, as in the past, envisaged as a process of power struggle which will bring in a new caudillo. The concept of the "just revolution" certainly is currently popular amongst the young, particularly those of socialist bent, and there is much optimism that the revolutionary process can cleanse society. Revolutionary parties in the Caribbean are the only ones raising serious questions about a new moral basis for political organization, about genuine peoples' participation and about putting mass welfare before conventional ideas of national growth. While there has not been much experience in the region with the situation created after such revolutions, there is some reason for concern that revolutionary governments themselves fall very rapidly into the pattern of arguing that the end justifies the means. Thus in the Caribbean there is increasing questioning of the moral posture of the new Grenadian government. Its leaders had been vocal advocates of human rights when in opposition, but themselves are breaching major civil and political rights now that they are in office. In defence they give the usual "reasons of state" argument — national security needs. But the "national" interest here is the defence and survival of the new government which has "captured" the state. The government is, of course, existing in a hostile international environment and so judgment has to be suspended for a while, particularly as it is experimenting with forms of popular participation and is dedicated to establish economic rights for the masses.

In the democratic states of the Caribbean there is, amongst elites and middle classes, the traditional Western pattern of putting, in practice, more emphasis on political and civil rights than on social and economic rights in assessing societal performance. But there is reason to suspect that the masses reverse the priority or at least have them on par. The prejudice in favour of civil and political rights has its origins in a global history of material inadequacy, and thus of a development of our philosophy and social sciences on premises of scarcity. It is the tragedy of our time that we have not adjusted our way of looking at the world to take account of the new reality — the ability of people everywhere in the scientific era to provide a world of plenty where all can have adequate welfare. This is no longer a matter of utopian political theory but of our actual capability.

Such a new historical reality has wide-ranging implications for political morality — it requires new perceptions and a new consciousness. Small states such as those in the Caribbean can do little to contribute to the recognition of the new reality and their experiments at establishing new domestic orders will founder, as in the case of Manley's Jamaica, as long as the international system remains under the control of the old morality.

It is thus important that an institution of such prestige as the church, which in the past has contributed significantly to developing the philosophical underpinnings of society, does pay attention to the issue of political morality. A great debate is needed, globally, on whether a new world is not possible without cataclysmic violence. The dominant morality of the day, and its philosophical underpinnings, assume that such violence is necessary. A phase in world history when a dominant minority establishment of power is being challenged by a dynamic emerging majority is necessarily one fraught with moral questions. It is, after all, the world order which is at issue.

Political ethics and the Caribbean church

The historic role of the Caribbean church

Traditionally the Caribbean church, coming as it does out of a wholly colonial history, did not pay much attention to political issues on the one hand and supported the established powers on the other.

At various times, however, individual church people — both clergy and laity — have stood up and fought the political authorities on matters of principle. This goes back, notably, even to the time of slavery. The institutional church however has always cooperated with and supported the "legal" authorities and has never questioned the fundamentals of the political system — even under colonialism. The exceptions to this have been a few non-conformist churches, especially in Jamaica and Guyana, which were characterized by their sense of cultural identity with the masses, e. g. the Baptist churches.

The Caribbean churches are reflections of Western society and accept its principles and mode of development. Christianity came, like other institutions, to the society as a higher given, and has been accepted unquestioningly for the most part. Since the societies were immigrant ones created by the West, there was no strong counter-culture which would counter the principles of Christianity. (Christianity was imposed on the slaves and their religions deliberately attacked and driven out.) Thus the style of church-state relations, the role of the church and the European attitude of the relation of religion to everyday life were internalized and accepted.

The result in colonial societies — which are, by definition, "non democratic" societies — was:
a) the development of a church focusing on the individual and the person's salvation rather than on the society and the role of its institutions;

b) the development of the tradition that Christian principles had more to do with personal ethics than with business ethics or affairs of state. Thus rapacious businessmen were, at the same time, "pillars" of the church, and mainstream political leaders were given pride of place and attention by the church. That European churches did, in varying ways and times, play political roles was not a conciousness transferred to the colonies.

The training which clergy received prepared them to be missionaries, conventional pastors, and teachers — and not to be social analysts or social activists. In addition, for a long time, most of the ministers were expatriates — this remains true today in some territories, e. g. Curacao — and the majority of these, particularly in the post-colonial period, were not prepared to get involved in "politics".

The "non political" role of the church was accepted by the people particularly as its welfare and educational work were meeting felt needs, especially for neglected sectors of the society. At best in terms of politics the church was a watchdog against "abuse" but even that posture was from a conservative point of reference.

The church and social action

The education system offered by the church fitted into, and was similar to, the state system. While it contributed to the modernizing of the people it was also conformist in character. Thus the church contributed to the reaction of a post-colonial elite which was not oriented to transformation and liberation.

When, from the seventies, serious challenges came to the "structures of domination" the churches were not close to and did not relate to the social and political movements which were challenging the established order. Indeed, till today, the churches do not have many links with urban grassroots or people's agrarian movements — admittedly there are few examples of these in the region.

It needs to be stressed that political conflict rarely is extreme in the Dutch, Commonwealth and French Caribbean (outside of Haiti). The military is not a vigorous political force and even where there was a military coup (Surinam) the style of the military is not abrasive and authoritarian.

There is no great desire for an alternative society — the people indeed yearn for the Western model, and only a small minority questions that. This is because there is no strong thrust of a counter-culture in these immigrant "New World" societies.

There is basic allegiance to the Western-type political and economic systems even though they have so far proved incapable of dealing with the ambitions of the societies. However it must be noted that the region (outside

Haiti) does not have the grinding poverty which is found in parts of Asia and Africa. In the Caribbean societies, where colonialism has fostered dependency, and which have no post-state identity to inspire self-reliance, there is a resignation which accepts that "the poor we will always have with us". The churches are, for the most part, of a similar view.

The contemporary effort of the churches

The phase of formal ecumenical institutionalization (the CCC was founded in 1971) also marks the period of serious attempts by the church to be active in social and political change.

In this period there have been a few cases of individual church people publicly bearing witness at trade union demonstrations or with peoples' movements, but this is still unusual.

Many of the established churches are verbally supporting the need for social change and some are questioning the direction of development of the society. However, for the most part, the churches remain divorced from political issues and are consciously apolitical. Thus, for instance, a council of churches in one state recently rejected a suggestion, from various civic groups, to organize and sponsor a public seminar on an important issue — the conditions for independence — with the statement "the issues were political and the churches should not interfere with the political". As far as international issues are concerned there is little interest as those matters seem far away from the Caribbean or not within the capacity of mini-states to do anything about. Thus disarmament, TNCs, the NIEO or ecology do not attract discussion in the church community. When the Christian Peace Conference recently made overtures, the churches were out of their depth.

The general problem seems to be not only that it is thought that the churches are not suited or equipped for handling the political sphere but, even more fundamentally, that politics is necessarily "dirty" business and its ethics "peculiar". It is clear that the church needs to understand, and come to terms with, the phenomenon of power — in particular, to appreciate that even its creative uses may have to involve the application of force.

There have recently been cases of direct challenges to the churches to adjust to major political change:

a) Grenada: after the coup of March 1979, the churches found themselves faced by a revolutionary regime of a Marxist character. Although the society and church welcomed the overthrow of the former petty oppressive regime, the church has not been able to accept the character of the new government. As a result, a far more serious rift is developing between church and state than under Prime Minister Gairy. The basic problem here seems to be that the churches put a higher value on constitutional ethics than on a "developmental ethic" which puts substance before form and which stresses the priority of needs before those of freedom of choice.

b) Surinam: the soldier coup in Surinam has so far only brought in a modest reformist regime although there is much verbalizing about "socialism". However, the Christian Council in Surinam had, for some years, taken an active role on social issues and had even submitted memoranda to the former government suggesting specific programmes of development for the country. They were thus well placed to deal with the post-coup government, which is dedicated to a policy of transformation. As a result there is an open dialogue between church and state on political, social and economic issues — unlike the Grenada situation.

c) Jamaica: over the last ten years political competition has reached very acrimonious levels in the vigorous two-party system of that state, with a regrettably high incidence of violence. Even more regrettably, some of the church leaders have become openly party partisan, with unfortunate results for the image of the church.

Ecumenism and political change

It is largely through the institutional ecumenical movement, the Caribbean Conference of Churches, that the churches have tried to engage the issue of political ethics.

The CCC has been a conscious agency for raising political awareness, attacking false social values, developing a liberating education programme, promoting concepts of distributive justice, and questioning the relevance of the role of the churches. It has emerged as a voice interpreting the problems of the poor and oppressed and as an agency which assists them towards self-reliance.

The CCC has started a debate on the role of order and of tension in the society and as to what is the meaning of peace. In this way it is seeking to move the society to think seriously about "political ethics" and about the possibility of fundamental change.

While the churches have always responded to individual human needs and have always upheld the cause of conventional human rights, the challenge of politics is significantly different — and demanding. This is particularly so in new states where the governments are jealous of their newly-won power and would prefer that the churches either remain in their traditional role or become subservient to the purposes of the government.

The task demands changes in the very structure of the church and in the education of the clergy. The simple fact is that, as constituted, the Caribbean church was not equipped to deal effectively with political ethics at a time of epochal social change. It is to the credit of the churches that they are currently trying to adjust to the task, with much internal debate, disagreement and emotion.

While, hopefully, the church will make a significant contribution to the creation of a new value system, that process is very much dominated by other estates — principally governmental, business and trade union — and influenced by the vigorous media network. Each of these estates is seen as related to areas where there are real, practical outcomes for the people. In the Caribbean, the churches need to commit themselves more integrally to programmes which directly serve the material welfare of the people, and redress the balance where "ethics" are seen as related essentially to the individual's personal and inner life.

In an era where violence, domestic and international, is on the increase, the church needs to develop and apply a practical theology on political change. Just as it responded to the demands of an earlier time with schools and hospitals and disciplined religious orders, today it has to find a relevant institutional style, e.g. alternative education, cooperative communities and animators. Governments today are under pressure from the masses to perform — given their inadequacies there is often the temptation to turn to repression. The church, which has far too often in the past been guilty of providing sanction and support for unjust structures, today, with an alert and aroused people, has to be true to itself. Caribbean politicians have long used religious themes for their own purposes — manipulative not educational. The debate about a just and participatory society is an entirely new one for the region and there is therefore a role for the churches to make a unique contribution to a society which has never asked itself basic questions about the nature of the social order and progress.

The churches have the opportunity to challenge the basic assumptions of freedom and order which we have inherited from the West and examine anew concepts such as justice, participation, power and its control, sustainability and the "supremacy" of the people in the context of the Caribbean — a bridge community between the West and the "third world.".

Conclusion

The modern political life of the Caribbean nations, small third world states off-shore a dynamic power like the USA, has been affected both positively and negatively by the influence of that state. This proximity meant that the process towards the establishment of real independence and valid societies has been delayed.

Caribbean states need to turn inward and find themselves out of their own resources and from their own inspiration. To this end it is necessary that they further implement the move towards regional integration which has been long part of their instinct and mythology. Regional unity is a material imperative, a cultural imperative, and an emotional one. In the modern world small states need to cooperate to deal with the pressures of the great states and of the international economy.

These states have a contribution to make to the ethical life of the New World; such a contribution depends on the serious belief that these societies can have useful and creative perspectives and values which the larger states might not have. This is particularly true as they are multicultural, non-white states and so can bring a unique sensitivity to their interaction in the world.

But, at the cultural level, much needs to be done domestically as integration and harmony is not deep enough. The specific contribution of the Hindu and Muslim populations, for instance, remains sectoral and parallel, rather than automatically defining and shaping the mainstream of the culture and thrust of the society.

The Caribbean has to move from societies dominated by the ethic of the West and the colonizer to a new synthesis of cultures representative of one meaning of the term "New World". In the Caribbean we have to learn how to respect the poor and weak, categories which are particularly miserable and scorned in colonial societies, and to respect ourselves. We have to learn democracy beyond the formalities and evolve into participation, through the imperatives of our situation, and our own societal view, rather than by following trends in the West. The challenge to the Caribbean is how to get a population, from a background of slavery and colonialism, to participate with self-confidence in the society and in the world; how to get various races to cooperate and participate fully in the society, and how to industrialize without automatically copying the amoral and immoral practices of traditional capitalism. This is the greatest practical and ethical task ahead of the region.

It is not easy for a society with such a past to evolve into a wholesome new polity, but the effort is under way. What is required is a whole new way of looking at the structure of society, its purposes and its methods — this "revolutionary" approach has begun in the region, particularly amongst the young. The most fundamental ethical imperative is for us to free ourselves from the burdens of the past.

Political ethics in the European context: the ethics of peace

WOLFGANG HUBER

The significance of the peace issue as an example

Since the end of the seventies, the discussion of basic questions of political ethics in Europe has centred again on the issue of our responsibility for peace. This has focused interest once again on an issue which has exemplary importance for the problem of political ethics. For in no political area is the connection and tension between ethics and politics stronger than in that we define as the politics of peace. The object of the politics of peace is one which is supremely binding on us ethically, yet the means to which it appeals are supremely questionable ethically. The attempt to solve this dilemma in the Christian tradition has taken opposite directions. From its very origins, Christianity has been a movement which renounces violence. At the beginning of the history of Christianity we find, therefore, Christians refusing to join the violent action of governments and this attitude has continued to claim allegiance right down to our own times. In the fourth century, when the church began to shoulder some responsibility for the fate of the Roman Empire, theologians tried to subordinate the use of force by the state — regarded as inescapable — to the goal of peace, and to develop criteria whereby to justify the state's use of force in certain circumstances. The result was the doctrine of the "just war". The development of modern means of mass destruction has intensified the controversy between these two classic positions. At the same time, however, it has become questionable whether it is any longer possible for Christians and the churches simply to accept the coexistence of these two positions side by side.

The reason is that in the present situation, the dilemma becomes intolerable. Peace is a goal which has a supreme ethical claim on us. But the military means which are supposed to secure peace are not susceptible of any ethical justification. They are weapons of mass destruction. If they were to be used, they would destroy what they are supposed to defend; they would cause long-term effects which go far beyond the framework of responsibility acceptable to anyone living today. Does this situation compel Christians, even those who do not regard themselves as absolute pacifists, nevertheless to affirm their "selective" renunciation of force in respect of these weapons of mass destruction? In other words, is "nuclear pacifism" the step they are required to take today? Or are they required by the development of weapons of mass destruction to re-examine the whole question of their attitude to violence as such? Or is it still possible, even in the present situation, to offer criteria for the conditions in which the threat and the use of military force can be justified? Above all, what is the relation between the decision called for here and the confession of the Christian faith?

Among the factors affecting the discussion of these questions in the European context is the development of the ecumenical political ethic. At each stage in the ecumenical movement, the ecumenical political ethic has been defined by some definite key problem, a leading idea (*idée directrice*). In the post-Amsterdam years from 1948 onwards, "freedom" was the key theme — in the overall framework of the concept of the "responsible society". Beginning with the programme on "rapid social change" and then more clearly after the Geneva Conference on "Church and Society", the question of "social justice" was the key theme. Fresh urgency was given to the question of peace already at the Nairobi Assembly in 1975, which initiated the programme against militarism and the arms race and for disarmament. This question has since then become increasingly urgent not only for Europe but also for the whole world.

The Nairobi Assembly called on the churches to declare their readiness to live without armed protection and to urge on their governments decisive steps towards disarmament. Behind this summons was doubt as to whether it was still possible for Christians to accept protection at the price of the threat of such weapons. The WCC Hearing on nuclear arms and disarmament in November 1981 considered this question and answered it in the following terms:

> The ethical question is this: Is the possession of nuclear weapons, the plan and the readiness to use them, to be condemned morally in precisely the same way as the actual use of such weapons? There is, of course, on the one hand a profound difference between intention and act, not least between their possible consequences. On the other hand, there is an element of ambiguity in threats, especially if their efficacy depends to some extent on uncertainty as to whether or not they will actually be carried out. It is impossible, however, to escape the conclusion that readiness to act unjustly is already tainted by what is reprehensible in the unjust act itself. It would be going too far to assert that the strategy of nuclear deterrence, together with the weapons on which it relies, is absolutely sinful in precisely the same way as actual nuclear warfare. But we believe that this

strategy and these weapons are sinful and that their possession and the readiness to use them are reprehensible in the sight of God and should be declared so by the church.

The question thus raised has at the same time been discussed in a number of the WCC's member churches. It was dealt with in exceptional depth by the churches in the Netherlands. The process of discussion in the Netherlands Reformed Church, a model of clarity and thoroughness, led to the conclusion that in the present situation the church must reject not only the use but also the deployment of weapons of mass destruction. For they are inseparable from the readiness to change God's creation back into the chaos from which it was rescued.

The Federation of Evangelical Churches in the Netherlands took up this question with great urgency. In autumn 1982, its Synod stated:

The threat to all living things which excessive armaments represent is a challenge to our faith. By tacitly accepting it, we set ourselves in opposition to God the Creator, for we have been commanded by him to preserve the creation and we are denied any right to destroy it. The question here, therefore, is whether we obey or disobey God. ... Can Christians share preparations for defence by means of nuclear weapons when it is beyond a peradventure that the "defence" destroys irrevocably what it is meant to protect? Can Christians share in the threat to use weapons which increase the probability of the very disaster they are meant to prevent? Can Christians and churches, faced with the inconceivable horror of a possible war, justify armed violence as a means of securing peace and defending the neighbour? In the long run, the answer to such questions cannot remain open.

In a memorandum entitled "The Maintenance, Promotion, and Renewal of Peace" (November 1981), the Evangelical Church in Germany (EKD) maintained that participation in military armament is *still* a possible mode of action for Christians. It thus retained an ethical distinction between the threat to use military force and its actual use. It still reckons with the possibility of Christians approving the stationing of nuclear weapons on the grounds that they can and should protect peace with freedom. But this possible Christian decision, confirmed once again for a period of transition, is hedged around in the memorandum itself by a series of incisive conditions. It is only a defensible decision in a situation in which all efforts are directed towards reducing the causes of war, developing methods of overcoming conflicts by non-violence, and undertaking effective steps to reduce the level of armaments.

In other words, the possession of nuclear weapons is made conditional on the deployment of every effort to make the nuclear deterrent and the threat to employ weapons of mass destruction superfluous by securing peace by political means. The continuation of the nuclear arms race in Europe is irreconcilable with this requirement. Even within the terms of the position developed in the EKD's peace memorandum, the only choice for Christians is a clear and unequivocal rejection of the continuation of the nuclear arms race.

Not all who have appealed to the EKD memorandum have drawn this conclusion, at least not with the requisite clarity. One reason for this is the way the memorandum — a people's church document — combines very different arguments. Greater certainty and clarity are found in the USA Catholic Episcopal Conference's draft of its Pastoral Letter on War and Peace, published by the bishops in the autumn of 1982. The American bishops — like the Anglican study on "The Church and the Bomb" — take their bearings from a classic model of Christian ethics, the doctrine of the "just war". From three angles, they point out that every use of nuclear weapons is irreconcilable with the criteria laid down by this classic doctrine:

a) The waging of nuclear war deliberately accepts its effects on the civil population. But "no Christian is permitted to carry out commands or strategies which provide for the slaughter of non-combatants".

b) Every "first strike" with nuclear weapons consciouly accepts that the response chosen is no longer proportionate to the nature of an attack. A strategy which includes a first nuclear strike must therefore be rejected by Christians.

c) Even were it possible to "limit" a nuclear war, it is impossible, once such a war has started, to predict the probability of success for such a "limitation" — still less to guarantee it. There cannot be any justification whatever, therefore, for exposing the human community to such a risk.

In the strategy of deterrence between East and West, all three possibilities are deliberately accepted. When the doctrine of the "just war" is applied to the present situation, therefore, it leads to the rejection not only of nuclear war but also of nuclear deterrence. Another specific ground for the rejection of the system of deterrence is that its acceptance as a provisional measure serves to justify a policy of increased arms production. The American bishops are obviously determined to undermine any such justification. They call for conversion; a conversion of the heart, which will necessarily imply a reversal of the arms race. Their purpose here is to guard against the misunderstanding which rejects only nuclear warfare in order to make the world "safer for conventional warfare". The task today is not only the prevention of nuclear war but the prevention of war altogether. This cannot possibly be done by continuing the arms race but only by reversing this race. The conclusion from this is that the question whether there is to be any possibility of a future for humankind is identical with the question as to whether conversion can assume a political form. The Catholic bishops remind us explicitly that the confession of sin, together with repentance, are essential dimensions of conversion. America's conversion, therefore, must include repentance for having dropped the first nuclear bombs on Hiroshima and Nagasaki.

In the Federal Republic of Germany, rejection of the threat to use nuclear weapons has come from the Executive Committee (Moderamen) of the Reformed Alliance in its declaration "The Confession of Jesus Christ and the Church's Responsibility for Peace". This declaration asserts that a political question, namely, the question of peace, is a doctrinal issue, a matter of confessing Christ. It insists on the impossibility of reconciling the development, deployment and use of weapons of mass destruction with the confession of the Christian faith. For, it says, these weapons can "destroy the humanity loved and chosen by God as his covenant partner and devastate the created world". As they see it, therefore, for those who stand on the Christian confession, the only possibility is an unconditional, unequivocal rejection.

Using a term which is open to misunderstanding, the Reformed church leaders describe this situation as a "situation calling for confession" (*status confessionis*). It would be clearer, perhaps, to speak of a "processus confessionis", the process of confession by the church. What we are required to do, in face of the question of peace, is to take a further step, a new step, in the continuing process of church confession. The question of the obedience of Christians and the church is inseparably part of this process of church confession. The word of God comes to us not only as gospel but also as law, not only as a promise which liberates us but also as a claim which lays a responsibility upon us. The church has to confess and attest its loyalty to its Lord not only by its faith but also by its obedience. For the church, the question of war and peace is a situation in which the obligation to confess the faith takes on a special urgency. It is impossible for the church to escape the obligation to draw political conclusions from its confession of faith in the God who is the "Lover of life". These conclusions have to be much clearer than they have for the most part been in the past. They must drive us in the direction of an effective halt in the arms race; they must require steps to introduce disarmament; they must encourage the respective governments to take even unnegotiated initiatives in this process. The churches in divided Europe have a particularly heavy responsibility to initiate and foster confidence building measures. Time presses.

The biblical dimension of political ethics

The reason why I have sketched the recent history of the discussion of peace in Europe is that it reveals something surprising and exemplary. The more deeply the question of the political responsibility of Christians and churches is probed, the more urgent becomes the deeper question of the biblical roots and principles of our contemporary responsibility. In his contribution to the European regional consultation in February 1981, Nikolai Zabolotski tried to develop from the Decalogue the principles of a contemporary political ethic. In other discussions an increasingly important role has been played by the question as to how far Christians can and should take their bearings from the Sermon on the Mount in their political decisions. In 1981, the Sermon on the Mount was even printed verbatim in the main daily papers in the Federal Republic of Germany; it became once more the public text it had been at the beginning.

When the question of peace is made the main question of a political ethic, the use of the Decalogue and the Sermon on the Mount as guides coalesces. For we thereby link up with the basic message of the biblical record, common to both the Jewish Bible and the New Testament.

The followers of Jewish religion and the members of the Christian church salute one another with the peace greeting: Shalom, peace be with you. In this greeting we pass on to one another the peace we have received from God. The peace which we owe to God becomes thereby a fundamental feature of human fellowship. When peace between human beings is threatened or destroyed, it is more than just earthly peace that is at stake. The threat to peace is most blatantly evident when human beings refuse one another the right to live. This helps to explain the incisiveness with which the prophets of Israel condemned the breaches of justice in their time: "You that turn justice upside down and bring righteousness to the ground, you that hate someone who brings the wrong-doer to court, and loathe one who speaks the whole truth... I know how many your crimes are and how countless your sins, you who persecute the innocent, hold human beings to ransom and thrust the destitute out of court" (Amos 5:10 and 12). Those who view social peace against the background of peace with God know that peace and justice are inseparable. For them there is no peace without justice, no justice without peace. They cannot divorce the question of peace between East and West from the crying injustice which dominates relations between the industrial nations and the countries of Asia, Africa, and Latin America. They cannot call peace a situation in which the present generation in the industrial nations increases its prosperity at the expense of the chances of life of future generations. Nor can they call peace a situation in which human rights and human participation are violated and destroyed in the interests of "national security". In the tradition of the biblical shalom, justice, participation and sustainability become central themes of political ethics. The hope of those who take their direction from the tradition of biblical peace — shalom — can never again be divorced from a common human life in which each promotes the others' rights instead of depriving them of these rights, in which each enriches the life of others instead of threatening it. Those who start from the peace of God will see peace as the fostering of the common life. No area of life is excluded from this. Life in the family is just as much affected by it as the sphere of education; the provision of health and food are just as much affected by it as the control of economic power and the just distribution of economic resources. In his contribution to the European regional consultation, Wolfgang Schweitzer listed themes which are especially important in the European discussion today. His list can be extended, but all these themes have a single context, when we look at them from the standpoint of the shalom tradition, which is at once a promise and a task for human beings.

For in all these areas the greeting — shalom, peace be with you — is heard. And for all these areas, the hope of a common human life in which violence is no longer automatic is unquenchable: a time when swords are beaten into ploughshares and spears into pruning hooks (Isa. 2:2ff.; Mic. 4:1ff.). This hope is at the very centre of the Christian faith; anyone who tries to excise it from that faith pierces it to the heart.

At the same time, however, the fullness of the peace expressed in such hopes demands too much from us human beings. Every step we try to take on the road to peace falls painfully short of our hopes. When we really commit ourselves to peace, we come up against the limits of our action at their most stubborn and resistant, against the defectiveness of our thinking and the sinfulness of our hearts. Really to engage ourselves for peace is to have our eyes opened to see that peace is grace and gift. This is the great theme of the New Testament. It does not cancel anything the Jewish Bible tells us of peace as the fostering of community. But a name is now given to the promise that despite all our lack of peace, God holds firmly to his peace — the name of Jesus of Nazareth. His cross becomes the sign for God's love of his enemies, a love which is stronger than all the enmity of our rebellion against him. The powerlessness of Jesus on the cross becomes the sign of the power of peace in which God comes to meet and greet us in our poverty of peace. The promise of peace seeks entry into our lives — not only in another world but in this world. This is why Jesus calls the peacemakers blessed (Matt. 5:9). God's love of the enemy seeks entry into our world of enmity; this is why Jesus invites us to love our enemies (Matt. 5:44). In no sense do these sentences of the Sermon on the Mount deny our lack of peace and our enmity; but they indicate a direction in which we may seek new ways of dealing with lack of peace, with enmity. Our century has experienced more painfully perhaps than any other that the old ways only lead into cul-de-sacs. Never was it more urgent, therefore, than now that we should as Christians tackle the task of establishing signs, pointers to these new ways of dealing with dispeace and enmity.

Political ethics in the one world

Every political ethics has its roots in the political, economic, cultural and religious context in which it is formulated. It is affected by the special problems of this context. In contemporary Europe, therefore, the need to formulate political ethics as an ethics of peace takes priority. All forms of theology and ethics are responses to a special historical situation and challenge.

Yet every theology and every ethics contains, as such, a truth which transcends its own historical conditions. The new forms of liberation theology developed in Latin America and Africa in recent years are particularly clear examples of this. The Min-Jung theology from South Korea is another. All these are conscious attempts to do theology contextually. Just because of this, they have an important message for other regions of the world — for Europe and North America, for example. Their insistence on the liberating power of the gospel, their conception of history as a process in which God acts as deliverer by his truth and love — these are insights which are important for Christians everywhere in the world; indeed they are of importance even outside the limits of the Christian community. So too the confession of Christ commits us to the "Shalom", to the peace of God, for which we hope and which inspires us to struggle actively for peace in the world. The confession of the faith gives us common perspectives, which open up channels of communication between Christians and churches in the different regions of the world. The consequences which follow from these perspectives may differ and they may require different forms of political action. It is nevertheless important that we should reach agreement within the ecumenical fellowship concerning these common perspectives.

To do so is more important today than ever before in history. For in our world today, even the destructive forces against which we have to struggle, the "powers of death", are not just local, national or regional forces. They are global powers, present at the same time in all parts of the world. Military might and the means of mass destruction, the exploitation of natural resources and the pollution of the biosphere, the ideology of national security and the concentration of economic power in the hands of the TNCs — these are all global phenomena. But they are also a special summons to us to redouble our efforts to achieve an ecumenical political ethic. They make us painfully aware of the fact that we have already been living for quite a time in "one world". But the "one world" for which we hope is a world which is not ruled by military might and oppression but governed by "shalom". Which is why we need common perspectives for our political responsibility and our political struggles.

Political ethics in Europe

The new elements in the European situation

A. The division between East and West Europe

The fundamental problem faced within Europe is the threat to peace across the division between East and West. There is a calculated build-up of tension and mistrust which is supporting the build-up of new weapons of mass destruction. The urgency of the problem is related to the installation of new weapons systems which hold out the possibility of a so-called "theatre nuclear war" in which Europe itself is the battleground for a nuclear confrontation between the major powers. Gradually people are being prepared for this situation and therefore we must give priority to removing the threat of nuclear destruction.

There are a number of ways in which we can approach this problem. *Firstly* we can affirm that nuclear warfare is qualitatively different from other forms of warfare, so much so that it is not a viable political means. *Secondly* we must reach for the underlying causes of this build-up of tension at the level of political economy — the arms race is profitable! This is not only true for the domestic economy of European countries. The misuse of technological development for the production of sophisticated weapons systems is also related to potential export sales aimed at bringing the balance of payments into equilibrium. *Thirdly,* many of the European countries are facing new internal problems, for example mass structural unemployment and the opposition to central governments from particular regions or groupings. In this situation, to build up a picture of an external enemy can serve to restore cohesion, divert attention from internal problems and justify tighter

---

• This is part of the summary of a European dialogue on political ethics which took place in Geneva in February 1981.

internal security. *Fourthly,* both major powers are seeking at this time to consolidate and expand their spheres of influence.

B. *The division between northern and southern Europe*

This is not the only level of conflict within Europe — we have our own division between northern industrialized countries and the southern region. The expansion of the European Community to include southern countries is aimed at stabilizing the southern flank of Europe and bringing influence to bear in the Mediterranean region. This expansion also opens up new areas for industrialization giving both cheaper labour costs and new markets. Already we see major companies transferring production south within the region where there are lower health and safety work standards and where trade union activity to control wages and the conditions of work is not as strong. At the same time we are also experiencing the continued migration of workers from the south to the north internally within Europe. This causes major injustices as these migrant workers are often outside the scope of national legislation and the provision for social security, employment protection and housing. It may be that the European Community membership of the southern countries will afford greater protection to such migrant groups.

Not all European countries are part of the European Community or within COMECON and we would have welcomed the chance for a more detailed examination of the possibilities of non-alignment within Europe to which such countries point.

C. *Europe and third world countries*

The European Community has meant the creation of a new powerful commercial and economic unit which is able to establish new neo-colonial relationships with third world countries, both to consolidate markets and to secure supplies of primary products and energy. (The Lomé convention is an example of this.) We have also seen a growing tendency for Japan, the USA and Western Europe to recognize their common self-interest (tri-lateralism). The Eastern countries of Europe are also pursuing policies of expansion and consolidation in the southern hemisphere. These are all instances of new relationships of dependence and impoverishment between north and south.

D. *Immigration and migrant workers*

Just as there has been internal migration within Europe, so Europe has recruited labour from third world countries, either through immigration from former colonies or through the system of migrant workers. This has produced new factors in the European situation. *First,* a new "underclass" of workers, usually in the lower paid unskilled jobs, has been produced. The legal situation varies but in all countries such workers are discriminated against and are vulnerable. *Secondly,* although immigration is useful at a time of labour scarcity, with growing unemployment the presence of immigrant, ethnic minority groups becomes a convenient scapegoat. So we see a rising tide of organized racist attacks in various Western countries, symbolic of increased racial tension. *Thirdly,* Europe is being challenged to recognize religious and cultural pluralism through the presence of substantial groupings of people who are members of different traditions and religions. In some situations even black Christians find themselves excluded from mainstream white churches. *Fourthly,* we have to attend to the question of politically induced migration on ideological or racial lines. Even within countries with strict immigration controls, certain groups are welcome. Furthermore in some countries with an offical ban on immigration, clandestine immigration continues.

E. The economic situation

In terms of the economy in Europe we can discern a number of new factors which challenge our ways of understanding and our political institutions. *First,* the economies of Western countries are increasingly dominated by major transnational corporations (TNCs) which neither existing state governments nor the trade union movement are able to deal with. Existing national institutions and organizations are unable to control transnational economic organizations and their activities. TNCs have developed global strategies and control systems which traditional political structures have been unable to comprehend. Nation states can have limited defensive impact, and they manage to exercise some control especially in northern countries but national sovereignty tends not to present an obstacle to the operations of TNCs. Also the production of arms and military systems on a large scale has turned the preparation for war into a profitable industry. *Secondly,* within Europe, the inherited economic systems are struggling to maintain viability. In the Western economies it was thought that mass unemployment had been defeated, but changes in the location of manufacturing industry and the introduction of new technology have produced growing structural unemployment, particularly amongst unskilled workers. The socialist countries also face new and unexpected problems of industrial production at the level of economic management, motivation and output. *Thirdly,* industrial production, constantly increasing in scale, produces new threats to the environment. We could give many examples of this from Europe but we feel that investment in the production of energy from nuclear systems not only poses short-term threats but also stores up problems for the future. At the same time such systems are linked to the production of raw materials for nuclear weapons and call for the creation of special internal security measures.

F. Political institutions and processes

Not only are the political institutions unable to cope with the reality of economic power and to respond to the demand for peace, they increasingly fail to command the allegiance of the mass of the people. This can be seen in a superficial way in some Western countries in the small percentages of people participating in electoral politics, and in the failure of people to use the structures for social action in socialist societies. Even at national government level, where electoral participation in the West may be highest, we can see the emergence of a new authoritarianism in some Western countries. For too long the participation of people has been tokenistic. In the East there has not been the anticipated new consciousness which would follow socialist transformation, whilst in the West growing inequality produces a reaction of nihilism or finds expression in a growth of fascist movements. We need therefore a dual strategy in order to both discover ways of taking advantage of existing representative political institutions and of discovering what new forms of political process can be created which will engage the issues and provide a motivation or imperative for action by the people. Indeed one of the key needs is for adequate social goals which will underpin democratic planning and development.

The urgency of the problems to be faced and the challenge of the possibility of nuclear war mean that we must find more effective ways of using existing political structures. We must find ways of calling government and economic power to account. It is in this context that we can see the importance of single issue political movements which occasionally cross major European and international divisions. Such single issue groupings are, however, no substitute for the work which is done through parties and existing representative institutions.

In both East and West, however, it was felt that there is need to work to build a new political infrastructure which will combat the current nihilism and allow far more effective participation in political and economic decision-making. We can begin to see how this might operate at local and regional levels. More effort is needed, however, to develop adequate understanding of the political processes and structures required. This effort creates the need for a new formulation of social and political ethics and imperatives.

On the level of political ethics these problems pose a number of new challenges. *Firstly,* we find ourselves in a situation where the need for action is urgent if we wish to share a common future presence. Inherited ethical theory, both Christian and secular, has not had to deal with this situation previously. Political ethics must be reformulated to take more serious account of the future. *Secondly,* there are demands for participation whilst at the same time control of government and economic life becomes increasingly centralized and powerful. This exercise of centralized power tends to frustrate people's participation and reinforces trends towards inequality. What we need to discover is a form of exercising centralized power, commensurate with the need we see for organizing democratic participation. Such centralized power is necessary in any move towards a just society. Such participation is necessary for each person to be freely involved in decision-making in a more substantial way than the present system allows. We are not, therefore, arguing against the exercise of power but are seeking to use power in the interests of justice and peace. *Thirdly,* traditional understandings of politics and the state are no longer appropriate in a situation where nation states cannot control economic and technological change. *Fourthly,* the link between the personal and the political is becoming clearer. On the one hand personal and group life is shaped in a political and economic context; on the other we can see that personal and political transformation must go together. Many of these insights derive from the women's movement and it must be taken as a new factor in its own right. From this we can begin to see how political ethics has paid too little attention to the processes of politics. Justice relates not only to goals but to processes as well.

G. The churches

Finally we face a new situation for the churches themselves. Whilst in many situations the churches seek, either by "neutrality" or by their actions, to remain uncritical or conservative, there are in most situations more critical elements within the church.

Some groups of Christians are able to act in advance of the institutional church on particular social and political matters. Although such groups may be discriminated against they are catalysts for change. We are, however, being faced with specific concrete choices as to with whom "we" cooperate and on what issues. Usually the "we" is an ecumenical group or a "base" group; sometimes it can be a national church which makes the choice. Single issue politics represents an opening for Christian groups and churches to find allies on particular campaigns. This must not, however, be the totality of Christian commitment to social change and politics.

We can however detect some tentative moves towards breaking the symbiosis in some areas. In relationship to policies on nationality and poverty in the UK, for example, the national churches have taken a more critical line recently. In the recent past the churches have tended to legitimize the status quo, their alignments and preferences reflecting dominant interests. Gradually we are seeing the emergence of a more critical relationship between church and state, but this has not yet resulted in changes in the internal structures of the churches. Furthermore, it is by no means clear how far such changes would command widespread support in the churches with their preference for private, personal commitment in politics. In some situations there is a need to develop a new understanding of the role of the church in a plural society.

We are concerned with the transformation of society towards justice. The implications of this vary from country to country according to the political and ecclesiastical situation. Generally, however, the highly structured European churches find it difficult to become committed to the processes and goals implied by JPSS. This problem is seen most clearly when the church is faced with moving from the moral discourse of the disengaged to having to choose sides in a conflict situation. The way towards a JPSS, however, necessarily will involve concrete choices, alliances and actions. Where we are unable to see this it is often because the membership of the churches is largely drawn from those not directly suffering.

What criteria can we bring to this situation?

We often tend to use the concepts "just, participatory and sustainable" in a static way, fixed on either existing structural patterns or on blueprints for a future society. It was felt that we should look much more closely at the political processes themselves to see how the concepts could be developed and expanded.

A. Justice

In the original version of the preparatory paper, justice was defined "as an attempt to minimize the suffering of the people". This is not the definition of a goal but of a task. We felt that this definition was not adequate for a number of reasons. *Firstly,* this definition was not a sufficiently positive and compelling vision of the process we were seeking to encourage; it does not describe what we are seeking to create. *Secondly,* the category of "suffering" was not the best for our purposes — suffering cannot be removed by social and political processes. Where so-called basic human needs are met, suffering still exists. *Thirdly,* we need to develop a wider view of justice because the meeting of basic human needs in one country is often the result of unjust economic and political processes in another. *Fourthly,* the definition could lead us to the false view that the promotion of justice did not heed the actions of the poor and oppressed themselves. We began in these ways to see that a concern for justice was not simply a concern for the distribution of resources but also involved the promotion of just processes and, therefore, was related to the necessity for the churches to enhance action and reflection on political ethics (both goals and means).

B. Participation

In the Eastern countries it was felt that channels of *participation* had been created for people but they did not use them. Major challenges are the "non-human" behaviour of human beings in a so-called human society and an emergent consumerism. In the Western countries we have seen many examples of "face-saving" participation which does not change the control and distribution of power or the access to power. This might lead us to two conclusions. *Firstly,* that the *giving* of channels of participation to people does not mean that they will use them; and *secondly,* that in many instances participation is simply tokenistic. Overall, however, in both societies we face the problem of disaffection from organized politics and in the West we have the problem of transnational economic power devoid of democratic control. The requirements of a just and participatory society are such that workers must have the right to participation in decision-making just as they do as citizens. Indeed the concept of democracy as commonly understood and practised is inadequate.

There are possibilities for developing participation on medium and lower levels but the churches have great difficulty in seeing this. First of all they are non-participatory themselves; secondly, they are tuned into the macro level; and thirdly in most societies they are made up of the relatively powerful. We should be urging a greater emphasis on responsibilities at local and intermediate levels, encouraging the development of processes which can develop people's power and democratic functioning. Participation should not be seen as simply having to do with participating in others' initiatives but also has to do with initiative-taking and control.

We should, however, take serious note of existing citizens' and workers' initiatives which point in this direction. Members of the consultation mentioned the growth of community organizing, black organizations, Burgerinitiativen, the women's movement, and workers' initiatives.

For European churches, theological thinking on political ethics has focused on church-state relationships conceived of in personal terms and operating at a macro level. We therefore find ourselves ill-equipped to deal with the question of the churches' relationship to political processes and people's organizations. Neither the churches nor politics have paid sufficient attention to participation by people at higher levels. It is the classic problem of representatives. Most so-called democratic processes do not yet require the active participation of the people. In this respect church structures reflect state structures. We can now see the development of people's participation as an aspect of human rights.

C. Sustainability

The issue of sustainability points us to another essential component of justice. To raise the question is not an excuse for not paying attention to the demands of justice. Non-sustainability may in fact destroy the basis for justice. Again we are pointed towards the future and the need to consider the intended and unintended consequences of our actions for ourselves and for future generations. Many of the central political questions of our time are related to the question of sustainability. The relationship of humankind to nature is no longer a peripheral concern (e.g. energy sources, nuclear, chemical and biological weaponry, environmental pollution). Governments so far have only exercised limited control over science-based technology by, for example, refusing to fund research and development. In the field of production and of consumption TNCs can, however, export dangerous processes or products to less "sensitive" countries.

D. Summary

In this section we have identified a number of key issues for future work if we are to develop adequate criteria for our involvement in politics. *First,* how can we develop more dynamic understandings of the concepts we use; *second,* how can we relate personal and structural change; *third,* how can participation be extended and control exercised over higher levels and in the economic sphere; *fourth,* how can we relate sustainability in a wider way to the sustainability of life itself. *Finally,* we noted that there are accessible theological concepts to deal with the questions of justice and sustainability but that our theological understanding of participation needs to be further developed.

What instruments are available for church action?

In our discussion we did not try to produce a definition of the church, preferring instead to develop a pluralist or conciliar understanding. On this basis we viewed the church as being made up of different groups and movements, including ecumenical groups and national and institutional structures.

Within Europe the forms of action will vary from country to country. For example, there are possibilities for action in some Western countries where churches can ally themselves with single issue groups. This removes the problem caused by the need to bind the identity of the church to a political party and its programme. Nevertheless the question of the relationship of national church structures to such parties and programmes remains an area of confusion and tension, not least because of the individualistic view of Christian political commitment. Furthermore, it is assumed that a church decision to ally with a particular programme would be imposed by authority on the membership rather than arise from an unconstrained debate amongst those involved. This is a reflection of the prevalent hierarchical view of both church and society.

The new factor we face, however, is the linking of political action to the fundamental reality of the church in hearing the gospel, conversion and confession. As long ago as 1954 the WCC affirmed that Christian confession and the support of apartheid are incompatible. This has been followed up in other church contexts. In this way a person's standing with the church is dependent upon a particular political, ethical and behavioural consideration.

In essence, of course, this is not a new problem. The church has always had to deal with the behaviour of its members (discipline) but this was not usually linked to a political stance. This kind of development will cause great problems for national churches who see themselves as having an inclusive ministry. Nevertheless we must grasp the issue because churches (as institutional churches) do have national political significance, often legitimating the persistence of poverty and injustice. Obviously racism is a key issue to highlight the possibility of the linking of political action to church discipline but we would wish to explore other examples. As far as the actual situation is concerned, this is a radical area to move into as, in Western Europe at least, it is by no means clear that the churches at an institutional level have recognized the political implications of their witness. The difficult period into which these countries have entered will, however, demand urgent systematic reflection on political issues and practice in order to strengthen the decisive social choices the churches will have to make.

A further confusion lies in the search for a distinctive Christian stance or for distinctive Christian action. We have begun to see that distinctiveness may not lie in the action undertaken (it will necessitate collaboration with particular groups, movements or parties); rather it lies in the *continuation* of action, confession, way of life and worship.

In looking at the modes of Christian action we can identify three classical instruments which the churches have used.

1) interpretation: where the church has interpreted to others the plight of the poor or oppressed;
2) intercession: where the church intercedes on behalf of others with those in authority;
3) intervention: where the church has acted directly for others.

All these are aspects of what has been termed "the church for others" and in certain situations they have great value. We need to move beyond these instrumentalities to efforts which enable people to:
1) articulate their own situation in their own way;
2) make their own legitimate "intercessions";
3) set up their own organizations.

In a symbolic way the PCR is an example of such a development providing a space for the race-exploited to become self-acting.

Such actions by churches, however, depend upon certain criteria. For example, are the oppressed willing to use the church? Are the churches willing to be used? Do the churches have the capacity for acting in solidarity? In the face of repression around the world, which has its own manifestations in Europe, the church has the opportunity to become a very important space for such activity. Of course again this will take different forms in different social political situations, but in each we will be looking for the changing effects of the gospel on people and communities leading to liberation, and the quest for justice.

The relationship of Europe to the world community

It has been impossible to neglect Europe's interdependence with the world community throughout this paper, but we felt that there were certain key features which should be highlighted because they recurred in our conversations.

Firstly, we are forced to recognize that many world problems have their origins in European history and current life. For example, the division between socialist and non-socialist countries has an impact on the world scene and the impact of the colonial past still is felt in the political, economic and religious life, both of Europeans and others.

Secondly, the churches and people of Europe are learning from their brothers and sisters in the southern hemisphere. This presents a challenge to the way we think and act in relation to the poverty and injustice of our own societies and on a global level. We in Europe are now having to re-examine the place of the poor in our societies and churches and to learn how our theology is limited by our political and economic history. We have also been faced with the way in which our economic viability has been built upon the exploitation of other races which now explodes as racism in our countries. The WCC Programme to Combat Racism is a case in point. Divisions which were exported from the North have been here readily overcome in the South, e.g. unity of church.

Thirdly, Europe has a major division between socialist and non-socialist countries and it has its own peripheral region and power centres. We noted that the effects, for example, in southern Europe in terms of both patterns of migrant labour and the movement of production, are very similar to global patterns. Also Europe has had to recognize a growing plurality of faith and ideologies which reflect the living faiths and ideologies in the world today.

Fourthly, we are seeing the emergence of new groups acting in solidarity with those suffering in southern countries on the question of human rights and economic exploitation. Examples would be Amnesty International and groups acting for economic justice. In many instances the churches have found ways of supporting and acting with such groups. The ecumenical movement, exemplified by the WCC, is a case in point.

Morality, politics and violence:
a Latin American interpretation

ORLANDO FALS BORDA

Origins of our ethos of violence

The sixteenth century brings forth in America an ethos of violent conquest
rooted in Catholic religion, which confronts an ethos of accommodation and
naturalness nourished by local animist religions.

How did it ever happen that a religion founded on the precepts of love and
peace should bless the acts of violent conquest in America? Reasons existed
already. The fathers of the church invented an adjustable principle concerning political morality, and in Greek philosophy they found two other principles equally malleable which could harmonize easily with Christian doctrine. Thus they invented the concept of the "holy war" or the "just war";
and adopted the old rules that "the end justifies the means" and that there
exists a supreme good above all individuals and their groups. Aristotle and
Heraclitus summarized these rules as follows: "A beast should be led to
pasture by blows"; because they believed that imposing this type of policy
was good for the sanity of souls and for the progress of the state.

The mediate and immediate precedents of the American conquest illustrate
fully such political morality of violence: the Crusades, which served so much
to consolidate the worldly power of the Holy See vis-à-vis the zealous successors of the Holy Roman Empire; the religious wars of central Europe carried out to defend various interpretations of Christian faith cohabiting with
secular interests of certain princes: and the conversion of the church into a
"kingdom of this world", a trend initiated with St Ambrose and Innocent
III, which culminates with Gregory XII as he punishes Emperor Henry IV in
Canossa, and focuses on the image of Pope Julius II riding on horseback in
armour to conquer the Romagna.

In Spain, congruent with the new Christian kingdoms, King Ferdinand of
Aragon had learned in his Italian wars to exercise a "pious cruelty" which, in
his time, Niccolo Machiavelli praised. Queen Isabella of Castille attempted to

take advantage of the discovery of America not only to save souls but also to become richer and to pay the many debts of the public treasury. The so-called Isabellian philanthropy was contradicted by that European genius who transformed Chinese pyrotechnics in deadly gunpowder and by a satanic utilization of technology to develop firearms. Since then, Christian nations took upon themselves the role of spreading violence in the world and they contributed to the destruction of all other civilizations, including the only one which, in this field, could offer some counterbalance, Islam.

With such political morality the violent elements from Europe had no difficulty or remorse in demolishing the American cultures whose ethos was inspired by a different life philosophy. Although in our hemisphere violence was known — and it had acquired a special political profile in the great mountain empires — the atmosphere prevailing here was one of a peaceful society, i.e. as producers of food and wealth, inventors of material and cultural elements, artisans of great architectonic and religious works — a society dedicated to normal trade and reproduction.

The contrast between the American Indian and the European invader was evident since Columbus' first trip, as stated in his diary: the Indians from the Antilles, he stated, were cordial, kind, open-hearted, curious, intelligent. In the same diary, the great Christopher — "bearer of Christ" — prayed to God that, above anything else, he be allowed to find gold!

According to many chronicles and anthropological sources, the Indian tribes were not prone to violence and much less did they ever use it for profit and enrichment. Conflicts between them were limited to adjustments urged by what may be described as evolutionary natural morality. Their weapons were tools needed for daily work. The groups of warriors easily became communities in peaceful occupation. On the whole, this tendency led them to accommodate and to produce rather than to fight and to destroy.

This unusual ethos of peaceful accommodation left the Indians helpless; they were overpowered by fear at the unpredictable and savage attitudes of the conquerors. As is well known, the Indians used counter-violence in order to survive and availed themselves of collective strategems of escape, such as pretending to worship the new gods, syncretism, amalgamation, emigration and suicide. There was bellicose confrontation on equal terms only in very few places.

Under those circumstances, the religion of the conquerors had no positive effect upon the political morality of the resulting society. On the contrary, cruelty was blessed and inhuman destruction of peoples and cultures was justified. However, the economic benefits sought by European political morality were secured as the Spanish dominated and exploited the Indians during that first stage of the world's capitalist expansion.

The Isabellian utopia was not entirely lost. It provided a glimpse of certain types of ideal societies proposed by some philosophers of the time. Thus the separate efforts of Las Casas and Vasco di Quiroga were followed by the attempts by Jesuits to build regional theocracies, and the efforts of others who dared to believe that the Indians did have a soul and that, therefore, they could be allowed to participate with the Spaniards in the whole effort of colonization. But the faith of those visionaries grew gradually weaker in the face of the violent ethos of the conquerors that permeated all their efforts. Several Indian tribes were trained in the use of the new weapons, that is, they were trained to become as violent as their European tutors. Utopian enterprise of that kind would not be seen in America again until the early nineteenth century after the convulsion caused by independence, thanks to the new lay religions which by that time appeared in Europe around socialism.

Once the empires became consolidated, other elements of political morality were encouraged, which were congruent with the point of departure offered by traditional violence. This morality may, in general terms, be summarized in terms of Machiavellism. There was, for example, the doctrine of the "greatness" (megalopsychy) of the rulers derived from Aristotle's advice to Nicomacheus. To this doctrine Machiavelli added the "prudence of rulers" as holders of power. Those were the times of the great enlightened kings and the learned autocrats who were never considered to be wrong, since their power was of divine origin. And if they ever did wrong, they could always disguise, or make their errors relative, by another Machiavellian principle: that of "reason of state" or "state secret". Such principles were applied widely in our hemisphere by the agents of the crown who, in this manner, encouraged alienation and increased the exploitation of the people.

But kings were quite soon overthrown by those who believed in the opposite theory of violence: the principle of "just rebellion". The ancient doctrine of the just war was turned upside down. As is known, the propositions of Father Vitoria concerning tyrannicide had found an initial dramatic application in Cromwell. In America the tendency was expressed more amply in the cry: "Long live the king, death to the bad government." The popular masses raised it during the eighteenth century. Subsequent conflicts demonstrated the applicability of *The Prince.* Statesmen were expected to combine the shrewdness of the fox with the strength of the lion. Hence, it was not surprising to see viceroys like Archbishop Antonio Caballero y Góngora in the New Kingdom of Granada using deceit to stop the justified rebellions of the Commons (1781) or to sanction the outrageous death sentences passed on popular leaders like José Antonio Galán and Tupac Amaru, or with a bad conscience to send to exile the translators of the "Rights of Man". In this devious manner the statesmen of the time attempted to stop what they called "subversion".

Seen from the angle of the exploited peoples whose ethos was being violently challenged, such historical "subversion" was a task which harmonized with natural evolutionary morality: it was a necessary moral task. It would yield political freedom for some twenty republics. Among such subversive champions of freedom there were freemasons and guerrilla priests (Hidalgo, Mariño, Sotomayor). They were like armed prophets who, luckily enough, had profited from the sad adverse experience of the unarmed Savonarola. The eventual triumph of those heroes seemed to justify the inverted theory of the just war, and the positive role of a properly understood counter-violence and "subversion". But once they were in power, these new heirs of political morality attempted to develop other principles of government which, inspired by alien ideologies, turned out to be utopian and ineffective.

Adaptations in liberal and capitalist morality

The national statesmen of the newly constituted American republics were not very original in their attempts to promote socio-political reconstruction. They discarded the primeval sources of the natives' non-violent ethos and resorted to the spiritual fountains of European rationalism, liberalism and romanticism. They did not notice that these were only a disguise for a new type of violence represented by the rampant capitalism of the time. Thus, new forms of state violence appeared which, in turn, referred to general principles of political morality.

Such principles may be summarized in three phrases: "the superior interests of society", "the myth of human dignity", and "the goals of collective wellbeing" elaborated by liberal philosphers. It is easy to see that they derived from the previous theses about the common good, now filtered through scholasticism and natural law. Thinkers like Hobbes, Locke, Kant and Rousseau tried, in this manner, to stem the spiritual crisis that followed the Renaissance and Reformation. These rationalistic, liberal and romantic principles of the political morality of the time were added to the ones mentioned above, both classical and Machiavellian. None of them lost their validity in the European context or in the colonies this side of the ocean.

The early patterns of exploitation and injustice, against which the peoples had revolted, continued unabated, since they were now reinforced by the expanding capitalist system. Even the slaves who became liberated through their own effort, like those in Haiti, tolerated black and mulatto exploiters who continued the former abuses in the name of a Voodoo-Christian empire. Although legally eliminated for the sake of the new liberalism, slavery continued in different forms, tolerated by society until early in the twentieth century. In addition, the Indians continued to lose their lands, and were forced to work for starvation wages.

Modern capitalism thus emerged at a regional level, sometimes supported by English, French or North American military interests demanding special privileges for their countries' trade agents or for Protestant missionaries.

In this manner there was a transition from the ethics of bloody profit-making of the Hispanic settlers towards a "redeeming neo-colonialism" in which accumulation of profits through work was seen as evidence of divine acquiescence in the individual efforts of the new entrepreneurs. It was an American version of Calvinistic ethics. Since entrepreneurs were already in power, it was easy for them to impose such ideas as the basis for a new and more convincing political morality: that of the "morality of justification of capitalist exploitation" which harmonized with European and North American trends of socio-political thought, mainly with Comtian positivism.

The main local adjustment of those imported theses which the Latin American statesmen made during that time took place precisely in the one concerning the great men: they gave it the specific context of "caudillismo" (bossism). There was no significant human or philanthropic progress in such transformation which turned out to be esoteric as far as the common people were concerned. On the contrary, the greatest bleeding of the popular classes took place when the period of civil wars started. Each leader could claim for his respective rebel cause an ethical justification represented by some disregarded constitutional principle, or the defence of moral theses. Quite frequently armies were organized with the cry of "Long live Christ the King", by soldiers bearing papal flags and rosaries, men who ostensibly fought in favour of social rights and church dogmas when, in actual fact, and without their being aware of it, they were defending the land and power of their respective leaders.

This unique development of political morality in Latin America during the nineteenth century became complicated when the new dominant classes became servile agents of foreign interests. Commercial ties imposed by European and North American capitalists — those of the "aggressive entrepreneurs" — many a time made puppets of the local bosses. It did not matter if they were stern tyrants dressed in black like Dr Francia, illiterates like José Antonio Páez, overpious like Miguel Antonio Caro, or technocrats like Porfirio Díaz: they were useful, provided they allowed the endless enrichment of the dominant European obligarchies which were the final benefactors of Calvinist redemption.

And when any deviation became apparent in such imperial accommodating patterns, the great powers had not the slightest conscience in intervening, whether directly or indirectly, in local affairs by contributing weapons — as occurred during the disastrous wars of Paraguay and the Pacific and during the empire of Maximilian.

Later this sacred policy of violent intervention would acquire the form of the "Big Stick". According to Presidents Monroe and Roosevelt and Prime Minister Gladstone, God was on the side of the Anglo-Saxon powers. There was a "manifest destiny" which Protestant missions of the time took upon themselves to emphasize in this part of the world, while they encouraged in the lower and middle classes mystical attitudes of renunciation of this world. This was adequate for the imperialist political aims and for those of the local proconsuls.

But the morality which justified the resulting capitalist exploitation was almost never questioned — by politicians or by missionaries — while lumber forests were felled, rubber resin drawn, gold mined, petroleum drilled, and local spices and medicines processed and exported, paying ridiculous prices to those who produced them directly.

The political morality of capitalist exploitation — which has led us, at a regional level, to a condition of economic, political and cultural dependency, and at a national level to a condition of poverty and human deterioration — has not changed much in Latin America since the last century, under the so-called democratic systems and under the successive military dictatorships. The greatest upheavals against it have occurred in Mexico, Guatemala, Bolivia and Chile, leading to ambiguous political processes or to catastrophes. In the Caribbean area, some new struggles for independence have followed paths different from the traditional ones, with marked utopian elements such as those proposed by Guevara for the socialist order in Cuba.

In this Caribbean region various patterns of political morality are being structured; for their examination it would be convenient to apply the criterion of differentiation in time suggested by Locke for ethical reasons. Whatever appears good on a short-term basis, he used to say, may become bad in the long run, and vice versa. Let us remember in this sense the dangers to which the Stalinist interpretation of Marxist eschatology has led. It will be necessary to evaluate step by step the march of societies towards the goal of general welfare among peoples who are today the victims of dominant systems. From this standpoint, it will be well to judge if respect and encouragement of life and culture are achieved, as well as the defence of human integrity and the creation of really philanthropic values as they emerge from the undercurrent of natural evolutionary morality.

From this point of view, the experiences of people's participation are important. Rooted within local realities, they were put into practice in Allende's Chile, retaken in Cuba through the constitutional mechanisms of popular power, and extended recently to Nicaragua. Here are some bases for a new positive moral subversion at hemispheric level, capable of moving groups, social classes and people of varied kinds into action (like the guerrilla priest Camilo Torres). They include other valued goals: the reduction of armaments, defence of ecological resources, fair distribution of wealth, popular welfare, and respect for human rights. They are components of that contemporary political morality which today tries to fight the immorality of the existing exploitation with its ethos of reactionary violence.

This struggle seems uneven because the ancient morality now appears rejuvenated, fed on all the traditional theses for the handling of politics which we have sketched. It is an astonishing accumulation of old ideas about how to manipulate, impose, oppress, harass and destroy the people who work and produce. But this is the political morality which is doomed to succumb sooner or later under the weight of its own historical ballast. It is the morality of the contemporary political class which has had to revert once more to another violent doctrine — national security — and to a totalitarian threat — the threat represented by rational technical control, mass media manipulation, and state repressions and terrorism.

Underlying the totalitarian doctrine of national security are old ideas about the use of armed violence with social and political purposes. In this manner, reactionary violence is being used to arrest the natural evolutive impulse of peoples towards necessary social change. The champions of national security (who hypocritically condemn violence while practising it openly or in its structural form) resort to a deceitful argument: they say that while fighting for national security they are defending a common patrimony, when in actual fact what they protect are vested interests of oligarchic minorities.

Besides, it happens that under this doctrine, a whole network of falsehood, bribery and abuse of authority is covered up by governments. Torture, murder, concentration camps, death brigades, counter-guerrilla movements and other deadly inventions proliferate among us.

We cannot finish this paper on a bitter note of pessimism. There still remain the forces of natural morality and of the non-violent native ethos in our continent. They refuse to surrender and can yet articulate a strong political resistance. In our milieu it can still be demonstrated that there exists for the public service the potentiality of a creative conjunction of interests (not conflict, but rather compatibility) between personal moral convictions and collective needs and urgencies. Humanitarian sectors of Christian churches have managed to articulate a theological position consistent with the need for the liberation of people. And several socialist parties and movements have abandoned useless sectarianism in order to approach the masses with a spirit of service and discovery and with a democratic mind.

Thus, it seems possible still to retake and to revive the long-standing moral theses of integrity of character and honesty which Plato attributed to Socrates in his famous "Apology". And, therefore, it will be no longer necessary to revive the advice about the art of government which Kirkegaard gave the handsome King Christian VIII of Denmark: "Become ugly, deaf and blind and don't say anything important."

Neither would there be any need for totalitarian controls and the implicit instrumentalities for standardizing society or for homogenizing cultures, nor for "political science" and "social engineering". Nor should we have to appeal to prescriptive planning or to continue courting the dangers of the Orwellian counter-utopia of the "Big Brother". We could act more in terms of freedom and personal responsibility, spontaneity and creativity, and the right to being different. In summary, we could think of encouraging and nourishing ample *vivencias* in human experience.

But to this end, it becomes indispensable to reject generalized violence as the only possible political weapon, to deny in practice Machiavelli's heritage, to struggle against the malformations caused by the ethical inconsistencies and wrong practices of our ancestors, and to allow ourselves to be guided by new political values of a moral nature, such as those proclaimed by the people's true participation.

Perhaps we will not continue to let ourselves sink in the vortex into which current political practices are leading us, although the advent of social change may be painful. Even if the new world being born under the circumstances already created by reactionary violence will require armed heroes and prophets, and martyrs sacrificed for the sake of the justice of their cause, may we then expect that the ancient cycle of war and violence will be broken by the new conscience of philanthropy which this final conflict may generate?

Aspects of political ethics in the Middle East

GABRIEL HABIB

Background

The Middle East, encompassing Turkey, Iran, Cyprus, the Arab-speaking states of the eastern Mediterranean seaboard, Israel, the Arabian peninsula, the valley of the Tigris-Euphrates, the Nile Valley, and Libya, has been on the world's agenda since the beginning of recorded history. Because of its geographical position between three continents, its lands have experienced a convergence of cultural influences. At the same time, while some parts have acted as transit zones for centuries, other areas of less accessible terrain (mountains, desert, swamp) have remained isolated, preserving ancient languages, religions and cultures. This contrast between seclusion and openness to outside influence is highly characteristic of the Middle East and explains why in some regions a modern outlook may exist alongside a traditional view of life with little change since biblical times. Rapid socio-cultural transition may thus coexist, within the same small region, with conservative traditionalism.

Religious divisions are strong in the entire region, and for many people religion and sectarian fidelity precede nationality. The uniqueness of the region, closely related to its geographical position as a meeting ground for cultures and peoples, is that it has been the birth-place of three great religions of the modern world: Judaism, Christianity and Islam. In addition, such religious movements as Zoroastrianism, Manichaeism, Mithraism, and the more contemporary Baha'i are associated with the Middle East.

This is why one cannot speak of political ethics in the Middle East without seriously taking into consideration the "living-together" of these three religions. In other words, a relational ethics of "coexistence" must incorporate the reciprocal rights and mutual duties of each, in order to be able to initiate and establish social justice and peace. Therefore, because of the complexity of the situation in the Middle East, and the coexistence (however harmonious) of Christians, Muslims, and Jews in many countries in the region, we cannot but speak in terms of a "Christian identity", a "Muslim identity" and a "Jewish identity" and about their different perspectives and problems which lie beyond the domain of nationalism (Lebanese, Syrian, Iraki, Egyptian, Israeli, Arab, etc.). To a great extent, in terms of these identities, the peoples of the Middle East have envisaged, and either solved or not solved, their main problems. Their history is marked by religion which embraces the totality of communal life, and is closely integrated into the very fabric of society. Therefore, the emergence today of a renewed awareness of what may be referred to as religio-centricity is not a strange phenomenon in the Middle East.

This does not mean that economics, social differences, secular ideologies and international policies do not also play an important role in the life and behaviour of the peoples of the Middle East. It does mean essentially that the Western political theories and criteria based on the humanist secular nationalist and materialist ideologies are not sufficient to understand the social and political behaviour of the Middle East peoples. Religious revelation, laws and traditions are fundamental.

On the other hand, the fact that three major religions inform the ethical sensitivity of the people of the region makes it difficult, but not impossible, to evolve sufficient common ethical perspectives within which the pursuit of justice, power, community, God-man relations, relationship of religion with the state and society, and many others can be faced.

The present situation

Today, the Middle East is one of the most tense and explosive regions in the world. Palestine, Cyprus, and recently Lebanon and Iran have witnessed the same phenomenon of destructive tensions between secular and religious ideologies and between what is universal and what is particular in people's ethical, cultural and religious traditions. The future societies in the region are being determined and shaped by the current tensions and events. The great powers, instead of helping to ease these tensions, have at times encouraged their development or used them for their own economic, political and strategic interests. This situation has led to immense suffering through violations of human rights, and through moral and physical violence. It is through these sufferings that the churches in the Middle East are called to witness to the resurrected Christ as provider of hope and peace to all peoples and nations. The gospel tells us that this can be accomplished through the proclamation of truth, the fulfilment of justice, and through genuine love that defies and destroys all barriers between individuals and groups.

While concerned with their spiritual and physical survival, the question is whether the churches could participate significantly with other religious and non-religious groups in making the future societies more respectful of human rights and more committed to peace? How can this be practically done, and what alternatives can they propose?

The socio-economic reasons

In spite of the fantastic revenue from oil, stark contrasts between rich and poor continue to prevail in the region. The oil income is not invested for the elimination of poverty, illiteracy and injustice in the Arab world. Unfortunately a high percentage of this income is spent on military build-up. Another high percentage is recycled into Western economy, and large sums are used in financing militias and wars by proxy. Of course, one should not deny the existence of very important developmental programmes, mainly in the Gulf States and a few other countries. And one should realize that sizeable funds are spent by Muslim leadership for the Islamic mission in Africa, Asia, and the West. However, an adequate and conscious policy for the use of oil revenues towards the fulfilment of social justice does not exist. Instead, and in addition to a growing spirit of selfish mercantilism among the rich groups, unbelievable amounts of money are irresponsibly spent on pleasure or on encouraging violence between individuals and groups as well as wars between nations.

Human rights

With the exception of two or three countries, most of the people of the Middle East are ruled by totalitarian regimes characterized by a one-party system. Democratic freedom, and in some instances religious freedom, is constantly threatened or denied. And the participation of the people in national decision-making is only theoretical, as these decisions are taken by the party or the military elite. At this juncture of Middle East history, when all elements of the present order seem to be in question, it is becoming increasingly important to affirm the unalienable civil, political and religious rights of every citizen and community.

The Gulf States, owing to their newly acquired and abundant material wealth, have suddenly found themselves in an extremely powerful economic position. They are, nevertheless, heavily reliant on and vulnerable to international military and political forces. Also the absence of an adequate native work force has forced Arab leaders to import large numbers of both skilled and unskilled foreign workers. The Gulf region is at present the scene of one of the most significant movements of migrant labour in the post-war period. While the movement of labour is a characteristic of industrialization, nowhere else in the world is the proportion of non-citizen labour in the work force and in the population higher than in the Gulf. Millions of workers are involved in this movement. Besides Arab workers from neighbouring countries, workers are coming from Asia (South Korea, Philippines, India, Pakistan and Bangladesh) and other parts of the world. These foreign workers might well earn more than they do at home, but this does not compensate for the exploitation or the discrimination and racism to which workers are exposed.

The West Bank and Gaza strip, which passed under Israeli occupation in the 1967 war, have about 1.5 million Palestinian inhabitants, i. e. one third of the total number of the Palestinian people. Statistics indicate that a number ranging between 90-100,000 Palestinians cross over each day into the Israeli territories where they are employed, either in the agricultural sector (12 percent of total), industrial sector (20 percent), service (18 percent) and construction sector (50 percent). The Israeli capitalists draw on this massive reserve of cheap and exploited labour.

Therefore the movement of workers to the Middle East from outside countries raises a number of social, economic and legal problems. The situation particularly in the Gulf is increasingly problematic.

The political conflicts

Because of its varied composition of different cultures, races, ethnic and religious groups living together in harmony or tension, the Middle East always had the potential for both great creativity and destruction. This made the search for identity through nationalism or religious affiliation a matter of considerable tension in the region. The struggle for Arabism, the conflict between Arab nationalism and Zionism or Israeli nationalism, the struggle of the Armenians, Palestinians and Kurds for self-determination and the Lebanese war are concrete examples of such tension.

Because of its strategic geographical position and its oil reserves, the Middle East has more than ever become the arena for international cold or hot wars by proxy. Palestine, Cyprus and Lebanon witnessed exploitation by international powers of their internal ethnic, religious and cultural differences. In addition, the Middle East has become part of the national security of the great powers. Thus it is suspected that the Western powers have been encouraging religious fanaticism in the region as a measure of security against secularist ideologies conducive to Marxist and communist influence.

In other words, the destiny of the Middle East people is not in their hands and is determined by foreign powers and interests. Would the peoples of the Middle East be able to unite and achieve together full independence? Since the death of Nasser of Egypt in 1971, such a possibility has been rather remote.

On the other hand, the continuation of the conflicts in the region, the arms race, and the escalation of tension between the two superpowers have been causing fear and despair, thus creating a situation where violence and physical liquidation of persons are increasingly becoming the norm in politics. Democratic procedures, dialogue, moderation and peaceful solution of conflicts are becoming increasingly difficult.

Religious developments and their effects on Middle Eastern societies

Of primary importance in this context and of particular relevance to political ethics in the Middle East is the contemporary return to religion — Judaism, Islam and Christianity — as the main or the only source for foundation of power, legislation and social structure.

Participation by Christians in the secular political life of the Arab East

The involvement of individual Arab Christians in the internal politics of Egypt, Jordan, Lebanon, Syria, Iraq and even Israel, both within and outside the accepted governmental framework, has been a feature of the Arab East since independence, and this involvement can be traced back over a century to the first stirrings of Arab nationalism, the original exponents of which were in fact Levantine Christians. At that time, many among the emerging ranks of Christian intellectuals rejected the Ottoman society, with its political-religious structure and Pan-Islamic outlook, in favour of a wholly Arab culture based primarily on the Arabic language, the greatest single tie linking Christian and Muslim in the Levant. Arab culture, unlike that of the Ottoman Turks, had Christian as well as Muslim origins, and it was felt that the renewal of its glory, accompanied by the religious tolerance that marked the early structure of its political embodiment — the Caliphate — would benefit all Arabs, regardless of their religion. As early as 1847 young Christian students in Beirut had begun to organize themselves in learned societies whose purpose was to initiate a renaissance of Arab learning, culture and society.

The Christian-sponsored nationalist movement continued to attract a strong following, particularly among the Orthodox and Protestant Arabs, and in 1875 a small group of Syrian Protestant College alumni organized a secret society aimed at spreading the ideals of Arab nationalism, and dedicated to the expulsion of the Ottomans from Syria. The society collapsed after less than a decade, however, having been unable once again to attract the necessary Muslim support. In the words of Faris Nimr, co-founder of an early Cairo newspaper, *Al-Muqattam,* the society "became convinced that between Christians and Muslims no understanding or agreement could be reached on the expulsion of the Turks from Lebanon" and therefore no unified action was possible.

During the remaining years of the nineteenth century, Arab Christians continued to advocate an Arab revival, and gradually began to attract a vital Muslim following. The oppressive rule of Sultan Abdulhamid, and the rapid decline of the Ottoman Empire, coupled with the spread of Western learning among a small but important group of Muslims studying in Europe, encouraged many to opt for the cause of Arab nationhood.

The first Arab conference, held in 1913, witnessed many expressions of Christian-Muslim cooperation and solidarity in the cause of the nationalist movement; indeed half the delegates, mainly Syrians and Lebanese, were Christian.

Not surprisingly, some of the prominent Arab Nationalist leaders of the interwar years were Orthodox Christians, and two in particular stand out as founders of important political parties and movements still extant today. These two movements are the Al-Ba'th (Renaissance) and Al-Hizb Al-Qawmi (Nationalist Party). But like so many Christian nationalists, they removed religion altogether from the realm of national action and based their social philosophies on a completely secular society, forgetting that most Muslims were not willing to cast off Islam so casually. For these Christian nationalists and intellectuals, Muhammad became a purely political figure, one to whom all Arabs owed primary allegiance as the founder of an united Arab nation. Thus, while it may seem curious to the Westerner to read of Christians in the Arab East advocating "with even more vehemence and eloquence than the Muslims that the relationship between Islam and Arab nationalism is intimate and that Islam should be the special object of veneration for all nationalists, no matter what their actual religion", it is a fact that they pointed out this relationship earlier and more frequently than Muslims. Dr Qustantin Zurayq, a Damascene Orthodox like 'Aflaq, made this point in 1938, 'Aflaq alluded to it in 1943, and the late Nabih Faris concurred in 1947 when he stated that "the birthday of the prophet is the birthday of Arabism." The ambiguity of this position for Christians was best illustrated by Makram 'Ubayd, a leading Coptic figure in the nationalist Wafd party in Egypt, during the interwar years, who once stated: "I am Christian by religion but Muslim by nationality." For the majority of Christians, however, some kind of commitment by Muslims to a purely secular nationalism was necessary before they would abandon themselves wholly to the Arab cause. This view was clearly set forth twenty years ago by Dr Charles Malik who, while acknowledging that "for the Christians of the Near East, Muslim culture... is in a deep sense their culture", and that "they cannot be too deeply interested in the development of their common heritage", felt strongly that there was a need for reciprocity on the part of the Muslim as well, for whom Christianity was an important part of the cultural heritage.

Thus while some Muslims could identify with a nationalism based on the "culture" of Islam, and rationalize away the religious context of both Islamic and Christian ideology, there was little indication that many Muslims were willing to do the same. Many Christians could accept Islam as "a response to Arab needs at the time of Muhammad...", but few indeed were the Muslims who would publicly accept such a limited view of their religion. For this reason, the majority of Christians on the eve of national independence sought to secure legal and constitutional guarantees of their political and communal rights, continuing to participate in the political life of the independent states as they had during the Mandate years.

A secularizing tendency was promoted by Ataturk of Turkey. He wanted to radically modernize Islam. Consequently, he replaced the Arabic alphabet by the Latin alphabet, changed the traditional dress of people, "unveiled" the women. These trends, first promoted by the Christians, continued until modern times through all the secular ideologies, such as Arab nationalism, socialism, Marxism, etc. and affected the development of constitutional laws in most of the countries of the area. The last most important Arab nationalist movement was the Nasserist movement that Colonel Ghadhafi of Libya is trying to revive today in a different form. The "Ba'th" parties in Syria and Iraq are continuing today under the leadership of Saddam Hussein and Hafez Assad. Therefore, the nationalist and secularist movements in the Middle East were promoted mainly by Christians, joined by Muslims and some Jewish intellectuals who have been in contact with European culture. These movements were based on the values of the Western humanist movement, the principles of the French Revolution and in some cases the Marxist philosophy and economic analysis; all of them aiming at a society based on equality between individuals regardless of their ethnic or religious background or affiliation.

In recent years, under the influence of secular nationalism, the course of change from the religiously structured Ottoman Empire to constitutional states in the Middle East under the influence of secular nationalism has been seriously challenged and to a great extent reversed. What really did happen?

The Israeli phenomenon

At one stage, because of the anti-Semitic movement in Europe and the emergence of Zionism, the Jewish partner decided to withdraw from the secular nationalist movement in order to form its own Jewish state, Israel. And, since the establishment of the state of Israel, divergent views as to the role of religion in everyday life and in relation to politics have influenced the socio-political development and have played a key role in Israel's attempts to come to terms with its own identity and relationship to its neighbours. An important objective of the Zionist movement since the beginning of Israel was to destroy the Arab nationalist movement and to prevent the establishment in the region of secular nationalist states. For such Western types of nationalist movement or state would have, in Israel's opinion, forced the Jews to assimilate into societies based on equality of individuals beyond ethnic and religious boundaries or to live a ghetto existence in a hostile secular environment which did not appreciate the special ethnic and religious character of the state of Israel. Therefore, in order to avoid being victims of a second holocaust which in their opinion would be perpetrated by the Arab nationalist movement, the Israelis are contributing to the transformation of the Middle Eastern national states into federations of communities ethnically and religiously identified. This is why Israel considered Nasser of Egypt the second Hitler and contributed to the destruction of his Arabist movement in the war of 1967. This is also why Israel refuses the Palestinian project of a Palestine/Israel where Jews, Christians and Muslims could live together in one secular and democratic state, and this is why Israel contributed to the destruction of Lebanon which served as a living example of coexistence between various religious communities in one state. Lebanon, under Christian influence, is a potential secular state in the region and if it works, it would be the defeat of the Israeli vision for the future of society in the Middle East.

Therefore, the Zionist movement and the Israeli phenomenon were the first challenge to the humanist movement and the nationalist ideologies borrowed from the West by the first promoters of nationalism in the Middle East. It was also a challenge to the spiritual vision of history and society based on St Paul's understanding that in Christ there are no Jews, Greeks or Arabs. "The Concept of Community of Communities" emphasized by the Jewish partner in the Christian-Jewish dialogue, organized a few years ago by the WCC, reflected Israel's understanding that the Middle East peoples should not be moving towards the goal Christians have always envisioned;

that is, instead of the Christian idea of becoming one community within the concept of a national state, they should remain a group of ethnocentric or religious communities, each one having its own source of inspiration, its own power, its own philosophy of existence and self-understanding.

Consequently, through imposing itself by force as a settler colonialist movement based on the Zionist interpretation of the Bible and the traumatic experience of the European holocaust, Israel did not only create the Palestinian question which has a tremendous impact on the political, social and economic life of the whole Middle East and constitutes a threat to world peace, but it also introduced political theories and ethics which are serious challenges to human rights and international law as understood and recognized by the international community. One of these is the policy of the fait accompli. Another is the right of self-understanding which justifies Israeli behaviour in disregarding even the best motivated criticism of Israel by non-Israelis. Most important is the divine right that Israel claims it has over the "Holy Land" over and against human rights or international law based on humanistic principles. "Nobody has the right to tell me whether I can stay in Judea and Samaria (West Bank and Gaza)", says Begin, since this "right is given to me by God the Father of Abraham, Isaac and Jacob". The same divine right seems to provide Israel with the power and the justification to carry out any aggressive or intimidating military action against any people or country. It is understandable that Israel should care about its security. Unfortunately, however, this concern for security and the fear of a second holocaust have made Israel intransigent. The refusal of the Palestinian State and the raid on the Iraqi nuclear plant illustrate this policy as does the invasion of Lebanon, with all the consequences.

The Islamic revival

Throughout most of their history, Christians and Muslims have lived together in a religiously pluralistic society in which the Christian minority existed basically by the tolerance of the Islamic majority. They joined hands against the Ottoman Empire through the Arab nationalist movement. Finally, Christians and Muslims in the Middle East shared together problems that came about as a result of the Western Christian impact on the Middle East either through the Crusades as a mixture of colonial, political and religious movements, or through the missionary movement which was aggressive towards Islam and often divisive within the Christian community on the local level. Recently, however, partnership in the renaissance and liberation of Middle East society has been challenged by new developments in Islam.

The Muslims gained economic power from the sudden rise in the price of oil, and acquired a strategic position in the economic world order. This new wealth permitted the Muslim leadership to invest large funds in Islamic education. The result was a new awareness that for centuries the Muslims have been an oppressed majority under the Western powers which they consider culturally and religiously Christian. They felt that this was the time to assert themselves as Muslims in the world community, to liberate themselves from Western culture, and to do their own mission through developmental aid as well as through liberation movements in the third world. On the other hand, Muslims also feel that the Western powers and the Christians destroyed their Ottoman Empire, and that through so-called modernization, they have imposed Western values incompatible with the Muslim faith. Christians, through their acceptance of both Western mission and secular nationalism separating religion from state, are considered by the Muslims as a threat to Islam itself, not only as a religion but also as a system of government, a political and ethical system and a style of life. The Muslims do not want to make the same mistake as the Christians who allowed certain values or theology to reach the point of even "killing God" for the sake of liberation of the human being and accepted the humanist movement and all its consequences including the values of the French Revolution and the Marxist Revolution. This is why Khomeini says that he wants to reverse what Ataturk had done in Turkey and why the Muslim revivalist movement in general is withdrawing from Arab nationalism which is considered as a Western secular movement. All these point to a desire to re-establish Islamic society based on the Koranic Law (Sharia).

Although Khomeini Shi'ism is quite different in its political objectives and revolutionary style from the Wahabi Saoudi Arabia conservative Islam, it is interesting to study some of Khomeini's statements which theologically can be shared by all Muslims. Upon his return to his home city, the Holy City of Qum, after 16 years of exile, the architect of the Iranian revolution delivered a speech in which he vowed to devote the remainder of his life to reshaping Iran "in the image of Muhammad". This would be done by purging every vestige of Western culture from the land. "What the nation wants is an Islamic republic," he proclaimed, "not just a republic, not a democratic republic, not a democratic Islamic republic. Just an Islamic republic. Do not use the word democratic, that is Western and we do not want it." In his book on the Islamic government, Khomeini denounces any form of distinction between temporal and spiritual leadership. This is "an apostasy imposed on Islam by colonialist powers... and the Islamic government is the rule of the *divine right.*'' The pressure of the Islamic revival is to reverse the secularizing process of nationalism and recover the Islamic structure of society.

Effects on the Christian communities

Today, both the Israeli philosophy of existence and the Islamic revival are opposed to the Christian post-Constantinian experience and theology expressed through the separation of the temporal and spiritual powers, and to the Western humanist movement accepted by the Christians and manifest in their culture and Western political ideologies. Consequently:

1. The process of transforming the religious society by way of the nationalist movement into a secular society where religion and state are separated, is now being reversed and *political power is being withdrawn from the state in favour of the religious community.* The recent war waged by the late President Sadat of Egypt against the Muslim powers in Egypt and Pope Shenouda III is the most recent illustration of this phenomenon. Because of the Christians' fear of the Muslims' power and their lack of confidence in the power of the government, they stood behind Pope Shenouda as the symbol of the power they should acquire for their survival in Egypt. For this reason, Muslim and Christian leaders who became a threat to President Sadat's power were imprisoned.

2. The peoples of the Middle East, including the Christians, are going through a new *crisis of identity.* Nationalism, with which people were trying to identify, after independence, and beyond their particular ethnic and religious backgrounds, is radically being challenged. Individuals and communities are therefore forced to redefine their identities along ethnic and religious terms.

3. Under these pressures, the Christian communities are experiencing a difficult time which is characterized by a serious concern for survival. They are presently faced with the following choices: They can leave the region out of fear and despair, and many are in fact emigrating to the West. In order to survive, another alternative is to opt for political power and political existence similar to that of the Jews or the Muslims. The third option is to continue the struggle towards a deconfessionalized society. Many, however, refuse the kind of political power offered to them, the same way Jesus Christ refused this power when it was offered to him. They consider that their power is the power of the Holy Spirit and of the cross, the power of the powerless of this world. For some, such an attitude leads to suicide while for others it leads to martyria. In Lebanon, young Christians with big crosses around their necks were taking up guns and killing innocent people in revenge and retaliation. Their argument is that the only language Islam or

Judaism understands is the language of power and of force. Such situations are making Christians raise the basic question of what in fact it means to be a Christian in the Middle East today. Is our faith the faith of power and therefore of institutions, of preserving our physical being, thus making compromises with the powers of the world? Do we relate to the Muslims and Jews only on the basis of balance of power, or is our power the power of sacrifice? How do we define our witness? Do we protect ourselves against the enemy who attempts to destroy our community or church by using power and armies? Or do we accept with courage to witness to truth, love, justice and peace until death, if necessary, for the sake of the resurrection of all? Do we accept an earthly kingdom, or do we long for the kingdom of God whose rule and power are of a completely different nature?

Towards a just and peaceful society

The poor

The witness of the New Testament to Jesus of Nazareth is not unambiguously clear at all points. But some things within the New Testament are indeed clear enough. The direction of Jesus' actions, the recurring patterns of his conflicts with the authorities, and his choice of disciples and companions all reveal his own declared self-understanding:

> The Spirit of the Lord has been given to me, for he has anointed me. He has sent me to bring the good news to the poor, to proclaim liberty to the captives and to the blind new sight, to set the downtrodden free, to proclaim the Lord's year of favour (Luke 4:18ff).

A theology of the poor or of the oppressed or the outcasts is not just one of several options which Christians may or may not choose, or use to counterbalance some other option. Jesus' own announcement *to* the poor and *for* them is no more an optional or dispensable item for Christian theology than is the cross. Discovering who the "poor" really are — speaking and acting in solidarity with them (and the "poor" exist on both sides of the lines of conflict and in all communities) — is a far higher Christian theological priority than trying to pick and baptize the eventual winner among the powerful forces at work in the situation. There is the game of politics whose rules are properly followed by governments. Christians ought to be fully aware of this game and its rules, especially in the conflicts of the Middle East. The rules of realpolitik do not have, in principle, any binding authority over Christian ethical responsibility. A theology of the poor puts Christians continually on the side of those who have lost and continue to lose according to the rules by which the powers of this world are playing the game. A greater awareness of this responsibility by the churches will lead them to correct their own practices and then to search for ways to alleviate the suffering of the poor and to work in solidarity with them for their rightful place in society and for justice to all.

Rights of minorities

It is observed that the status of the various Middle Eastern minorities, whether religious or ethnic, is put to test by the politico-religious developments in the region. The growing tendency on the majority's part to enforce its own specific laws on minorities spreads a feeling of uncertainty and at times unrest among the minorities. The majority must be helped to realize that, in the final analysis, it is its action or inaction which will impose intercommunal peace in the region. The minorities, however, must realize that there is no future for them in isolation from the majority groups. An important question is how can churches establish understanding between communities in the Middle Eastern multi-religious society towards a *common concept of citizenship based on equality, mutual respect and freedom.*

Politico-religious reconciliation

The church, by definition, is committed to a faith that "seeks understanding" and not merely to a faith which seeks "advantage" or even "victory". Understanding Islam and Judaism is today one of the imperatives of the struggle for justice, peace, and a sustainable society in the Middle East.

The Christians have been for a century in the forefront of Arab national rebirth. Today, if the fragmentation of the Middle East into ethno-religious groupings is seen to mean the destruction of Arab cultural ethos from which a spiritual renewal might emerge, Christians should rescue "Arability" as the common message with the Muslims and the promise of humanization. For it is to the extent to which the common action of Muslims and Christians is developed along the path of Arability for the sake of all the outcasts of the earth that a real Islamo-Christian understanding and cooperation becomes possible.

The historic connection between the holocaust and the foundation of the state of Israel has exposed a whole range of theological-psychological-spiritual issues which should be explored seriously. The fear of a second holocaust is in the background of the Israeli ethical behaviour and strategy. The-end-justifies-the-means and the Massada complex are expressions of this ethic. The Christians, therefore, should help the Jews go beyond these complexes by re-evaluating the practice of reading history from the holocaust in the light of the cross and the resurrection. Not only *suffering* should inspire the power of Israel and its behaviour; it must be also hope in a better future between Israel and its neighbours, if Israel listens to its prophets of justice. How could the Christians of the Middle East contribute to this end? In political terms, reconciliation of the Arabs and Israel implies that Israel does not build its security at the expense of Palestinian rights and security, but does help the Palestinians recover their identity and human dignity. Self-determination for the Palestinians and all the other stateless peoples of the region is the door to peace with justice and reconciliation between the three monotheistic religions. Israel should therefore make the necessary concessions to the Christians and Muslims, if it seriously wants peace in Jerusalem, the City of Peace.

This paper does not in any way deal profoundly with all the aspects of the search for a just and participatory society in the Middle East. Neither does it deal directly with the biblical and theological basis of the Christian political ethics in the Middle East. It is an attempt basically to show that Christian participation and the political ethics involved in this process should be recognized in the light of the churches living as a minority in a multi-religious society where Islam is the majority and where Israel as the modern Zionist version of Judaism has an important and direct influence. This is the particularity of the Middle East in comparison with the other regions of the world.

Nevertheless, despite the fact that the context is different and the priorities and the partners in the struggle are different, our witness is to the one and the same Jesus Christ and the mandates of our faith remain the same. Accordingly, the churches need to take greater risk in identifying with the people's struggle for justice, unity and peace beyond their ethnic or cultural boundaries without forgetting that the church should never be reduced to any political system or ideology. Also, Christians in their involvement should realize that power is not the only valid criterion for resolving international and inter-religious conflicts.

Towards an ecumenical political ethics: a marginal American view

ALAN GEYER

My disqualifications for being an American representative in a global forum on political ethics are most impressive. I have been on the losing side of most electoral and legislative contests which really mattered to me in the past 15 years — which means that my theology of hope has increasingly been based on the evidence of things unseen. Moreover, the ascendant religiosities and moralisms of American politics, blatantly displayed in the campaigns and elections of 1980, have rudely frustrated my own agenda of justice and peace. So I write out of a deepening sense of alienation from both my political and religious environments. Moreover, my present academic title as "Professor of Political Ethics," if useful for this assignment, is of dubious legitimacy and uncertain meaning in all three realms which are vocationally important to me in America: religion, politics, and higher education.

American problems with politics and ethics

We have an old cultural problem in the States concerning the meaning and value of politics itself — a problem greatly compounded by religious attitudes. The anti-political prejudices of our business civilization which have infused our churches and our universities have made it peculiarly difficult to develop and sustain a healthy, humane view of what government is all about. Perhaps no major industrial nation is more deficient in its sense of the common good or more disposed to demean the vocations of politicians.

If this is an old problem, it has been profoundly aggravated by our political misfortunes and mediocre presidents of the past decade and a half. In fact, our two most recently elected presidents have attained their office largely by damning their government and its politicians. One of Ronald Reagan's favourite lines is: "Government is like a baby's alimentary canal, with a healthy appetite at one end and no responsibility at the other."

One reflex of this downbeat view of politics and politicians is the tendency to define political ethics itself in terms of personal morality rather than public philosophy or policy. Congressional ethics committees and executive ethics officers are preoccupied with such matters as bribes and conflicts of interest.

Recently I spent a day with a select group of civil servants in Washington, newly organized into an elite Senior Executive Service. My assignment was to discuss ethics and public service for professional bureaucrats. Most of these officials were quite prepared to take a much broader view of political ethics than that imposed upon them by official regulations. Indeed, some testified to profound conflicts of loyalties and values which were untouched by any professional code of ethics. One official whose primary responsibility is legal counsel for his agency confessed his distress in being also obliged to be "ethical counsel". The nub of his distress was that he had to function as policeman with regard to "Mickey Mouse matters of bureaucratic conduct" instead of providing guidance in coping with serious moral dilemmas about his agency's functions, policies and priorities. So the very definition of political ethics is hardly well-established in the US.

Pulp novels, TV, movies, and often the news media wallow in the personal peccadilloes of politicians rather than subjects of larger social import. Electoral campaigns become obsessed with Chappaquiddicks. Personality politics obscures social justice.

If popular prejudices thus reinforce the cultural distance between religion and politics in a country where, paradoxically, religious influence on political institutions has been profound, there is yet a deeper intellectual split which reflects the dualism of the American character. It is the split between moralism and materialism, or between messianism and pragmatism, or between idealism and realism. For decades, sophisticated discussions of ethics and world politics have tended to pit the so-called "realists" (such as Reinhold Niebuhr, Walter Lippmann, Hans Morgenthau and George Kennan) against a variety of "idealists" (not as easy to identify) who may also be denominated internationalists, liberals, legalists or crusaders. In the process, generations of students and clergy have been left with a rather schizoid view of relations between ethics and politics. The typical polarity, too often posed in terms of mutually exclusive choices, has been the "national interest" vs "morality". This polarity has severely inhibited the thoughtful articulation of national goals and purposes.

For a variety of reasons, then, the first challenge to political ethics in the US is to establish its own definition and legitimacy. That challenge confronts politics itself as a vocation. It confronts the academic study of politics in both universities and theological schools. And it confronts the churches with special imperatives.

A preliminary formulation of the inevitable connectedness of religion and politics — a formulation which grows out of a lifetime of having to explain and justify this connectedness to American audiences — is the following set of six propositions:

1. Politics has to do with all of life.
2. Religion has to do with all of life.
3. Therefore, religion and politics interpenetrate throughout all the tissues of personal and social life — a reality which our misinterpretation of the good principle of church-state separation often obscures.
4. To isolate religion and politics is schizophrenia: it literally threatens our mental health and obstructs social justice.
5. Yet to combine religion and politics thoughtlessly and uncritically threatens both the integrity of faith and the freedom of the political system.
6. Therefore, the discernment of both the *actual* and the *right* relationships between religion and politics requires much thought and study.

If these propositions are lacking in positive ethical content, they nonetheless may help to define the context in which Christian faith must express itself politically.

The late Archbishop William Temple once declared: "To religion the sphere of politics is never neutral ground. The state is an exposed sector of that mysterious struggle between *civitas Dei* and *civitas diaboli,* which is the central issue in world history."

From theology to politics to ethics

Professor Theodore Weber of Candler School of Theology, Atlanta, has offered an outline for a theology of politics which points towards a more adequate political ethic in the North American context than the political theologies of J.B. Metz, Jurgen Moltmann, and Dorothee Sölle. These German theologies (along with some of the Latin American liberation theologies) Weber finds to be "insufficiently political" — which is ironic in view of their insistence on the centrality of politics. They fail to "develop a political theory which clarifies and gives organizational expression to the basic and constant patterns of political society."

At the 1978 inaugural consultation of the Churches' Center for Theology and Public Policy in Washington, Dr Weber set forth an outline of the theology of politics in terms of five major elements:

1. *Comprehensive reflection on divine activity in relation to politics and the state.* Here Weber begins with the theme of redemption: "God the Healer at work in the fallen creation (both history and nature) to renew it and make

it whole." Then Weber proposes inquiring into "political work of God the Redeemer who is also Creator, Sustainer and Judge".

2. *A concept of Christian political vocation or responsibility that corresponds to the understanding of the political work of God.* Here the crucial theological focus is "the correlation of Christian selfhood and action with the confessional understanding of divine activity".

3. *A theological anthropology that acknowledges the historic Christian insights into human nature.* Here Weber's emphasis (echoing Reinhold Niebuhr) is on "the persistent ambiguity of human nature in politics" — especially between rationality and sinfulness.

4. *A systematic development of the phenomenology of politics that reflects the theological understanding of political reality.* Here Weber (again following Niebuhr and citing Jacques Maritain and Helmut Thielicke) insists on a profound examination of "the constant structural and dynamic elements which comprise the phenomenology of politics" — including the problems of authority, representation, law, and the distribution and limitation of power.

5. *A philosophical analysis of political reality which moves towards normative political philosophy.* Here Weber takes special note of the overlay in "Western" political thought between the Greek concept of *polis* and the Roman concept of *societas.* Each has its ethical vitality and limitations. *Polis* is holistic, organic, integrative, participative — but can be taken to totalitarian excess. *Societas* is associative and pluralistic, making the important distinction between society and state — but risking an excess of individualism.

Weber's framework, again, is for a theology of politics which can serve as the foundation of Christian political ethics. This is not a scheme for political ethics itself.

Subsequent to the Inaugural Consultation mentioned above, a continuing study group drafted a "Provisional Agenda for a Theology of Politics". That draft begins with a paragraph which pinpoints the distinctive contextual challenge to North Americans:

> A continuing North American study group on the theology of politics must not only be open to liberation theologies and other political theologies which are indigenous to other societies: it must deal concretely and experientially with the special features of politics in "advanced", "developed", "democratic", and "industrialized" societies. Such a focus will not only be concerned with vertical issues of justice — how to lift up the powerless and the oppressed — but with horizontal issues of justice among multiple centres of power.

Implicit in this statement is a recognition of the fundamental difference between two contrasting cultural situations. In some cultures, a ruling oligarchy excludes most of the people from significant political participation, represses civil liberties, and frustrates mass aspirations for economic justice. There is a potential for revolution because large elements of the public do not accept the legitimacy of the prevailing polity. Force and violence may be widely regarded as necessary means of liberation from oppression.

In other cultures, the achievement of revolution or social transformations in the past has led to a relatively stable polity in which groups continue to struggle for power and the satisfaction of their interests — but opportunities for political participation are broadly based and most groups accept the legitimacy of the prevailing polity, even if they believe they are victims of substantial injustice. In this second case, words like "revolution" and "liberation" may be more metaphorical than precisely applicable. The primary categories of political ethics are likely to be terms like "public interest", "consensus", and "compromise".

These contrasting cultural situations may be viewed as *ideal types* in the sociological sense: they are models or images of social systems which may help to highlight diverse characteristics. Perhaps most societies are actually strung along a continuum somewhere between repressive oligarchies and representative democracies.

These significant qualitative differences among political systems make a truly ecumenical study of political ethics extremely difficult. In some societies, Christians are rightly preoccupied with radical social change towards a more humane political system. In other societies, Christians are rightly concerned to conserve, improve and redeem an existing political system so that it may serve the common good more adequately. It is the wholesale transfer of an ideologically fortified ethic of one political situation to a fundamentally different situation that must be rejected. Too often, Americans have attempted to export if not impose their own models of constitutionalism or political parties on cultural environments in which those models are inappropriate or untimely. Similarly, some Americans have attempted to import models of revolution or liberation which are not responsive to indigenous political culture in the USA.

To speak of political "imports" and "exports" is to recognize the reality of international transactions which may be problematically related to domestic political values. Some societies have achieved democratic and/or socialist polities at home, yet have exported imperialism, repression, and massive violence abroad. Some American liberals practise a consensual ethic at home and patronize a liberation ethic for the third world. The obverse is the disposition of some conservatives: a consensual ethic for the US but an ethic of authoritarian repression for much of the third world (for the sake of "stability" or "containment"). The point here is not to propose a rigid uniformity of political designs for all societies: it is simply to highlight the difficulty of basic consistency in political ethics.

It is this boundary-crossing aspect of political behaviour, so extensive during the past century, which compels a reorientation of most inherited Christian political thought in the West. Political philosophy has traditionally been the philosophy of the state and its internal institutions, not a philosophy of its external life. Church-state theory has tended, all too similarly, to locate the church within a single state or society and has rarely hinted at the multitude of states or the claims of a world community.

The quest for a fully ecumenical political ethic must somehow do justice to both the internal and external behaviour of political systems — and beyond all national systems to the international system as a whole.

To speak of large-scale systems, however, is to risk speaking of impersonal abstractions in which any sense of moral responsibility may be diffused if not dulled altogether. Political ethics must therefore always be prepared to return to the decisions made by particular persons and groups. It must be an ethics of responsibility.

A mature and responsible ethic has at least four irreducible components: goals, motives, means, and consequences.

To have goals is to ask: What values do we want to achieve?
The question of motives asks: Why do we want to achieve these goals?
The question of means asks: How shall we achieve them?
The question of consequences asks: Are those values actually going to be achieved or destroyed? What other values may be achieved or destroyed?

If you fix on any one of these four components of ethics in a political situation, to the exclusion of other components, a problem of reductionism is likely to result.

Those who are absolutely fixated on *goals* are fanatics. (The philosopher Santayana once defined a fanatic as "one who doubles his speed when he has lost his way.")

Those fixated on *motives* may be innocents who naively suppose that purity of feeling is the essence of political responsibility.

Those fixated on *means* are perfectionists if not egomaniacs: persons who insist on only one way of doing things (usually their own way) so that they can't compromise, bargain, negotiate or mediate. Yet compromise is an essential political virtue, too often demeaned by moralistic Christians.

Those fixated on calculation of *consequences* tend to become cynics: persons who lose the capacity even to measure results by meaningful moral norms.

These four components of an ethical approach to political decision-making have no specifically Christian content. If they are broader than Christian, however, they are much narrower than the proper agenda of ecumenical political ethics.

A lush agenda for political ethics

In 1967, in the annual Raymond Walters Lectures at the University of Cincinnati, I made a comprehensive attempt to define the nature and scope of political ethics. (The overall theme was "Christianity and Political Ethics: Design for a Discipline".) While I now repent of some foolish things I said on that occasion, I shall draw on the framework of those lectures in this section. The tasks of political ethics, I said then, "add up to a long, lush agenda of concerns which must be brought into an integral relationship with one another". That agenda was set out in terms of twelve tasks, which I recapitulate here with some modifications:

1. *To appropriate the historic teachings of Christian faith concerning the meaning of political life.* God's justice as Sovereign Lord of all nations, the coming of a Prince of Peace whose government shall have no end, security as part of the promise of liberation, wrestling with principalities and powers, being subject to and dragged before the governing authorities, the beastliness of empires, loving even the enemy, the ministry of reconciliation overcoming the dividing walls of hostility — these and other biblical motifs will continue to inspire Christian political thought for as long as the church itself has life. Their extension through the centuries into doctrines of the City of God, orders of creation, a holy commonwealth, the Beloved Community will always give some fruitful guidance to the mind of the church.

2. *To encounter the politically significant teachings of other world religions.* If so-called universal religions were neatly restricted to particular territories and if they were devoid of political significance, this would be a needless task. It is because religious hostilities are all too typically at the heart of political conflict and international violence, however, that inter-religious communication has become a precondition of world community.

The great Hindu thinker, Sarvepalli Radhakrishnan, once lamented:

> It is one of the major tragedies of the world that the great religions instead of uniting mankind in mutual understanding and goodwill divide mankind by their dogmatic claims and prejudices. They affirm that

religious truth is attained in this or that special region, by this or that chosen race, condemning others either to borrow from it or else suffer spiritual destitution.

The challenge to Christians in that lamentation is not to foster syncretism among world religions: it is to understand the incarnation itself as a revelation of common humanity and the universal work of Christ. Dag Hammarskjold offered such testimony at the Evanston Assembly of the World Council of Churches in 1954 by declaring that "the cross, although it is the unique fact on which the Christian churches base their hope, should not separate those of Christian faith from others but should instead be that element in their lives which enables them to stretch out their hands to peoples of other creeds [for the sake of] a world of nations truly united".

The political discourse of Christians requires three different languages: (1) the language of Christian faith which must be revivified and clarified; (2) the language of common faith with other religious communities; (3) the language of common humanism in a pluralistic world. All these languages are *theologically* important.

3. *To engage in dialogue with secular political philosophies and ideologies.* Because modern ideologies have become the functional equivalent of religious faiths, Christianity is vulnerable to both conflicts with and manipulation by political belief-systems. At the same time, most ideologies serve as vehicles of moral values, often values with which faithful Christians can identify. Joseph Roucek has described the essential features of a vital ideology in terms of

its completeness and internal coherence,
its gorgeous vision of the future,
its ability to hold men's imaginations,
its pretence to provide a universal frame of reference of good and evil,
its consistency,
its convincing criticism of the present and picture of the future,
and its ability to circumvent counter-criticisms.

Ideology in some sense has become indispensable to the work of communication and consensus in all political systems.

Dean Charles West of Princeton Theological Seminary, a veteran of Christian-Marxist dialogues, has declared that political ideologies are useful and necessary — but "nowhere else is the temptation so great to justify human power serving special interests with arguments claiming ultimate and universal validity". Covert religions may "masquerade under the title of the laws of economics (capitalism) or of history (Marxism), national self-identity, individual liberties, people's solidarity, or the mystique of the small-town ethos". But all such cases represent an effort "to sanctify and make ultimate some particular human interest".

No substantial political ethic can justifiably claim to be non-ideological. No Christian ethic should be uncritically identified with any ideology.

4. *To interpret the fundamental categories of political experience in terms of their moral significance.* Interests, power, authority, coercion, controversy, compromise, consensus — these are some of the perennial and irreducible raw materials of political life with which ethical study must deal. (This task roughly corresponds to Theodore Weber's plea for a phenomenology of politics that reflects a theological understanding of political realities.)

A principal difficulty in political ethics, however, is precisely to describe just what those political realities are. Ethics is not simply an argument about what *ought* to be: it is an almost uninterrupted argument about what *is*, what *has been,* and what *will be.* The facticity of public policy is often more problematical than the choice of ethical principles. Whose reading of history, which theory of human nature, which social analysis, whose worldview, which intelligence data shall we choose as being empirically sound? How do we decide what is true to the political experience of humanity?

Great as our indebtedness to Reinhold Niebuhr surely is, Niebuhr allowed some of his dogmatic preoccupations to disqualify some of his claims to "political realism". In the view of political scientist Kenneth W. Thompson

> Niebuhr's application of the concepts of realism and idealism is so inconsistent, polemical, and vague as to drain them of much of their content, meaning, and usefulness. Realism at one time or another is said to imply... policies ranging from preventive war to naive demands for a peaceful settlement..., or from indifference to the ideological dimensions of conflict to an exaggerated awareness of national deceptions and pretensions. In fact, for Niebuhr political realism refers to conduct on a continuum ranging from cynicism to sheer utopianism.

So: there is no ethics-less, value-free method for determining just how we shall perceive political reality. Perception, as well as choice, is at the heart of political ethics.

5. *To share in the creation and transformation of political ideas which inspire public action.* Goals and purposes are at stake in all national and international action whether or not they are articulated in terms of political philosophy. There must be a positive philosophical creativity in political ethics.

One of the reasons for the ascendancy of conservative politics in the US and other countries in recent years is the failure of liberal and progressive movements to generate significant political ideas. David S. Broder, one of our most perceptive political columnists, has observed that the Democratic Party, long the engine of social change, has ceased to function as an "idea factory". The Carter administration was animated by a welter of positive moral impulses which were never thought through with sufficient clarity or coherence, nor were they persuasively articulated to the public. The heightened emphasis on human rights was full of potential and apparently encouraged more liberal measures in some countries — but it also led to invidious discriminations among countries and was not clearly connected with other goals like national security, detente, and economic justice. It has been commonly observed that Jimmy Carter himself failed to achieve many of his policy goals because he was essentially a technician trying to solve problems piecemeal, instead of educating the public to a vision of what he wanted to achieve and mobilizing the political resources to do so.

To the extent that liberals have been wedded to pragmatism and its "problem-solving", "cost-benefit" style, they have found it increasingly difficult to confront a rather new intellectual and moral moment in American life: a moment when profound systematic maladjustments have been exposed, large-scale problems increasingly linked to one another, and piecemeal "solutions" become new problems. In such a moment, basic assumptions must be clarified, priorities must be reordered, and new visions inspired. Ideologies become the necessary bearers of political ethics. Pragmatism is not enough.

Charles West has said that we must "not be afraid to have a philosophy of the common good and a programme based on that philosophy. Not to have such a directing vision is to surrender [government's] forming, reconciling and peace-making functions to the arbitrary decisions of special interests as they compete and compromise in the political sphere."

Every morally vital political philosophy articulates a distinctive conception of justice. A faithful Christian ethic will ground justice in the loving purposes of the Creator. It will articulate the meaning of justice in relation to such precious political values as peace, freedom, equality, community and order.

6. *To examine the technical issues of public policy in their bearing upon human values.* Every realm of public policy reveals an interpenetration of technical and ethical factors. With a decent respect for technical expertise, Christians must always be prepared to discern the thrust of ethics into the design of a highway system, patterns of health care, green revolutions, price structures in the world market, research and development for new strategic weapons.

To have an incarnational ethic is to *humanize the technical* in every area of governmental activity. It is to recognize that it has become fatally irresponsible to confine the ethical task to the promulgation of abstract principles, leaving the actual engagement with technical matters to others. It is to *demystify* the claims of expertise which too often are invoked to silence political discussion.

In a recent monograph published by our Center titled "Technology Assessment: Some Political and Theological Reflections", Catholic ethicist Ann Neale has written:

> In assessing a technology one must look at the impact of the end to be achieved as well as the impact of the means by which the end will be achieved.... TA is more than a narrow cost-benefit analysis which attempts to translate all effects into monetary terms. TA involves a comprehensive assessment — economic, social, political, ethical — involving all the implications of all the aspects of the technology to everyone involved. Not only the technology itself must be assessed, but also the state of the society into which it is introduced — the context — must be assessed.

7. *To articulate the ethical implications of theory, research methods, and findings in political science and related disciplines.* Surely those whose very profession is the full-time study of politics should be accorded some special place in political ethics — not that all of them would welcome such a place! In fact, the dominant behavioural and scientistic fixations of North American political scholars have provoked a humanistic rebellion during the past two decades.

In a provocative essay on the nature and scope of political science, Hans Morgenthau deplored the tendency of that field to "retreat into the trivial, the formal, the methodological, the purely theoretical, the remotely historical — in short, the politically irrelevant". Morgenthau, who died in 1980, belonged to a lively minority within his field who agree with David Easton that "the inspiration behind political science is clearly ethical". Morgenthau wrote of the "moral commitment" of political science in

> telling the truth about the political world... telling society things it does not want to hear. The truth of political science is the truth about power, its manifestations, its configurations, its limitations, its implications, its laws. Yet, on the other hand, one of the main purposes of society is to conceal these truths from its members. That concealment, that elaborate and subtle and purposeful misunderstanding of the nature of political man and of political society, is one of the cornerstones upon which all societies are founded.

There is much wit as well as wisdom in those sentences.

There are, after all, substantial contributions from the literature of political science to ethical discussion. A very short list might include studies of political alienation, opinion studies revealing attitudes of trust or cynicism towards government, case studies of decision-making, policy studies highlighting the impact of government programmes on communities and families, analyses of the images of enemies, analyses of bloc politics and power structures in the United Nations and related institutions like the World Bank, international relations theory which posits the emergence of an international system in which every part is dynamically related to every other part, examinations of the causes and consequences of political violence, modes of conflict resolution and peace-making.

8. *To investigate the value systems of various political cultures and movements.* Political ethicists also need the assistance of historians, anthropologists, social psychologists, and others whose disciplines may equip them to interpret the empirical reality of ethics. There is a distinctive cluster of political values in every community and society which gathers up not only the fruits of religious doctrine and of professional philosophy but the myths of its political history and the moral impacts of such forces as technology. This is what we mean by a *political ethos.* It is here that a great deal of demythologizing needs to be done in every society. There is all to much truth in T.H. Huxley's dictum that a nation is "a society united by a common error as to its origins and a common aversion to its neighbours".

My first book, *Piety and Politics,* was an attempt to analyze the "Puritan ethos" and its impact upon US foreign policy. That book modestly set forth the "Geyer-Freudian theory" which asserts that no nation exhibits more of a founding-father complex in its domestic and international politics than the United States of America.

Harold P. Ford, Presbyterian layman and CIA official, has urged that a theology of politics must become a theology of politics-and-culture. A radical critic of the "Canaanite culture" of North Americans, Ford goes beyond the usual harangues against materialism in pleading that we recognize "the enormous degree to which we unconsciously worship the god of Technology, and how this tends to cut us off from a sense of transcendent imperative, and from compassion and concern" for our fellow human beings. As one who was involved in Pentagon war games during the Vietnam War, Ford came to believe that US policy in Indochina increasingly exhibited a "compassionless, technical over-confidence". Another element of the American ethos identified by Ford is "visceral self-righteousness".

Whatever the ethical liabilities of a political culture, political ethics must also discern whatever ethical treasures there may be in our political heritage. More of this later.

Studies in cross-cultural communication have become increasingly vital to wise diplomacy and the effective management of international institutions.

9. *To engage in the critical analysis of the structures and processes of political decision-making.* Many of the world's most morally earnest people have a fixation on issues which simply take the present structures and procedures of government for granted. The radical frontier of political ethics is that point at which the structure itself becomes the issue in the struggle for justice and peace.

Given the increasingly bureaucratized structures of decision-making in virtually all societies, the fundamental imperative of truthfulness has taken on new complexities. While much attention has been devoted to ways in which bureaucracies may become insensitive to personal grievances and even unresponsive to their own managers and policies, it is the frequent gap between the psychological environment and the operational environment confronting decision-makers that aggravates the problem of truthfulness. Harold and Margaret Sprout give us a rather grim picture of this truth-problem:

> The higher one moves in the hierarchy of a great power's government, the more one is impressed by the remoteness of executives from the operational environment in which their decisions are executed. What passes for knowledge of the situation at the higher levels consists mainly of generalized descriptions and abstracts, several degrees removed from on-the-spot observations... To what extent is a top executive a virtual prisoner of the civil and military officials who provide data for him?

Thus does the political structure itself often give the lie to the claims of top policy-makers that they alone have all the facts. Again, it is the *perception of reality* rather than the choice of moral principles that may be the crucial element of political ethics in some contexts.

At the WCC-MIT conference on "Faith, Science and the Future" in July 1979, I presented a list of 18 propositions analyzing the impact of military technology on political institutions. The comprehensive picture that emerges is of the most fundamental changes in the structure and style of government, even of the purposes of government — changes of constitutional importance which have taken place through extra-constitutional processes. Moreover, these changes have had profound consequences for international relations:

The impact of military demands on science and technology is not only to distort the priorities and perceptions of "developed" societies: it is to intensify the pressures of domination upon "developing" societies. The pattern of domination is one in which economic, military, intellectual and cultural interests are closely inter-related. Some of the poorest of "developing" societies are increasingly militarized through collaboration between indigenous elites and the military-industrial-scientific elite of "developed" societies. The distortion of developmental priorities (educational, technological and social) thus increasingly mirrors the misplaced values and interests of richer countries — but at the heavy cost of frustrating the most elemental human needs of poor countries and even undermining their authentic security.

(That paragraph and the 18 propositions are to be found in the Section IX report from the WCC-MIT conference, titled "Science/Technology, Political Power and a More Just World Order".)

10. *To perceive the operation of ethical factors in the character and behaviour of political leaders.* All Christian ethics is finally incarnational and biographical: it moves beyond abstractions like ideas and institutions and seeks embodiment in the life and work of individual women and men. Theologians, political scientists, historians and psychologists have common homework to do here. Personalities as diverse as Woodrow Wilson, Mahatma Gandhi, John Foster Dulles, Dag Hammarskjold, Martin Luther King, Golda Meir and Ayatollah Khomeini reveal the ultimately personal mixtures of politics and morality.

Some Americans continue to find in Abraham Lincoln an incomparable sense of transcendence — a man who could say, in the middle of a bitter war:

> We have forgotten the gracious hand which preserved us in peace and multiplied and enriched and strengthened us, and we have vainly imagined, in the deceitfulness of our hearts, that all these blessings were produced by some superior wisdom and virtue of our own. Intoxicated with unbroken success, we have become too self-sufficient to feel the necessity of redeeming and preserving grace, too proud to pray to the God that made us. It behoves us, then, to humble ourselves before the offended Power, to confess our national sins, and to pray for clemency and forgiveness.

There have been moments in recent years when national leaders have been deficient in such a sense of grace, with tragic ethical consequences.

11. *To scrutinize the styles of political action in which the churches are involved.* It is the task of political ethics not only to bring religious perspectives

to secular politics: it is also to bring secular perspectives to what the churches are doing in the world.

As Theodore Weber notes, it has been the way of political theology and liberation theology to make the church "aware of its inescapably political character, to disclose its political captivity, to set in stark contrast the gospel message of freedom and vicious circles of oppression in society, and to delineate the political commitment to freedom as the only authentic mode of Christian discipleship".

Depending on one's definitions of freedom and politics, that could seem to be a reductionist concept of discipleship. But if totalitarian states cannot tolerate the autonomy of a free church, the political character of the church in "free" societies is typically denied or disguised. Disguises may include: (1) Melting Christian identity into a civil religion. Edmund Burke praised religion as "the public ornament, the public consolation". But he made it quite clear that this ornamental status of the church ruled out any political controversy about or within the church. (2) Sectarian withdrawal from what is believed to be the corrupt and sordid world of politics. (3) Withholding Christian involvement except on "great moral issues" — traditionally conceived as issues of personal morality like sex or temperance rather than issues of social justice. (4) Absorbing all the energies of the people in intramural church programmes so that they are deprived of the opportunity for political participation. The effect of all these moralities of disengagement is to forfeit the freedom of the church to the political status quo, a result not totally different from the totalitarian context after all.

12. *To expose the internal politics of the churches, especially as it affects the churches' influence upon society.* This task was well-performed in an introductory way by Keith Bridston's 1969 book, *Church Politics.* Bridston wrote somewhat colourfully of the "political pathology" of church leaders, the reality of "the church as a power complex", the "camouflage of political processes" in the church, and "ecclesiastical tycoonery".

If we had a political science of religion, as we have a sociology of religion and a psychology of religion, there would be more empirical data on the churches' own lobbies, party systems, gerrymanders, rotten boroughs, slush funds, propaganda mills, intelligence operations, colonial empires and bureaucratic empires. The ethical attitudes of Christians towards secular politics might become much healthier if they had a more candid understanding of church politics. The fact is that these internal struggles for power within religious institutions largely determine the capacity of churches to be a redemptive power in the outside world.

Some priorities

The foregoing twelve tasks do not prescribe the content of an adequate political ethic for Christians. They do suggest the subject matter for continuing study.

This paper concludes with an enumeration of priority issues in political ethics for the 1980s, from one American vantage point. Some of these issues have been anticipated in the preceding pages. All of them have international implications.

1. Issues of political culture

The traumas of the American people since the early 1960s have made our very definitions of nationhood and historical identity more problematical than ever in this century. Some have regressed to a primitive chauvinism which once again magnifies the moral gap between the American public and the rest of the world.

The 1980 elections and the resurgence of militarism both testify to the force of this chauvinism. Reactionary movements like the Moral Majority and their more sophisticated neo-conservative intellectual counterparts have tended to define the terms of public debate over ethical questions — a debate for which liberal and moderate Christians seem ill-prepared.

A counter-trend, responsive to the same national traumas but with a sharp tilt to the left and a revulsion at the new chauvinism, is to be seen in those who have become alienated and radicalized to the point of national self-hate. Thus the ethical importance of positive nationhood — nationhood devoted to the common good and to a constructive role in world affairs — has been understated by too many liberals and progressives.

Dag Hammarskjold once suggested that persons who seek to become revolutionaries by totally repudiating their national heritage are bound to become purveyors of hate and violence. They do not really help the people. "To separate himself from the society of which he was born a member will lead the revolutionary, not to life but to death unless, in his very revolt, he is driven by a love of what seemingly must be rejected, and therefore, at the profoundest level, remains faithful to that society." That reads like the odyssey of Dietrich Bonhoeffer: driven not simply by Christian imperatives but by a profound commitment to German nationhood even in its most humiliating and despicable days.

When radical Christians in America forfeit the competition for national symbols and stories to those who seek to obstruct racial justice, or promote special economic privileges, or impair civil liberties, or lobby for more aggressive military policies, they are likely to be morally irrelevant and politically ineffective.

No American has better understood all this than Martin Luther King, Jr. For he came to a moment of truth in the 1960s when he knew that justice in America could not be separated from peace in the world — and that there would be no peace for Americans at home unless there was justice in the world. When Dr King spoke of his dreams for America, he was at once a force for liberation and national reconciliation.

To have a positive view of nationhood can have vital implications domestically as well as internationally. The "Provisional Agenda for a Theology of Politics" addressed this concern in pleading for the renewal of a philosophy of "positive government", a term which flourished in the Progressive Era early in the twentieth century:

> The anti-political animus of American political culture makes the restatement of the case for *positive government* a prime task: that government really can and must serve the people in that range of human need which will never be justly served by private action. What a mature religious faith must do is not only to offer prophetic principles from which to criticize government: it must lift up the most creative human possibilities of achieving the common good through government action. The positive functions of government require a new normative understanding. In particular, the *nature and meaning of security* as a governmental function requires a new theological and ethical basis. The belief that security is an essentially quantitative matter — more weapons, more dollars, more growth — is now being challenged politically and must also be challenged theologically.

2. Issues of political economy

One does not have to be a Marxist to recognize symbiotic relationships between political and economic institutions. These relationships provide an inescapable subject for political ethics.

A second "provisional agenda" from the Center for Theology and Public Policy has to do with political economy, an old and classical term now enjoying a revival because of these symbiotic relationships in industrialized societies. While the full text of that document is appended, one paragraph particularly highlights the problems of ideologies and myths in prevalent notions of political economy:

> The most serious economic disorders of our time have exposed the severe limitations of all inherited schools of political economy — classical, Keynesian, Marxist and other varieties of socialism. Moreover, while comparative studies of these inherited options are ethically and

theologically important, we must ask increasingly whether industrially advanced countries generate common human consequences.... We should also explore new modes of interpreting the economic history of our own society, being prepared to uncover the myths that may have obscured the objective record and the moral meaning of that history. We must also be prepared to demythologize our understanding of the actual dynamics of our present economy.... The renewal of ideology is a fundamental task for those who seek to inquire deeply into the relationships between theology and political economy.

Later paragraphs in that document highlight questions of transnational interests, the military-industrial complex, economic growth, concentrations of power, freedom, welfare, and the rights of women — all questions in which economic and political issues intersect.

Here again, we must recognize the moral significance of political culture. It has been the habit of much democratic political thought to dissociate itself from the dynamics of the economy. Yet American political culture tends to be captive to the capitalist ethos without articulating the imperatives of economic democracy. In some "socialist" states, which trumpet the rhetoric of economic democracy, the pre-revolutionary political culture remains a powerful if not dominant reality in national life.

3. Issues of world politics

Early in this paper, an appeal was made for a reorientation of political ethics to include both the internal and external conduct of political systems — and beyond all national systems to the international system as a whole. The traditional domestication of both political philosophy and church-state doctrines makes it extremely difficult to view international conflict in theological and ethical perspective.

At our Center's inaugural consultation in 1978, Sister Helen M. Wright's paper on ecclesiology and politics declared that "political theology needs a global perspective". She hoped that the church itself, as a transnational institution, would "encourage the development of a political theology in every part of the world so that many peoples of the most diverse cultures and socio-political situations will feel called to look critically at their particular situation and place it over against the gospel message for reflection and interpretation in order to find in their faith meaning and direction for the future". Sister Helen proposed the radical participation of base communities in many countries, along with the world church's encouragement of "some kind of synthesis, some way of looking at the inter-relatedness of issues, some way of creating a global view no matter how tentative and changing that view may be".

My own studies in the international field in recent years have concentrated on nuclear disarmament and economic development. When one views these topics from the perspective of multilateral institutions like the United Nations rather than from the unilateral base of one's own foreign policy, a whole set of novel ethical questions arise.

Under the Non-Proliferation Treaty, for example, the renunciation of nuclear weapons by 110 countries in return for the sharing of energy technology and effective measures towards disarmament by the nuclear-weapon states is a solemn covenant of the most fateful kind. A coherent global nuclear policy, on which the survival of earth itself depends, requires increasing equity in the international power structure: there must be real and substantial compensations for any discrimination between nuclear "haves" and "have-nots" if there is to be any hope of international security. The Final Document of the 1978 UN Special Session on Disarmament strongly emphasizes the rights of all nations to share equally in negotiations which "have a direct bearing on their national security". An earlier, unofficial version of this principle is the slogan of the non-nuclear states for the past three decades: "No annihilation without representation."

The failure of the SALT process and the Non-Proliferation regime to make substantial progress towards disarmament and to be responsive to the protests of non-nuclear states is an issue of political ethics which is second to none in importance and urgency. Yet it has been the habit of most political and ethical discourse to view nuclear issues in a nation-centric rather than a global context. There has been a preoccupation with "nation security" dogmas like nuclear deterrence rather than the scenarios of peace-making, with the characteristics of military hardware rather than the qualities of political institutions, with unilateral applications of "just war" doctrines rather than systemic justice in the family of nations.

In the field of economic development, the chronic tendency is to take a shortsighted view of national interests, profits, and even benevolence rather than focusing on the power structure of the world market, banking, finance, investments, and insurance. The role of multilateral institutions tends to be trivialized. Church food programmes too typically are examples of cheap grace in failing to face up to the systemic causes of poverty and hunger.

Once again we see that our very notions of justice as the core principle of politics are inseparable from our angle of vision. *Perception is as crucial as principle.*

One of our leading political theorists, Stanley Hoffmann of Harvard University, years ago suggested that we need to turn our conventional thinking about politics inside out: "If we were to put the primary emphasis in the study of politics on world affairs, and to treat domestic politics in the light of world affairs, instead of the reverse, we might produce a Copernican revolution even bigger than the change that transformed economics when macro-analysis replaced micro-analysis."

Political ethics, if it is to have a firm grasp on reality, must not be preoccupied with micro-analysis. As it moves towards macro-analysis in world politics, it also improves our possibilities of becoming more responsible and more faithful Christians.

Appendix 1

A provisional agenda for a theology of politics

A continuing study group gathered around the topic "Theology of politics" has been meeting periodically since the inaugural consultation of the Churches' Center for Theology and Public Policy in April 1978. This brief working paper is a provisional agenda for the group's work but is now also shared with a wider public for any appropriate use and response.

A. Some assumptions

1. A continuing North American study group on the theology of politics must not only be open to liberation theologies and other political theologies which are indigenous to other societies: it must deal concretely and experientially with the special features of politics in "advanced", "developed", "democratic", and "industrialized" societies. Such a focus will not only be concerned with vertical issues of justice — how to lift up the powerless and the oppressed — but with horizontal issues of justice and order among multiple centres of power. (This was a major concern of Theodore Weber's paper at the inaugural consultation, the title of which was "Beyond Political Theology: Towards a Constructive Theology of Politics in a Democratic Society".)

• This document first appeared in *Center Circles*, June 1979, published by the Churches' Center for Theology and Public Policy, 4500 Massachusetts Avenue NW, Washington DC, 20016.

2. Issues of justice are not only issues of *power,* they are also issues of *cultural values* widely shared by a majority of the body politic. Harold Ford and John Langan both insisted at the consultation that a theology of politics must be developed into a *theology of politics and culture.* Ford spoke of a "Canaanite culture" underlying United States policies — a political culture which is urban, sophisticated, materialistic, and marked by "compassionless technical overconfidence". Unconscious nationalism and "visceral self-righteousness" are important basic identifications for most Americans.

B. Prime issues

1. The churches themselves typically seem preoccupied with their essentially private interest to the neglect of the common good. In part, this preoccupation suggests that the *churches' concerns in the public sector* (such as issues of justice and peace) are not high priorities for church leaders at present. In part, it reflects the anti-political orientation of the Protestant subculture. An adequate theology of politics must articulate a normative approach to the churches' priorities in relation to the public sector and the common good. We need a new typology of church-political relations (perhaps developed from H. Richard Niebuhr's *Christ and Culture* and Alan Geyer's *Piety and Politics*) in which the dimensions of both involvement and over-againstness are vivified. Such topics as the political ministry of religious vocations and the church as a source of moral wisdom for public policy require fresh formulations.

2. The anti-political animus of American political culture makes the restatement of the case for *positive government* a prime task: that government really can and must serve the people in that range of human need which will never be justly served by private action. What a mature religious faith must do is not only to offer prophetic principles from which to criticize goverment: it must lift up the most creative human possibilities of achieving the common good through government action. The positive functions of government require a new normative understanding. In particular, the *nature and meaning of security* as a governmental function requires a new theological and ethical basis. The belief that security is an essentially quantitative matter — more weapons, more dollars, more growth — is now being challenged politically and must also be challenged theologically.

3. A critical topic just now is the relationship between *public and private centres of power.* As confidence in government has declined in recent years, the political process has more and more come under the sway of special interests and single-issue lobbies — groups which often have a vested interest in

deepening the alienation between public and private sectors. But government by piecemeal policies and private manipulation can hardly do justice to the common good. The relationship between *political and economic power* is a particularly critical frontier for theology today.

4. Political cynicism has deepened so severely since the mid-1960s that the anti-political traditions of our culture and our religion have been powerfully reinforced. Issues of *political vocation, citizenship,* and *participation* require vital new expressions in Christian thought if cultural prejudices are to be overcome and justice to be done. A doctrine of positive politics is a prophetic necessity. Political action must be dignified as an expression of human nature and selfhood. We should reflect on recent studies which suggest that blacks and other minorities have greater expectations and confidence in government than do whites. To what extent is white middle class cynicism a reflection of the fact that government may, indeed, be effective in promoting social justice in some respects? To what extent is current political cynicism abetted by the propaganda of business interest which have always expressed anti-political attitudes, even while seeking to dominate and manipulate government?

5. It has been the tendency of American liberals and pragmatists to view social evils largely in piecemeal and non-ideological terms. As some analyses of cultural crisis have increasingly focused on systemic breakdowns and linkages among major social problems, theological reflection confronts a new ideological question. To what extent are the greatest social evils (racism, classism, sexism, ageism, materialism, violence, imperialism) products of particular political systems and ideologies? Is it possible to view basic political realities in non-ideological terms? Typically the moral dilemma is not simply a conflict between principle and politics: it is a choice among competing views of political reality.

6. Christian thinking concerning the state has typically been domesticated and unilateral — as if the church were contained within the state. The increase of external claims and pressures on the state, especially with the emergence of a whole array of global survival issues, calls for a new *transnational context* for an adequate theology of politics. The United States is simultaneously caught up in patterns of increasing interdependence and patterns of dominance over those societies — economically, culturally, militarily. Church-state doctrines must be reconstructed for this new transnational reality.

7. Another underlying question concerns our *theology of history.* Issues of God's action in history, religious and cultural identity, inherited obligations, intergenerational justice towards the future, discerning signs of the times —

these and other topics appropriate to theological reflection on politics are rightly grounded in our theologies of history.

8. Underlying all these topics is a basic methodological issue for the theology of politics; what is our *style of thought,* especially in relating *engagement* to *reflection*? If engagement is a precondition of an adequate theology of politics, what place must be accorded to politicians themselves ("politicians" here taken to mean both government leaders and non-governmental activists)? How do we do our most faithful and creative thinking theologically about politics?

Appendix 2

A provisional agenda for theology and political economy

During 1979 a study group on theology and political economy was gathered at the invitation of the Churches' Center for Theology and Public Policy. The study group plans to continue its work on a number of topics mentioned below and remains open to new participants. This brief working paper is a provisional agenda for the group's work but is now also shared with a wider public for any appropriate use and response.

Virtually every area of public policy has both economic content and economic consequences. The mutual interpenetration of political and economic institutions appears to be a feature of every known society, notwithstanding compartmentalized ways of thinking about politics and a certain tendency in US society to draw too sharp a boundary between the "public sector" and the "private sector". The range of governmental responsibilities for economic policy is extensive and complex.

Economic life is also at the heart of Christian efforts to interpret the world theologically. From the first century on, some Christians have sought to avoid this task by over-spiritualizing the Christian message or by thinking only of that time when God would bring an end to history and inaugurate the reign of Christ. But the mainstream of Christian thought has rejected such irresponsibility, emphasizing that the created material world is God's world in

---

• This document first appeared in *Center Circles,* June 1980, published by the Churches' Center for Theology and Public Policy, 4500 Massachusetts Avenue NW, Washington DC 20016.

which God's purposes challenge human faithfulness. Theology has been and is challenged to relate the great themes of Christian thought such as creation, sin, Christology, grace, redemption, liberation, love, eschatological hope, stewardship — to economic realities. Insofar as theology deals with actual human existence in a real world, these themes have substantial economic importance.

During certain periods of its history, the Christian church has addressed economic life forthrightly and creatively. For instance, the American churches in the late nineteenth and early twentieth centuries gave major attention to economic justice and welfare as a part of the social gospel movement. The origins of social ethics in our theological seminaries and the early impetus to the ecumenical movement can also be traced largely to Christian response to economic issues. For nearly a generation, however, economic issues, have been relegated to remarkably low priority among theologians, ethicists and church programmes. During these same years, we have had growing apprehensions of the human costs of systematic poverty in both the US and the world's poorer nations. Moreover, the quality of life in all societies has been exposed increasingly to the creative and destructive possibilities of industrial technology.

The tentative agenda offered here represents an effort to focus concerned Christians' thinking upon a clearly defined set of critical issues of political economy. All Christians have a contribution to make in helping to think these issues through in relationship to the gospel and their own existence as people who wish to live a Christian life in difficult times. Christian teachers and church leaders are challenged by the economic issues of this period of history to give creative new leadership and to develop imaginative new church programmes expressing a renewed commitment to economic justice.

1. *Theological method.* Most theological doctrines and most forms of theology can be related to economic life. But the intensely productive theological work of the past half century has not been as carefully related to economic issues as it needs to be. In particular, greater attention must be given to theological method. To what extent and how should biblical material be formative of conceptions of economic justice? What is the enduring contribution of natural law ethics, and how can it best be formulated in theological terms? How should theology make use of the social sciences, including economic science? What authority should be attributed to Christian tradition, ecumenical councils, ecclesiastical pronouncements of various kinds?

2. *Ideologies and myths.* The most serious economic disorders of our time have exposed the severe limitations of all inherited schools of political

economy — classical, Keynesian, Marxist and other varieties of socialism. Moreover, while comparative studies of these inherited options are ethically and theologically important, we must ask increasingly whether industrially advanced societies generate common human consequences, whether in capitalist, socialist or communist states. A pluralistic approach to basic economic paradigms should be explored, with a view towards cultural and developmental differences. We should also explore new modes of interpreting the economic history of our own society, being prepared to uncover the myths that may have obscured the objective record and the moral meaning of that history. We must also be prepared to demythologize our understanding of the actual dynamics of our present economy with regard to such matters as competition, inflation, unemployment, profits, and the dynamics of the market. The great significance of ideology, as the organizing perspective on the basis of which we assess particular problems, challenges us to profounder ideological reconstruction. The renewal of ideology is a fundamental task for those who seek to inquire deeply into the relationships between theology and political economy.

3. *Growth.* How shall we value the various aspects of economic growth? What norms should guide intentional, planned growth? What options are there in the relationship of economic growth to Christian doctrines of vocation and stewardship and to Christian concerns for conservation? If we project a no-growth or a slow-growth economic future, how shall we deal ethically with the pressures to redistribute income in our own society? How are the interests of the poorer nations affected by alternative approaches to the ethics of growth?

4. *Equity.* By what theological and ethical criteria do we determine the just distribution of goods and services and the just division of wealth? What are the relative claims of need, merit, market forces, and equality as governing principles? When hardship and suffering result from economic changes, how shall such costs be apportioned? Who is hurt most by inflation? Recession? Industrial shutdowns? Court-ordered desegregation? Affirmative action? Increased competition for the high costs of environmental protection technologies? What is a just policy approach to the increasing debt service burden of most poor countries? How shall inequities in the tax and incomes policies of our government be rectified? How should the economic benefits of the global commons—such as the seabeds—be developed and distributed?

5. *Power.* If much centralized planning has become inevitable in economic life, what patterns of public and private participation in planning decisions are ethically imperative? How can the power of ordinary people to control their economic destiny be assured in a world of giant corporations and imper-

sonal government? Are regularory agencies and the play of competition sufficient safeguards against irresponsible power? What public policies can help
local communities retain a significant measure of economic autonomy over-
against the non-local decisions of conglomerates? How can smaller and
poorer nations be helped to retain economic autonomy over-against the
powers of transnational enterprises? How shall we evaluate the patterns of
dominance-and-dependence in the world market? What are the most com-
mendable power relationships in the control and transfer of technology,
especially between richer and poorer nations?

6. *Freedom.* What are the moral bases and limitations of freedom in
economic life? To what extent is freedom in economic life essential to other
forms of human freedom, and to what extent has economic freedom of the
powerful contributed to the loss of freedom by weaker members of the community? What forms of regulatory control are needed to assure that the
freedom of large economic institutions will not be used to exploit workers,
consumers, and the environment? What responsibilities does a democratic
government have to preserve the housing options of its citizens in view of the
damaging effects of inflation of housing costs in many areas of the country?
How shall the freedom of the labour movement be balanced with the public
interest and the special needs of unorganized workers and the unemployed?

7. *The military-industrial complex.* While many studies have demonstrated
that the US civilian economy can generate more than enough aggregate demand to sustain economic growth and general prosperity, many regions and
enterprises are heavily dependent on the military budget. What is the appropriate role of the government in facilitating economic conversion to
civilian needs? To what extent is the current crisis of productivity in the
American economy a result of a gross misallocation of research-and-
development technology to the military sector, and what changes in public
policy might alleviate this situation? To what extent is general inflation attributable to high levels of military spending for the past two decades? How
are the principles of a free enterprise economy affected by patterns of
defence industry and procurement? What are the moral and economic effects
of international transfers of weaponry?

8. *Welfare.* Whether the "welfare state" is here to stay, or can yet be un-
done, or has yet to be achieved is an inescapable controversy for Christians
seriously concerned about genuine human welfare. Welfare policies,
however, are viewed by many as the consequences of inadequate economic
policies in such matters as employment and incomes. To what extent would
altered economic policies actually reduce government expenditures which
now maintain a costly welfare system — and could such policies actually im-

prove the social and psychological circumstances of millions of persons now on welfare? Should basic income needs of welfare recipients become an entirely federal responsibility, and should the United States adopt a form of "negative income tax"? What are the implications of current economic realities for the maintenance of a basic livelihood for all people? Are we approaching the time when the relationship between work and income will have to be reordered?

9. *Economic rights of women.* In the current wide-spread reordering of the relationship of women and men, many issues are basically economic in character. The traditional division of labour which has placed women in the roles of mother and homemaker while men are the "bread-winners" has come under increasing pressure, with profound ethical and theological issues not yet wholly resolved. Is there, in fact, any basis in a Christian doctrine of creation for insisting upon the maintaining of those traditional roles? Do these roles carry subtle overtones of inferiority/superiority? What economic losses has society had to bear as a price for neglecting the creative contributions of women? In what areas do women need special protection and how can special protection be provided without vitiating the equal dignity and rights of women? How can the widespread patterns of unequal compensation for women be overcome? To what extent are policies of affirmative action needed to open up job opportunities for women in areas traditionally closed to them?

10. *Economic and non-economic institutions.* Economic institutions interact with other institutions than the government. A broad theological approach to political economy should raise questions of justice, freedom and the common good wherever economic interests appear to dominate and manipulate other human interests and needs. Health care, higher education, the arts, religion itself are all subject to massive economic pressures in American life. To what extent do these pressures compromise the integrity and autonomy of such institutions? To what extent are the gross materialism, pervasive violence and sexism, stress and anxiety so widely perceived in American culture attributable to the aggressive pursuit of economic interests? How can public policy properly cope with such problems?

11. *International economic relationships and world order.* What theological considerations can be offered in support of the national economic interest when this is in conflict with wider human economic interests? Is the present framework of international economic order substantially favourable to the interests of wealthier, more powerful nations? Do transnational corporations enjoy substantial freedom from accountability to any nations? To what extent is the economic prosperity of the wealthier countries a function

of the dependency of poorer countries? To what extent is inflation and recession within a country caused by international forces beyond that country's political or economic control? What new international economic institutions are needed to facilitate the emergence of economic justice on a world scale?

12. *The churches.* What is the churches' proper role in support of just governmental economic policies? While churches in contemporary America profess to be hard-pressed economically, they remain in possession of greater wealth than the churches of any other nation. To what extent are the institutional resources of the churches (amounting to tens of billions of dollars in properties, equipment, investments, and related institutions) allocated with reference to norms of economic justice? The churches operate many institutions and programmes specifically directed to the health, welfare, education and food needs of millions of people. To what extent are such efforts a philanthropic distraction from the basic issues of economic justice? The basic arena for most church members' opportunity to witness to their religious concerns about economic life remains the world of work and vocational groups. Yet the ministry of the laity, as the apostolate to the world of work and citizenship, remains a chronically underdeveloped doctrine of the American churches. How can the ethical dilemmas and the public responsibilities of the laity be given a central place in the worship, nurture, and witness of the churches?

Political ethics in Vanuatu

FRED TIMAKATA

Background of Vanuatu

Captain Cook is said to have "discovered" the islands we now call Vanuatu, although when he first sighted them in 1774 he named them "the New Hebrides". Our islands had been navigated in part long before this time by Spanish and French explorers from as far back as 1606, and yet it was not until the nineteenth century that Europeans began to pay attention to them, mainly with a view to exploiting our resources.

Prior to the invasion of the white "settlers" — as we shall call them — life in our islands, as in so many others in the Pacific region, contained many of the elements of a just, participatory society. This was in spite of the fact that culture varied from island to island; languages were — and still are — many and different (no less than 110 plus English, French and our lingua-franca Bislama). Dancing, singing, marriage ceremonies and feasts, funerals, land use, the grading of the chiefly line of leaders — many of these show large variations in practice and yet there was an overall harmony as our people did not rape the land or the sea, but maintained a delicate balance of the whole which manifested itself in some measure in a "just, participatory and sustainable society".

When the traders and missionaries came, over 150 years ago now, the culture of Vanuatu began to disappear in many cases; and in others, it started to lose much of its value. The intrusion of cultures from the West, from the white man, and later from parts of Asia, began seriously to erode our cultural values which we had cherished for the previous 5,000 years of our habitation of these islands.

From the moment the first ni-Vanuatu stepped ashore onto our islands, land has been an essential element of their very existence. Not only did ni-Vanuatu work and till the land to produce the food they needed for survival in a largely agricultural society but, like many other islanders and aboriginals, their links with the land were such that they were part of each other like a mother and her baby.

For ni-Vanuatu, land was not, and never will be, a portable, disposable commodity which can be bought and/or sold as in many Western societies. While others may, for the time being, have the use of land, the custom owner always retains the right of ownership and the sole authority.

When this aspect of our society is understood, many other facets of our culture can also be grasped.

To press the example of land a little further, during the last 150 years, land has been alienated, largely through fraudulent dealings by outside settlers and dealers. Other holdings were just appropriated, while still more land was "bought" for liquor, tobacco, guns, trinkets, etc. People were enticed to give up their land, some were gradually killed off and then their land taken over on the basis that payment in kind — liquor — had been made.

About one-fifth of all our land was alienated, owned variously by French, British individuals and/or companies, missions, the French government, native trusts/boards, ni-Vanuatu. The remaining four-fifths is still customary owned land, somewhat inaccessible, although very fertile.

My government has now set itself the task of doing something positive and constructive on the issue of land as many ni-Vanuatu rightly demand the return of what is theirs by birth. And so with the advent of independence we see the beginning of land reforms, tenure, registration, survey and administration in order to restore at least one major aspect of what was for us at one time an element in a "just, participatory and sustainable society".

The effects of population movements

Coupled with the coming of the foreign traders, missions, and various ethnic groups, especially during the nineteenth century, there came exploitation, sickness, disease, death with a subsequent reduction in the population.

Notable among those exploitative traders who first came to our shores were the sandalwood traders. They literally wiped the islands of Tanna and Erromango in the south clean of sandalwood, so that today very little is left for local use, much less for overseas trade. Most of those who came in the early 1800s were nearly all bad characters with little regard for the local people, the land, justice, or any other quality of life.

And of course, the inevitable occurred in Vanuatu as in other islands of the Pacific. With the coming of the white man there came the introduction of his diseases, and very soon many epidemics were rampant in the Southern Islands.

In addition, in about 1840 the Queensland and Fiji canefields began to suffer from a shortage of labour and the recruiters came to Vanuatu. It is conservatively estimated that between 1847 and 1880 some 20,000 people had gone from our islands, mostly taken by force.

So the two events, the advent of the white man's diseases and the abduction of our people, reduced the population so dramatically that only now have we come close to the number that was fairly accurately estimated back over 100 years ago — 1874. The attached graph gives statistics only. It does not enumerate losses due to Western diseases like measles, influenza, etc. It does not tell the story of "blackbirding", but it is a commentary on our personal experience during a dark period in our history when we lost our customary justice, when only those who raped our land and our people participated, and when all elements of a sustainable society almost disappeared from the face of Vanuatu.

GRAPH SHOWING CHANGES IN POPULATION SINCE 1874

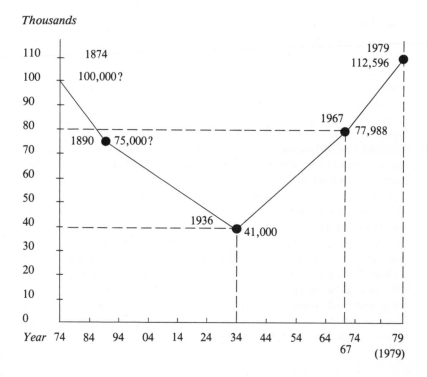

While the above account tells of our losses, there have been some gains which have also added a variety of cultural mixes to our country. A century ago, fewer than one hundred Europeans had settled in Vanuatu, mostly on plantations. Then for a time we had a large population of Asians, mostly Vietnamese, who had been brought to the then New Hebrides as Tonkinese indented labour to alleviate the acute labour shortage on the French-operated plantations. Others who have since come include those from the Wallace and Futuna Islands who were attracted to work on the manganese mining project which is now defunct due to the depressed world market. By 1929, the year the world depression began, there were 5,974 Tonkinese labourers in Vanuatu. Since the end of the war in Vietnam many have been repatriated and a recent census figure lists them as representing 0.5 percent of the population.

To close this section of my account, let me just add that that same census indicated 0.3 percent Chinese; 1.6 percent Polynesians and Micronesians; 2.5 percent Gilbertise (ni-Kiribati), Fijians, Tongans and Wallisians. The European population at that time was 2 percent, a figure now requiring revision.

The effects of missions

During the period I have outlined, the so-called traders' "plundering" period, missionaries had also been settling in Vanuatu. The first to be sent was the Rev. John Williams of the London Missionary Society. After his arrival on Tanna in the south, he visited Erromango Island nearby where he was murdered in 1839.

The Rev. John Geddie, a Presbyterian, started work on the southernmost island of Aneityum in 1848, while Bishop Selwyn of the Anglican Church founded the Melanesian mission in 1849. The Roman Catholic Church, through its Marist Brothers, visited Vanuatu in 1849 but did not establish their mission until 1887.

From those early beginnings, the Christian church was established throughout Vanuatu, reaching from the south to Santo in the north during the following years. Today, the Presbyterian Church, of which I am a member and pastor in good standing, represents over 30 percent of the population, claiming some 45,000 members. Anglicans number almost 11,000. Other groups include the usual "sects" which seem to use the Pacific Islands as a "hunting ground" — Mormons, Jehovah's Witnesses, SDAs, etc., with such other "custom" religions as the Jon Frum movement, animism and the "Royal Church" of the Nagriamel movement (a reactionary political group, active as secessionists prior to independence).

The effects of the early missions here are similar to those in other parts of the world: the establishment of schools, hospitals, clinics, churches, missions, and the gradual handing over of the educational and medical institutions to the metropolitan powers, keeping only their churches and missions. This is except in a few cases where some of the schools are still run by the churches and, of course, the Roman Catholic Church still maintains its active interest in and support of its educational programme as in other countries.

This side of independence, the churches in Vanuatu are playing an important part in the nation's development and in the restoration of a "just, participatory and sustainable society". For example, I am one of seven ordained ministers of the gospel who are members of the Representative Assembly. There are also three elders holding high governmental positions, while a prominent member of the Roman Catholic Church's priesthood is in the opposition.

The government has made a deliberate choice, which is reflected in the preamble of the constitution of Vanuatu, pledging allegiance to "Faith in God, Melanesian values, and Christian principles", a statement which, of course, commits us to the development of participatory methods as we attempt to build a new way of life, a just society.

The churches today have come a long way from those early days of the coming of Christianity to our islands. The early evangelical zeal of those first missionaries has been extended now to include a new development in the area of maintaining the centrality of the gospel as more and more villages throughout Vanuatu, of which there are some 2,200, extend political independence to the heart of their small self-managing communities.

Nowadays, as a travelling Minister for Home Affairs, I marvel at the way many of our small village communities are accepting the responsibilities of their new political independence as a new awareness emerges, showing realization as to just how far our people can go as self-sustained communities. And further, at their awareness that such communities are a gift from God, even though for a long period in our history this gift was hidden from our eyes, suppressed and thwarted by the metropolitan powers.

This new awareness is already being felt in other countries in the Pacific. And although many island nations in the Pacific are not using words like just and participatory, nevertheless Pacific identity and solidarity are emerging as strong factors throughout the churches which make up Melanesia, Micronesia and Polynesia, expressed in the forum of the Pacific Conference of Churches.

Signs of hope

Japanese theologian Kosuke Koyama, in his book *Three Mile an Hour God,* reminds us of God's promise to Abraham: "Go from your country and your kindred and your father's house to the land that I will show you" (Gen. 12:1).

We ni-Vanuatu have at last come into our own land, which God promised to our forefathers long ago, a land which we are in the process of making a just land, a land in which every citizen can participate to the fullest extent of his capabilities, a land which, by God's grace, will grow to become more sustainable as the years go by.

Koyama reminds us that the Promised Land has an interesting geographical location at the point where Asia, Africa and Europe meet and he goes on to say to his readers that the promised life is not one of isolation, but one of daily encounters as one lives at the intersection of life.

For us in the Pacific, especially in Vanuatu, we feel that we are at the intersection of the busy, developing life of a large group of scattered islands stretched right across the Pacific — small atolls, tiny islands, extinct and active volcanoes dotted over the largest mass of ocean in the world.

As we struggle to wean ourselves from colonization, we are conscious of the marks left by that experience. We are conscious that during that time, many of our prized cultural values and heritages were all but eroded because of the values of other cultures imposed on us. So today, in our search for the recovery of those original values we cherish so much, we are "rediscovering" and "restructuring" in the hope that our children will learn what it means to participate in a culture blessed by God, enriched by nature and in which there is justice for all. We are also beginning to learn that for us, the Western model is not the one to follow: materialistic, technically advanced society based on growth and scientific and material progress does not seem to contain the elements of "just, participatory and sustainable" groups of Pacific islands.

Since our own independence, we have become acutely aware of the fact that there is a new, more insidious form of colonialism exerting its influence and without any regard for the delicate balance in which the whole of the Pacific ecology is held. Many powerful Western nations have used our region as a place to spew their refuse and excrete the manurial wastes of their nuclear experiments. Some advancing countries in the East are planning to do the same.

So while we have high hopes for the future of the new politically independent Vanuatu and other neighbouring islands within our region, we know that other forces are at work around us.

We feel that while nuclear testing continues in that part of the Pacific called French Polynesia and the dumping of radio-active wastes goes on, our hopes will disappear in the mushroom clouds of another catastrophic disaster, which, if allowed to persist, will ultimately annihilate us all.

Our current history in Vanuatu still bears the scars of recent rebellion, of the French reluctance to leave, right up to the eve of our independence. But let us not forget our near neighbours in French-run New Caledonia — rich in nickel and other minerals. For them, their natural resources will ensure a fully sustainable society; but under the present colonial domination, justice and complete participation are scarcely possible.

And while we all know of Japan's constant threat to use our islands and ocean as their nuclear waste dumping ground, let us not overlook the fact that Australia, Canada and New Zealand all engage in the active pursuit of the nuclearization, militarization and commercialization of our Pacific region. In the face of these threats, most of us in the Pacific islands — nations, churches and other communities — have actively and loudly voiced our opposition to such activities; yet, the big developed nations with their multinational corporations and technological plans for future "growth" will nakedly persist, at the expense of our hopes for a sustainable Pacific.

If we are to sustain our society in such a way that it can be transmitted to our successors in an unsullied condition, then it is obligatory for us to continue to raise our voice for justice, for peace, and for a sustainable society, both for us and for our children's children.

But how do we confront the whole reality of sin in the world today — and in the Pacific in particular? Not only the greed, selfishness, self-centredness and unjust attitude of individuals, but also that which exists at the national levels of our society. That which almost seems to precipitate multinational corporations into a frenzy of activity which has no regard for anyone or anything else except the god of profit. How shall we in Vanuatu, and all of us in our countries and regions, act with all due care and responsibility in such a way as to critically address ourselves to such a frustrating, impossible, yet vitally important job?

When those first exploiters of our islands landed on our beautiful shores, they did not find a political vacuum on the beach, or the reefs, the hills and mountains of our islands. Rather they found a well-organized, self-sufficient group of communities with their ordered villages, graded system of rule and chiefly authority, all designed for the maintainance and wellbeing of their inhabitants. Evangelical zeal and colonial imperialism all but destroyed all this.

The reason we are rejecting many of the imposed colonial values at the point of gaining our freedom through independence is that the individualistic

Western approach which appears to be the foundation of a culture is not our culture. We have little to do with the Western culture which, in spite of its so-called "Christianization", shows very little evidence of those values of justice, participation and sustainability which are basic to the gospel. Part of our hope is that the day will soon come when we in the Pacific can come to the "developed" countries of the world with our "missionaries" and share some of our cultural understanding of the gospel.

Appendix 1
Towards a method in political ethics

ROGER HUTCHINSON AND GIBSON WINTER

Following the CCPD consultation in Cyprus, several of us reviewed our experiences there. We came to the conclusion that the paradigm of reading a text could be useful in reviewing the work of the consultation and anticipating work to be done. (See Appendix for an exposition of this method.) No attempt is made to attribute particular perspectives and content to members of the consultation, but the materials are drawn largely from the work groups and plenary reports.

Selection of the text

In developing the paradigm of the text as a method for interpreting political-historical process, no attention was given to the selection of the text, i.e. what in the totality of human dwelling is taken as the subject matter for interpretation (see Appendix). Does one look at a sacred history, a confessional tradition, or Christ and Culture with H. R. Niebuhr? Such a selection is decisive for the work of political ethics. The consultation seemed to come to a consensus that the text for political ethics is the People's story or socio-biography. The text of political ethics is the politico-historical life of the People in the context of faith. Any attempt to shortcut the People's story by imposing a programme from the top violates this understanding of political ethics, adding one more oppression to the existing structures. The People's story is a praxis, an historical-political struggle for liberation from suffering and oppression. This gives a particularity to a People's story. Different peoples are engaged in very specific struggles, though they share a common work of liberation. This means that political, ethical and theological interpretations and proposals are qualified by the contingencies of the People's story.

"People", as a term, has been capitalized in these preliminary remarks. This signifies that "People" is a central symbol in the work of political ethics. There seemed to be a consensus that the "People" are those who are excluded from subjecthood, depoliticized and dehistoricized by oppressive forces. These are the silenced, those who are made invisible or marginalized. It is the socio-biography of this People that constitutes the subject matter of political ethics. They are the bearers of hope for the larger community. Through their struggles the communities may find their path towards justice and peace.

The guess

We do not tell our story or hear a story without some sense of the "story". Whatever the narrative, it unfolds as more than a concentration of meaningless happenings. Even the recent anti-novel presupposes the novel as the frame of meaning against which it rebels. Much of our time at Cyprus was wisely spent in hearing the stories of many regions. This is the beginning of ecumenical understanding. In this dialogue, a dramatic interpretation of the common story began to emerge, a drama of the pain of the oppressed. Undoubtedly other guesses or images were working in the various work groups and plenaries, some drawing from the Exodus narrative of liberation, others from Jesus' liberating and healing ministry. These paradigmatic stories furnish an anticipation of the "sense" of the People's story. The test of their credibility is the degree to which they actually illumine and empower the People's struggle. The sense is in the story. The People know that sense, directly if not reflectively. Their folk-tales, dramas, tales and socio-biography unfold that sense. The guess is drawn from that sense but also brings that sense to awareness, illumining and sensitizing the People in its struggle. By the same token, the guess can misconstrue the story, confusing issues and actions. Only the People's experience can test a particular way of hearing the story. The guess is the way we hear the story.

The Enlightenment tradition drew its paradigmatic sense from the autonomy of reason in its emancipatory drive, freeing the human species from error, superstition, religious traditions and authoritative institutions. Christian theology has tended to project the sense of liberation in terms of redemption from sin and eternal death. Politico-historical liberation of the People draws on these and other traditions but brings them to focus in the struggle to liberate a People for responsibility in their own history. Thus the drama of oppressor/oppressed seemed to be the persuasive guess, guiding reflection in the telling and hearing of the stories.

Explanation

As a People assumes responsibility for its story, analysis can be useful in tracing patterns of oppression and identifying strategies for extending the

People's participation in shaping its own future. Various analytic models may be useful in tracing the sequence of oppression and liberation, but no model or style of analysis can lay claim to finality. In this sense, social scientific interpretations have their own ideological bent, distorting as well as illumining possibilities of justice and peace. For the most part, analytic models have issued from a Western pattern of thought and action, usually ignoring the People's responsibility for interpreting their own experiences. In this respect, all styles of analysis are open to a hermeneutic of suspicion. Hence, a dialogue of perspectives and interpretations is fundamental to the explanatory moment in political ethics. Different understandings deserve to be heard. The wisdom of the People is central to the unfolding of the story and empowerment of responsibility.

Dominant styles of human science are not very useful in enabling People's movements. The human sciences, for the most part, accept a theory of empirical science which makes truth accessible only to the experts. Understanding, prediction and control provide the criteria of such a human science. This approach excludes 99 per cent of the People from policy, planning and strategy. It elevates a priesthood of professionals who hold positions in bureaucracies and lay down the programmes of public policy.

There is no clear way, at present, to integrate professional expertise with the struggle of the People. Antonio Gramsci struggled with this problem, proposing that organic intellectuals were those who identified with and shared in the struggle of the People. He designated traditional intellectuals as those who served the established powers. This basic distinction may be useful, but it still requires that styles of human science be descriptive, testable by the wisdom of the people and accessible to critique by those engaged in the struggle. In the field of economics, for example, this would suggest something like a "needs-based" economics in which the People would have a major voice in determining needs and sharing in the organization of the processes through which those needs are met. This is to say that economics is the "science" of a human process and is scientific only insofar as it illumines the human struggle for a just economic order. Whatever the liberating path to the future may be, it seems that a fundamentally new paradigm of politico-economic process will be required.

In the thinking of the consultation, the People seems to be the proper matrix for the fashioning of such an economic paradigm. This would imply that the work of professionals will not be very helpful unless it is anchored in the struggle of the People. This applies to ethical and theological work as well as to inquiries in the human sciences.

It would be naive to assume that professionals can be lured away from the academic and bureaucratic institutions of the establishment into such a costly and risky enterprise as the People's struggle. Nevertheless, where this occurs and where historical, descriptive approaches take precedence over scientism, new ways towards justice may be found. Dialogue would seem to be the proper method for such inquiries. The People's struggle is a dialectical engagement: contradictions, conflicts, challenges and persecutions are the stuff of this process. Where structures of subjugation are demystified, they become open to challenge from below. The work of political economy is to help the People in charting a way beyond economic exploitation. Such a science involves implicit ethical understandings and theological background which can be made explicit in a full-blown political ethics.

The ethical disciplines of the establishment have proved to be about as useless in the People's struggle as most of the human sciences. The ethics of a society always projects the authoritative order of the established powers. It is often assumed today that ethics deals only with principles and rules that illumine a natural or reasonable order of justice. The politico-historical realities are quite the contrary. Equality of opportunity in the United States is a crucial principle for maintaining the advantage of the powerful over against oppressed People who have for centuries been excluded from the market of "just exchange". This ideology of legitimation sets the stage for serious political ethics. It illumines the importance of doing political ethics in the context of the People's struggle. It raises very serious questions about the academic ethics that dominates the literature and institutional life of the over-developed societies of accumulation. It means that the wisdom of the People provides the one sure resource for creative ethical work. The People constitute the ethical reality of the total society, for they are bearers of the possibility of overcoming oppression in the name of justice and peace. The empowerment of this People thus constitutes a first step towards fashioning a political ethics. Human science and ethics are of a piece in this task, though the former has the primary task of a descriptive tracing of possibilities of political responsibility for the People, while ethics has the reciprocal task of bringing to light the pathways of justice. The distinction between description and evaluation is useful so long as it is viewed analytically and not substantively. Human sciences deal with human life and thus presuppose the valuative aspects that inform all human experience. Ethics deals with personal and public action and thus presupposes the empirical situation of action. In this sense, ethics is the deepening of social scientific reflection with reference to normative issues.

Comprehension

The discussion of political ethics in the consultation challenges theological work on at least two fronts. (1) By identifying the People's politico-historical struggle for justice as its subject matter, political ethics raises significant questions for the legacy of symbols. To what extent do the symbols challenge systems of exclusion, hierarchy, oppression and domination? To what extent do they reinforce structures of social class, racist, sexist and imperialist oppression? Symbols conceal and cripple as well as reveal and empower. This is as true of political and economic symbolizations as of confessional and communal symbols. Hence, symbols demand critique as well as new appropriations. (2) Furthermore, symbols coalesce in configurations which furnish religio-moral and politico-economic horizons. The way sacred symbols are lived empowers particular modes of politico-historical action. Similarly, economic arrangements and political organization live out or distort sacred symbols. The global system of capital accumulation and domination of nature, thus, lives out a distortion of the symbol of creation. Institutionalization of individual and collective greed undermines communities of care and solidarity. Theology of the People has the task of forging a new appropriation of the symbolic legacy. Nature and humanity are now being threatened with total destruction by these distortions of a sacred legacy.

The oneness of confessional and political symbols does not mean that religious and governmental institutions are one. The relation of confessional and governmental institutions is always problematic and contingent upon particular historical contexts. Because of the symbolic coherence of the sacred and political, at least in the biblical heritage, confessional institutions always embody one or another stance to the political. They are never politically neutral. The same holds for the governmental stance towards the sacred. For example, the national security state in its various forms is a declaration of war against its own citizens and a vehicle of a condition of universal and constant warfare. The global merchandizing of armaments, one of the few growth industries of the accumulative societies, is the economic expression of this security state. It is, at the same time, an institutional expression of the meaning of power in creation, power as domination in a zero-sum game: only the powerful shall inherit the earth, and from those who have not, even that which they have shall be taken away. The People are "weeds and grass".

In view of this contingent, historical character of the interplay of confessional and governmental communities, it would be difficult to argue for any universal arrangement. In societies that profess an atheistic faith, the confessional communities would have a particular set of possibilities to explore. In putatively "Christian" or "Islamic" or "Jewish" societies, another more critical or prophetic role may be more appropriate. It would seem that the crucial question for political ethics would be how the confessional community and its institutions can contribute to the political responsibility of the People in shaping its future. Within such a stance, the confessional community may also serve as a critical and prophetic voice within the struggle of the People, challenging its own aberrations. Needless to say, religious institutions usually want to play this critical role in relation to the People without sharing their struggle or understanding their oppression and suffering. Only so far as the confessional community is a part of that struggle and suffering can it have a valid prophetic function.

The bridge to politico-theological reflection, then, is participation with the People, recognizing the transformative power of the divine Mystery amidst their suffering and struggle. This means that the People's struggle is the revelatory matrix of theological appropriation of the legacy of symbols. The forgiveness and illumination of grace work within this matrix. The empowering grace of new life and hope moves in this medium. This is the moment of comprehension, the moment of spiritual renewal and transformation. Within this horizon, the practical tasks of policy and strategy, however limited the objectives, can be entertained and tested by the wisdom of the People. Here political ethics comes to fruition in decision and risk.

Problems for further exploration

One of the obvious problems for political ethics is the right and dignity of the included members of the society. If the People are the excluded, what place do the included have within the divine economy? It would seem that the hope of the included is borne by the liberation of the excluded. In this sense, there is no salvation except through the suffering of the People and their deliverance from pain and death. However, this question requires much further reflection and praxis.

Another question is the multiplicity of religious and cultural heritages that now shape the politico-historical horizon. The Christian heritage is but one among many confessional legacies. Moreover, the Christian movement has been very much a part of the Western, imperialistic domination of peoples and cultures. In this politico-historical context, ecumenical can only mean the coming together in a common struggle of many faiths and traditions. Ecumenical solidarity, then, is the sharing of this struggle and suffering through hearing one another's stories and bearing one another's burdens.

In consultations and actual praxis, the paradigm of reading the text can furnish some guidelines for the raising of consciousness and development of policy. The first step is unfolding stories, hearing and heeding. This beginning in ecumenical solidarity can establish a common future in hope.

Appendix: Reading the societal text

Ricoeur (1976) has made an important advance in founding interpretation by unfolding a dialectic of explanation and understanding. A dichotomy of explaining and understanding has plagued hermeneutics and the human sciences for over a century. Explanation was identified with natural sciences and the development of laws of process. Only objectifying science of behaviour attempted to achieve such a causal analysis in the human field. Understanding, on the other hand, was identified with an intuitive process of empathic comprehension for which the slogan was to understand authors or figures better than they understood themselves. Thus, understanding was thrown into a psychologizing subjectivity, somehow getting to the "intention" of the author or actor. Ricoeur argues from the gap between "saying" and the "said" in the speech-event that discourse involves a precipitate of the "said" which poses the question of understanding and explaining in its own right. In the speech-event, this work of interpretation is carried out between speaker and hearer through question and answer, showing, gesturing and explaining. In the written text, this gap is extended and the text (the "said") achieves a semantic autonomy, transcending the author's intention and calling for interpretation in its own right. The objectivity of the text becomes the problem for interpretation. Ricoeur poses the question of how this objectivity can be made productive for understanding. His path to this productivity is the dialectic of objective explanation (penetrating the grammatical infra-structure of the text) and subjective understanding (grasping the text as a whole and moving with it into a comprehension of the world of the text, its referential projection of possibilities). From the perspective of social theory and religious social ethics, this is the most important move that Ricoeur has made in his theory of discourse, since it opens the way, by analogy, to an integrative approach to interpreting societal process. So far as the notion of the text (i.e. the work of art) is appropriate to interpreting

• This appendix is excerpted from "A Proposal for a Political Ethics" by Gibson Winter, *Review of Religious Research,* Vol. 21, No. 1, 1979, pp. 87-107.

a people's praxis, the way opens for a comprehensive discipline of social interpretation.

This theory of interpretation involves three moments or steps which are interwoven in any actual reading of a text: (1) *guessing* the structure of the whole; (2) *analytical explanation* of the sense of the text; (3) *comprehension* of the referential meaning of the world the text projects. The first and third moments are non-methodic in the sense that they involve interpretative understanding. The second moment is methodic in the sense of a scientific, analytic explication of the inter-relation of parts. In Ricoeur's problematic of the text, moments (1) and (3) are semantic interpretations, while moment (2) works from a semiotic of the text of the kind that stucturalism has explored.

Guessing

Guessing, or preliminary construing of the text, concerns the work as a whole. It is not an arbitrary procedure, as is suggested by our common use of the term "guess", but rather a move comparable to "insight" in Lonergan's work (Lonergan, 1957). Guessing involves something like a *gestalt,* a sense of the whole which furnishes a context for the parts. Shifts in this preliminary sense have marked major turnings (e. g. in biblical criticism from interpretations of biblical materials as "myths" and legends of a pre-scientific people, to investigations of primitive histories, to inquiry into the structure of confessional formulations). Guesses, as Ricoeur notes, are not simply arbitrary, but can be validated by various modes of converging indices and subjective probabilities. The importance of this first moment is that it locates the text by genre, prescribing the kinds of coding that generate the text as a whole, hence the analytic procedures which are relevant to explore the deep structures of the text. Further, the guess dictates the horizons of sense which define certain aspects of the text as relevant for inquiry while excluding others. The guess is prescriptive as well as descriptive.

Explanation

The explanatory moment investigates the deep structure of the text through analytic method. Ricoeur takes the structuralist approach as appropriate to this process, using the example of Lévi-Strauss's work on myth. This approach to the sense of the text abstracts from author and hearer, world and history. Here the text is treated within the structure of language as having its sense from grammatical coding. Ricoeur argues that such explanatory inquiry presupposes existential conflicts which it traces through in the logical oppositions of the text; hence, understanding is presupposed and implicitly guides the explanation. In this sense, abstracting from referential meaning to immanent sense actually is suppressing the guess and the presuppositional understanding which guides explanation (Ricoeur, 1976, pp. 78f.). Hence, in Ricoeur's interpretation, methodic explanation of the infra-structure of a text draws, implicitly or explicitly, on understanding. Furthermore, explanation discloses a horizon of world that is mediated in the text and borne within the immanent sense of the text. For example, he notes that Lévi-Strauss understands myth as "making men aware of certain oppositions and of tending towards their progressive mediation" (Ricoeur, 1976, p. 87). In this way, the penetration of the depth structure through explanation opens the way to the referential meaning of the text — the kind of world it projects — even though explanation stops short of this task of comprehension.

Comprehension

Comprehension depends upon the guess and the explanatory unfolding of the structure of the text. Where explanation has found its entrance into the text through the objective, distanciated autonomy of the text, the contemporary meaning of the text remains to be fulfilled. This subjective appropriation is more an appropriation to the disclosure power of the text. Hence, appropriation is not taking possession or control of the text — an obvious danger of explanatory method — but being appropriated to the world of the text. This is not a question of the author's meaning taking over, nor the mind of the original audience displacing contemporary appropriation. It is the disclosure power of the text now as it addresses a people, unfolding possibilities of their being.

Ricoeur understands guessing, explaining and comprehending as culminating in the event of interpretation. Hence, he aligns his view with Gadamer's notion of a fusion of horizons. This alignment with Gadamer's position suggests that the text is not the atemporal, ideal object of the explanatory inquiry, but the horizon of interpretative reproduction through which the text has lived and continues to live so long as it mediates disclosure power (Ricoeur, 1976, p. 93). For example, the notion of the canon of scripture, or of any textual tradition, would have to be reinterpreted to mean the ongoing horizoning of a text in its reproductive process as history, always demanding critique and renewal, but never the "same" text in that process. Interpretation and representation are continually bringing it into a people's dwelling. The Pauline texts, for example, never will be the same in the Western world after their appropriation during the Reformation in Luther's works, not to speak of the subsequent history of Protestant faith and life.

The text lives as temporal event in this interpretative work, though, at times, Ricoeur seems to want to stress the semantic autonomy of the text to the point of weakening this contemporary dimension of horizoning and representation. Gadamer stresses the reference to the original drama, the work of art, as furnishing a criterion of a correct reproduction, but he does not mean this in the sense of going back and doing the drama in original costumes, as though its history of interpretation and our contemporary horizoning of a world could be cancelled. The text lives from its history of interpretation as well as original disclosure by confronting our world with its disclosure power. Since interpretation also selects and conceals, the original does have a dialectial role in this history.

This contemporaneity and subjective horizon of appropriation — not in the subjectivizing or psychologizing sense of the older school of *Verstehen* — enters already into the guess. Guessing is located historically in a particular, contemporary horizon. Why, for example, did historical criticism move towards confessional formulation as genre for scriptural interpretation in the latter part of this century, in the context of the neo-orthodox attempt to transcend the problems of historical criticism and the dominant mode of rationality in the modern world? Was this turn to confession already prepared by personalism and subjectivism of faith? Why, for example, does structuralism move in the realm of oppositions and a logic of binary unfolding — a method with such close affinities to the mathematical and scientific procedures of the contemporary world? These existential understandings are embedded in the preunderstandings that come into play in the guess. As Gadamer has shown so well in his exploration of preunderstandings, these guesses are not to be discarded or avoided, since they are unavoidable (Gadamer, 1975). They are to be brought into encounter with the horizoning of the text as the horizoning of our world. Here the term "fusion of horizons" may obscure the event, since it is difficult to give precise content to this notion. However, "fusion of horizons" is true to the encounter of worlds which occurs where there is appropriation to the text.

This summary of Ricoeur's recent work on interpretation of a text furnishes guidelines for a political hermeneutics. The three moments of guess, explanation, and comprehension furnish a model for interpreting a people's dwelling. Political ethics is, in this sense, a critical reading and reconstruction of the societal text (Winter, 1981).

REFERENCES

Gadamer, Hans-Georg, *Truth and Method,* London, Sheed & Ward, 1975.

Lonergan, Bernard, *Insight: a Study of Human Understanding,* New York Philosophical Library, 1957.

Ricoeur, Paul, *Interpretation Theory: Discourse and the Surplus of Meaning,* Fort Worth, Texas, Texas Christian University Press, 1976.

Winter, Gibson, *Liberating Creation: Foundations of Religious Social Ethics,* New York, The Crossroad Publishing Co., 1981.

Appendix 2
Report of the Advisory Committee on "The Search for a Just, Participatory and Sustainable Society"

(CENTRAL COMMITTEE, 1979)

I. Mandate and work of the JPSS Advisory Committee

The Advisory Committee on the JPSS programme emphasis was established by decision of the Central Committee of the WCC in August 1977. The Central Committee suggested the following functions for the Advisory Committee:

1. To offer advice on programme plans of units and sub-units in order that ways be found by which their contributions to a coordinated concern for JPSS might be strengthened.
2. To discover appropriate ways to stimulate theological and ethical reflection on the JPSS programme emphasis.
3. To oversee the preparation of a 25-30-page working statement on the substantive ideas which would "define" the JPSS.

Two or possibly three meetings of the Advisory Committee were foreseen prior to the next meeting of the Central Committee, when the experience and value of its work should be reviewed. The first meeting was held in Geneva, 11-14 December 1977. A preliminary report was prepared, summarizing the discussion (printed in *The Ecumenical Review*, April 1978). The report was then shared with the Executive Committee of the WCC at its meeting in February 1978. The Executive Committee offered a number of important observations for the further work of the Advisory Committee. It recommended in particular that the report be shared with the WCC commissions and working groups directly concerned with the programme emphasis with the request "to relate their specific programmes to the tentative framework and the theological reflection offered by the Advisory Committee, spelling out in particular their contribution to the clarification of the Christian vision of a 'just society'". The Executive Committee also suggested that, at the second meeting, the Advisory Committee should give particular attention to regional perspectives on the search for a just, participatory and sustainable society.

The second meeting of the Advisory Committee was held in Geneva, 12-15 September 1978. The Committee considered a great variety of regional statements as well as responses from many sub-unit commissions and working groups of the WCC. It now submits the following report to the Central Committee of the WCC for its meeting at Jamaica in January 1979.

The members and consultants of the Advisory Committee who participated in the work were:

Members: Prof. José Miguez-Bonino, Argentina (Moderator); Protopresbyter Prof. Vitaly Borovoy, USSR (only first meeting); Mr Gabriel Habib (for Metropolitan Hazim), Lebanon (only second meeting); Ms Janice Love, USA (only first meeting); Bishop Dr Henry Okullu, Kenya; Dr Koson Srisang, Thailand; Mrs Marie Assaad, Egypt (only second meeting); Bishop Dr Manas Buthelezi, South Africa (only second meeting); Prof. André Dumas, France; Dr Eberhard Eppler, Federal Republic of Germany (at first meeting replaced by Dr Jan Pronk, Netherlands); Prof. Masao Takenaka, Japan; Bishop Dr Karoly Toth, Hungary.

Consultants: Dr Kim Yong Bock, South Korea (only first meeting); Mr Nicholas Maro, Tanzania (only first meeting, for Bishop Buthelezi); Dr Jørgen Randers, Norway (only first meeting) replacing Prof. Charles Birch; Prof. David Rose, USA (only second meeting).

II. A developing debate

1. Origins

Throughout its history, the ecumenical movement has sought to reflect not only on the unity and mission of the church, but also on the basic Christian convictions which could guide the people of God in the struggle for a better society. It was not an arbitrary choice when, in 1976, the Central Committee of the WCC adopted the search for a "Just, Participatory and Sustainable Society" as one of four major programme emphases for the work of the Council in the period following the Fifth Assembly at Nairobi in 1975. This emphasis has grown out of the dynamics of the ecumenical discussion beginning with the Oxford conference on "Community, Church and State" in 1937. While Oxford emphasized economic planning and justice in the "free society", and Amsterdam 1948 introduced the concept of the "responsible society", the development debate since the Geneva conference in 1966 and the increasing relation of the WCC through its programmes to the struggles for liberation and for human rights have rightly laid the major emphasis on justice in society. This has led to the present attempt to identify the concerns and specific issues that must be faced today in the shaping of a just society and to look at them in the light of the biblical witness to God's kingdom.

2. Starting from the present, historical reality

The purpose of this programme emphasis is not to elaborate and present a blueprint or a Christian programme of an ideal society which would be just, participatory and sustainable. The search rather starts from the present historical reality of our societies of which the churches are an integral part. The situation differs from region to region, yet an increasing number of societies are characterized by structures of injustice, lack of participation and the threat of unsustainability. Local approaches, appropriate as they may be, do not necessarily get to the root causes. The responses of the people must include the global perspective of justice, people's participation and responsible shaping of the future of all humankind. In fact, there are signs everywhere of an awakening of the people, affirming their selfhood and defending their rights and dignity and calling for self-determination. There are movements of people challenging structures of alienating power which control economic, political, as well as technological developments and decisions. To start from historical reality, therefore, means to be primarily concerned with this process of struggle and its dynamics as it impinges on the structures and ideological presuppositions of society.

3. Voices of the people

The people do not speak with one voice; sometimes their voices are conflicting or in tension with each other. This is an essential aspect of the historical reality and it emerges clearly where the different regional perspectives in the search for a just, participatory and sustainable society are taken seriously. Thus, justice in terms of the realization of primary economic and social needs is the central concern of the people in Africa, Asia and Latin America, and participation is understood as an integral part of the struggle for justice. The internal problems and conflicts in many countries are exacerbated by foreign political, economic and military intervention. Specific issues in the struggle concern the dominating influence of transnational capital (Latin America), land rights and land tenure (Pacific), human rights understood as people's rights (Latin America, Asia), the extension of authoritarian systems and the implications of the doctrine of national security (Latin America, Asia). In much of the Northern hemisphere the issue of sustainability appears as central in terms of the needs for industrial redeployment, self-reliance in the use of raw materials, alternatives to the present op-

tions of energy and military technology, solutions to structural unemployment. In regions of the Southern hemisphere the quest for the sustenance or
sustainability of life is more urgent, while in socialist countries the priority
would be placed on the maintenance of peace and peaceful coexistence
without which it would be inconceivable to envisage sustainability, participation and justice in a global context. In all regions, however, the sometimes
conflicting claims of sustainability and social justice need urgent attention.
Finally, there is a pressing concern among many people for the sustainability
of their corporate identity, culturally and spiritually.

4. A challenge to the churches

Christian churches are part of this historical reality. They cannot remain
neutral regarding the struggle of people for greater justice and participation.
But the crisis of human society is reflected in many churches as well. In some
situations, the churches need to adjust to a growing minority position
without privileges and influence. Many of their members experience a crisis
of faith while others are being overwhelmed by feelings of impotence and
anxiety. This finds its expression in an inability to manifest concretely their
Christian obedience in increasingly complex situations. There are also those
who are not convinced that it is part of their Christian discipleship to participate in the struggle of people around them, or see no possibility of being
involved meaningfully. Some consciously support the existing structures in
the name of their Christian faith, feeling called to manifest a fundamental
loyalty. For some Christian communities, which live as minorities in societies
or states shaped by other faiths or ideologies, participation can be limited by
the values and norms of the majority. Others again have made a clear choice
and committed themselves to the struggle of the people as an expression of
obedience and faithfulness to God's call for justice. Given this diversity of
responses, we must ask the question: how can the churches arrive at a common understanding of historical reality and become significantly involved in
this struggle through their life and action, their witness and service? How can
they understand the nature and modes of their participation in the creation of
a new society? How can they be helped, through their fellowship in the
ecumenical movement, to learn from the insights and experiences of the
people, to listen to new voices within the ecumenical fellowship, to renew
their own lives and to readjust their self-understanding in the light of the present historical reality? Thus, the purpose of this programme emphasis is to
promote Christian participation in and Christian contribution to the process
of historical transformation towards more justice, dignity and fulfilment in
human societies.

III. The aim: justice and society

1. The promise of the messianic kingdom

Christians believe that the whole world is God's creation, continuously being renewed by the power of redemption and living under the promise of God's kingdom, the reign of peace and justice. Christians believe that all human beings are part of a dynamic pointing towards the messianic kingdom. This conviction is neither an exclusive Christian property nor imposed upon anybody: it is an invitation, offered freely to all people. While Christians claim no monopoly, they live under a special call to obedience, to engage with other people in a search for the common aim: justice on earth, manifested in peaceful community of all humankind in which every human being finds true fulfilment of life. The biblical witness refers to this final aim as the "kingdom of God" which embraces the two dimensions of redemption of the whole of creation and personal fulfilment for each human being.

As Christians we are called to "search for the kingdom of God and his justice" (Matt. 6:33). But we cannot use this central biblical concept without some further clarification. We call this kingdom "messianic" because we believe that Jesus, as the Christ, i.e. the Messiah, has brought, lived out and inaugurated the kingdom on earth, within space and time. Without this Christological manifestation the kingdom would be an abstract utopia, a dream embracing all the unaccomplished desires of humankind. In speaking of a messianic kingdom we also make two other affirmations: it is already at work, therefore not a futuristic or spiritual escape, but is not yet fulfilled, indeed beyond historical achievement. The messianic kingdom, while having entered history, transcends it; it is present for the eyes of faith, and yet it remains the object of hope. It is operative in human reality and still we are waiting for it. Waiting without action would be a denial of the historical coming of Christ. But action without waiting would be a denial of the second coming of Christ. Our bodies, indeed the "body" of history, derive their inner power and strength from this active and waiting presence between the two comings, one historical, the other eschatological. The Spirit of God binds together history and eschatology, faith and hope. In this manner we are animated as human beings by a unity in tension, which reflects the unity and the tension of the trinitarian life of God hiself.

In the light of this aim, i.e. the messianic kingdom, Christian faith understands the present struggles and contradictions as a part and a manifestation of a dynamic in history pressing for eschatological fulfilment, thus defending history against both pretension and discouragement. Christians will always be faced by two temptations: either to escape history by means of a premature eschatology (enthusiasm and illusions; pietism without responsibility; activism without realism), or to eliminate eschatology by way of a self-sufficient history (conservatism without hope for change; cynicism as a caricature of wisdom; self-confidence without self-criticism). The messianic kingdom calls for a present response in human life and action through powerful decision, and at the same time for the attitude of expectancy, searching for that which cannot be seen, with patience and powerful prayers.

2. Justice, a messianic category

The messianic kingdom of God is the fulfilment of the promise of a new heaven and a new earth — "the home of justice" (2 Pet. 3:13) and the fulfilment of the hope of those "who hunger and thirst to see right prevail" (Matt. 5:6). The kingdom is "not eating and drinking but justice, peace and joy, inspired by the Holy Spirit" (Rom. 14:17).

Justice, therefore, is a messianic category. It embraces both God's righteousness and fidelity and his will for a right ordering of human community. Jesus proclaims justification of the repentant sinner before God and justice in society. Justice takes the form of punishment and prophetic judgment as well as compassion for the guilty and release of the prisoner, liberation of the oppressed. Justice is the historical, penultimate embodiment of love. We cannot put one against the other. It is a mockery of the biblical witness to appeal to love and at the same time to deny justice. The eschatological reality of the kingdom of God is the coming of love in the form of justice and righteousness and of justice with love. The inseparable relation of justice and love finds its dramatic expression in the cross and resurrection of Jesus Christ.

Justice is today at the centre of the aspirations of people in their struggles all over the world. How does justice as a messianic category actually relate to the historical struggles of our time? Christians are far from being clear and united in their response. The foregoing affirmations need to be tested in mutual dialogue and actual experience of struggle for justice in society. In this context it is important to recall the full biblical meaning of the search for justice: the search for the abolition of oppression as in the Exodus story; the fulfilment of personal and collective security as in the establishment and defence of the ordered life of the people of Israel; the judgment over sin as in the deportation into exile; God's forgiveness and fidelity, as in the return from exile and the restoration of the people. Seen in this biblical and in its human context, justice is the criterion of human life in relationship with God as individuals and in community. Justice is the gift of fully being oneself without egocentric indifference or alienating dependency. To achieve justice is the historical task given to human beings and the eschatological goal of God's righteousness. Justice is to be received from God, but also to be realized and shared out by us. In this sense, justice is both a gift and a task; it aims at a change of heart, as well as at changing structures.

Justice is the first characteristic of the new society for which Christians together with people of other beliefs and convictions are struggling. We do not pretend to have the monopoly of the concern for justice. But we trust that faith helps us not to confuse justice with our own interests, whether personal, collective, national or social. We also believe that hope helps us not to withdraw in resignation from this continuous struggle. Justice calls for the active participation of all.

3. Participation

It has become increasingly clear that participation constitutes a necessary condition for the full realization of social justice. Those who possess and exercise power must not treat others who are dependent on them and affected by their actions simply as being on the receiving end, expected to implement plans and decisions prepared for them in the offices of government or management. Participation calls for a recognition of everybody's right to be consulted, to be heard and understood, whatever their political, economic or social status may be in society. Everyone must be involved in planning and action, giving as well as receiving. Participation means that each one takes initiative in formulating or changing policies and becoming involved in directing their implementation.

The call for full participation concerns not least the church in its life and structure, beginning with worship and extending into the daily "liturgy" of service to others. The church is to be a participatory community enabling all, men and women, old and young, weak and strong, clergy and lay people, to share, participate in and contribute to the common life according to the gift of each.

A good example of such participation is given in the symbolic definition of the workings of the different parts of the body (1 Cor. 12:14 and 27):

> Yes, the body has many parts, not just one part... Now here is what I am trying to say: all of you together are the one body of Christ and each one of you is a separate and necessary part of it (*The Living Bible*).

This participation must embrace every sphere of life: political — in being allowed to exercise full political rights — economic, social, cultural.

Justice will be achieved only in a society where people are regarded as subjects able to transform by their own resources their political, social and natural environment and to establish and maintain relationships of equality with one another. Thus, respect for the human — civil and social — rights of everybody is an essential condition for justice in society. Sometimes it is argued that there exists a dilemma or a "trade-off" between the goals of social justice in the sense of equality and civil and social liberties in terms of people's participation. In messianic perspective, participation is an essential manifestation of the true *koinonia* in which there is no domination of one over the other, but where all are mutually accountable to one another. The alleged dilemma finds a clear resolution if viewed in the light of the struggle of the people.

According to St Paul, love is the normative factor in equal participation in human affairs. It is the enabling, the energizing effect of love which makes it possible for each part of the body to give due regard to other parts as being of infinite worth, and thus makes the whole body function together in perfect harmony (1 Cor. 13:1-4).

4. Sustainability

The concerns for justice and for participation are highlighted today in a particular way in the context of the problems of the sustainability of the whole earth and of personal life. The concept of sustainability is relatively new in the ecumenical discussion. It is connected with the discussion on the limits to growth, with the growing awareness of destructive potential, of the irresponsible expansion of cost both for the poor and for exploited nature. Sustainability in the Bible is expressed by the faithfulness of God to his lasting covenant. God blesses continuously his creation, preserving it from destruction and leading it to the fullness of life abundant. We have received God's earth as our common inheritance, not as privilege for some and a source of frustration for others. We are today becoming more conscious of the fragility of sustainability if we remain in a situation where the distribution of the fruits of the earth and of products of technology is unjust, and if we do not achieve a participatory approach to information, decision and enjoyment. Sustainability is therefore related to the possibility for everybody of having a sense of belonging, and having access to work and to education. The long-term concept of sustainability is also becoming more and more a concern for our generation. We know more about the dangers of purely technocratic attempts to master a future which is ultimately beyond human control. But this long-term sustainability would remain an abstract concern if it were not accompanied by the concern for the present sustainability of all men throughout the world. Here also we have to connect present history with responsible stewardship in long-term perspective.

IV. Issues in the struggle

We have started from describing and understanding the historical process of struggle and social transformation in which people all over the world are engaged. We have tried to interpret this process and its goals in theological terms as "messianic", i.e. as pointing towards a final eschatological transformation of all things. It is important for this approach to maintain the integrity of the spiritual dimension of the struggle, and to take seriously the specificity of the Christian message over against the inherent dangers of a purely secular messianism.

Speaking in terms of a struggle implies the recognition of tensions, of setbacks, of defeats, as well as breakthroughs. The messianic perspective of the kingdom allows us, however, to understand all this as part of and as phases of one dynamic process. The struggle requires a constant review of immediate and long-term objectives. In this context, we are faced with a number of issues on which Christians engaged in the struggle do not agree. The JPSS programme emphasis is an invitation for open debate of these issues, so that a common sense of purpose can develop. There is need to spell out concretely the basic convictions which sustain Chritians in the struggle.

1. People, the subject of the struggle

Who is the subject of the struggle? We have referred to the "people" as the subject of the witness through the struggle for justice in society. The ambiguity and frequent misuse of the notion of the "people" in a totalitarian or in a populist sense is one of the issues calling for clarification. The people are defined in terms of their historical and cultural biography and identity, and more specifically in terms of the prevailing structures of power, state, class, caste, etc. In concrete terms: the vast majority of the people are young, children or adolescents, the "lost generation" of their societies who elude any "strategy" or "programme" but who will increase in numbers focusing more clearly yet the brutal realities of poverty. The biblical messianic perspective focuses on the poor, the sick, those in need without voice and power, those who are humble enough to benefit from the messianic prophetic witness. Where mutually exclusive interests are at stake the church must take sides on the basis of the criteria of justice and love. Participation in the struggle means understanding reality on the basis of a commitment, a fundamental option for the poor, recognizing that there can be no human development and change without their being a part. Their poverty in most cases is not of their own making but is a result of injustice; poverty has become institutionalized, generating more poverty, and can only be overcome if the poor become aware of their situation and identify their strength. It is their struggle, and Christians are called upon to struggle with them irrespective of whether there are Christians among them or not. The church itself is called the "people of God", the "poor in the Spirit", who are empowered by the Holy Spirit to deny themselves in overcoming their self-interest and to break through the captivities of given structures of power, class, caste, nation.

2. *Common struggle with people of living faiths and ideologies*

Christians are engaged in a common search together with people of different beliefs and convictions. It is important to affirm this basic solidarity in the struggle. There is, however, also the need to assess together again and again the nature and shape of the society in which we live and to agree on the basic principles of the society which we struggle for. In various situations, it is at this point that the solidarity and cooperation of Christians with people of other living faiths and ideologies encounter difficulties. There seems to be today an increasing trend towards revival of cultural particularism as well as ethnocentric religious and even theocratic principles of society. From this perspective, Christianity is seen as claiming universal values over against the ethnic and religious rights and values of particular people. However, in many societies one can notice also another trend towards marginalization of important sectors of the population from decision-making processes. This is the case, for example, for popular cultures, ethnic or religious groups, including minority Christian communities. Christians and churches have to ask themselves self-critically whether they have not taken for granted too easily that there is universal validity in all cultures of the model of a "secular" state and society and even encouraged an apparent identification of Christian values with a secularized, pluralist type of society. In witnessing to their neighbours of living faiths and ideologies, they have to face up clearly to the dilemma inherent in this situation. This includes determining more specifically the basis of cooperation in the struggle.

3. *The reality of power*

The struggle is a struggle about power. Among Christians there is a basic ambivalence regarding the attitude towards power. The critical attitude towards power is, however, not enough. It must be realized that power is an essential instrument of change. It is also a basic element of the relationship of persons in community. It can be exercised by the use of force to achieve obedience whether the cause is just or unjust. The sword is the symbol of this form of power. It can also be exercised through authoritative and sometimes charismatic leadership. Throughout history there have been efforts to exercise power on the basis of public consent and participation. Under no circumstances should the church seek and accumulate "temporal" power for itself. Yet the various forms of the ministry of the church mediating divine grace are in themselves power-generating by strengthening and empowering people (cf. 2 Cor. 12:9). That is so whether we think of proclamation or witness through suffering or pastoral care. For instance, to comfort means giving power to the one from whom it has been drained by despair. Courage is the necessary power for continuing in an endeavour. The same applies to power-generating forces of prayer, intercession and fasting. The experience of solidarity in powerlessness is also power-generating. Shared powerlessness is a lighter burden than the one experienced in solitude. Empowering the people, however, also means sharing the power, e. g. funds, resources, expertise, which the church may have.

Solidarity is therefore a power for endurance and determination. Today power is exercised increasingly in an anonymous way through and in complex social and technological systems. In biblical perspective power is both demonic, perverting human relationships, and liberating for the preservation of human life. This has led some to regard power as neutral, or functional, placing the emphasis on its good or bad use, while others have established a radical metaphysical distinction between sinful, selfish power and the good power of God. Again, in the perspective of the messianic struggle, we discover that the principalities and powers of this world are unmasked by the power of the kingdom. The liberating power of Jesus Christ and his Spirit enables people to challenge existing structures of economic, political, military and scientific technological power. The essential objective in the struggle should therefore be to render all exercise of power accountable to God and accountable to the people who are subject to it. The universal tendency towards demonic self-glorification of power needs to be corrected constantly through the critical participation of the people and preaching of God's word. Equally, Christians have to guard against the temptation of considering all physical power as "evil" seeking refuge in the realm of "spiritual" power and thus avoiding the difficult task of engaging in the stewardship of power.

4. Structures of participation

People's participation obviously is a central issue in the struggle since in many situations social, economic, and political structures are such that people are largely excluded. The call for people's participation is rendered problematic by the fact that the major components of power in social life, especially technocratically organized economic and military power, are structured globally and thus are beyond the political control of the people. The people are divided into various political units, i. e. nations, states, etc. Even when there is a strong conviction about democratic participation, its effectiveness is severely limited by the global power reality. In the light of this situation, Christians and churches have to reflect on the following basic questions. What are the spiritual resources of the Christian faith and also of other religious traditions that would enable humanity to break out of the present structural captivity? What are the foundations on which a new order, characterized by more justice, more participation and sustainability, can be built? What is the role and contribution of the churches and the ecumenical movement in this process? What insights can be gained from the experiences of the various people's movements around the world?

It seems clear that participatory structures need to be developed at *all* levels, rendering the exercise of power more accessible and accountable to the people, and building confidence between people of different faiths and ideologies. At the same time, it is clear that only a global perspective and approach to the questions of world order and peace can mobilize the necessary power of control. More thought is needed on the issue: which structures of participation are appropriate to different levels of power and in different cultural and religious contexts?

5. Modes of action

The issue of participation leads directly to the issues concerning modes of action and methodology. Modes of action are not merely questions of means related to a specified objective or goal. If the final aim is the kingdom of God and his justice, then the basic criterion for a Christian methodology is love, not as an emotion but as action. The end, therefore, defines the means; i.e. we are engaged in an adventure of justice and love, reaching out towards the final reign of justice in the kingdom. Can we say that people's participation is the methodological criterion in a struggle for justice and sustainability?

The methodology of participation encounters difficulties in situations where different traditions and ideologies try to assert or even impose their own way. We have to acknowledge the limitations of our methodologies, including the present emphasis in ecumenical programmes on inter-relating action and reflection. Searching for appropriate modes of action may lead to new discoveries. In the light of the reflection on JPSS, it appears that a new methodology should take the following elements seriously:
a) the historical, cultural and religious heritage of the people;
b) the contemporary power structures of human society;
c) the commitment of faith to search in hope for the messianic kingdom where justice and fullness of humanity will be "realized".

Such a methodology will in practice take its clues from the "stories of the people" struggling against oppressive powers. It will take seriously the rediscovery and articulation of religious symbols and meanings, the need for a caring relationship to nature as creation, programmes of concrete action for justice and peace expressing both the critique of existing power structures and the faith and hope that the messianic power of Jesus Christ will in his own time bring about the kingdom of God.

6. Interaction between global and national issues

Increasingly the question is being raised as to whether the struggle should focus on justice in the context of a given society, or whether priority should be given to issues of a new world order. We have to understand more clearly how the demands for justice internationally and nationally relate to and condition each other. The disillusioning experience of two development decades strongly suggests that the struggle for justice must focus on the basic needs of the people — in developing as well as in developed countries. The New International Economic Order will not simply come by government decisions; the people themselves have to demand it of their governments. For the developing countries this implies that development policies need to be oriented not only towards but elaborated together with the poor. In the developed countries it means changes in the production structure and employment policies which will only be possible through a certain "socialization" of decisions that have so far been taken autonomously on the basis of interests of the private sector. Tackling the specific problems of social justice and equality in industrialized countries is a condition for establishing a New International Economic Order (NIEO).

7. Science and technology

Knowledge is a gift of God; science, along with other arts, tells us of both the glory and exquisite subtlety of God's creation, and therefore is at least a conditional good. Technology in its modern form is the application of scientific method to perceived social needs. We have free will, also given by God, to use this technology for good or bad — that is, to be good or bad stewards of this part of creation over which we have been given dominion. The concept of the necessity of careful stewardship is deeply rooted in the Christian tradition, as it is in many others; but too often we have been bad stewards, and like bad worker, have blamed our tools. We have used technology to exploit resources as though they were limitless, leaving behind a detritus of environmental ills that a seemingly infinite earth would absorb, and leaving behind a residue of social ills. The most blatant example of this misdirection of technology is the concentration of increasing resources on military research and development.

All that must now change; God's judgment is upon us; there is need for active repentance. The finiteness of resources and increasingly apparent limits to the absorptive capacity of the earth now affect us all — the industrialized countries as they face the need to adjust radically their technological bases, and the developing countries as they see before them increasingly clearly a world in which the available technological options become unexpectedly limited.

These circumstances call for much more international cooperation and coordination than hitherto; to have one half of the world wasting resources and the other half doing without them will lead to the collapse of all. Worse still, it is wrong; the power of modern technology is so strong that it can be (and has been) used to capture resources from those who are technologically disadvantaged, and past exploitive economic principles tended to drive such activities, thus dividing the world more and more into sectors that seem increasingly rich and others that certainly remain poor. Thus arises the need to develop a delicate combination of sectoral self-confidence and independence. The first is needed to prevent exploitation, and the second is to stimulate universal attitudes that it is better to belong to a cooperating world than to try to overthrow it.

V. Some affirmations about the life of the church

1. Solidarity and identity

The concern for a just society is shared by people of different faiths and ideologies. Christians participate in it together with others, without claiming any privilege or leadership role. At the same time, as Christians we share in that common quest in the obedience of our faith and bring to it all the resources and insights which this faith provides. The church, therefore, needs to be aware both of its solidarity with all people and of its Christian identity, the integrity of its biblical faith.

2. A common humanity

In solidarity with people of different faiths and ideologies we gratefully confess a common humanity which we believe to be grounded in God's creation. The Spirit of God awakens in human life and society the vision of and the impulse towards a renewed humanity. This has found and continues to find expression in many living faiths and ideologies. As Christians, we share in this movement of the Spirit: we wait and work for a new creation, not for a new "Christendom". The ecumenical movement should continuously strive to identify new partners and constituencies among Christians and others. It should draw into the debate those representing people in the struggle, e.g. people's movements, trade unions, but also people who have experience in exercising power, such as scientists, business people and others in decision-making centres.

3. The witness of redemption

Yet, the kingdom of God is for us not only a common search, an expectation or a vision: through baptism we are redeemed from the powers of sin and death and incorporated into the one body of Christ. In celebrating the eucharist we share, by the power of the Holy Spirit, in the life of the new creation. Thus, we are constituted into a particular people who have experienced in Jesus Christ the presence and the power of "the new age" and who know that he who has begun the renewal of the world and of humankind will bring it to its fulfilment. Therefore, we do not look at a new society merely as a dream or a utopia, but as a reality that is present and active in history through the power of the Spirit moving to ever new and fuller manifestations of true justice, participation and responsibility for creation. We cannot rest satisfied with any of those achievements because we know that they will never realize fully God's new creation. Yet we commit ourselves to them with joy and hope because we live with certainty under God's promise.

4. The form of servant

In manifesting its solidarity and its identity, the church must be ready to follow its Lord in his "kenosis". It will not try to become itself an autonomous realm of power, but to inspire and sustain in the people — particularly in the poor and the oppressed — the hope and the courage in the struggle for a just society. This calling to live in the form of a servant has given rise to various models of Christian life in community throughout the history of the church. Today we see "base communities" of Christians springing up in many parts of the world which may foreshadow the shape of the church as it participates in this quest: i.e. a church, increasingly formed as a network of communities spread throughout the society, proclaiming and witnessing to the transforming power of the kingdom and participating with the people in their struggles.

5. A "living sacrifice"

The participation of the church in the creation of a new society is not a secondary or derivative dimension of its existence. It begins at the very centre in the celebration of the sacraments as an anticipation of what the world is to become, in the proclamation of God's judgment and love for his whole crea-tion, in the liturgy of adoration, intercession and prayer which the church of-fers on behalf of all people and which sustains it in the struggle. In the centre of its life the church is the fellowship of the Holy Spirit, that koinonia of cor-porate love and faith in the triune God which, as a sign of the kingdom, seeks to expand itself and to penetrate the total life of humankind and of the world, to transform the human "mind", values and relations, to reshape structures and institutions according to the mind of Christ.

6. The structured life of the church

The church should not seek to retain or to regain a position of temporal power. Yet, it exists as a distinct body, as a witness to and sign of a perfect consummation, a witness that cannot be dissolved into humankind until that time in which "God will be all in all". As such, it penetrates the life of socie-ty, according to times and circumstances. Its structured life must itself meet the criteria of justice, participation and sustainability if it is to be credible in its functions in society. It has a function of proclaiming the good news to people and society and of announcing God's judgment over life and history. More specifically, it has a pedagogical function in the conscientization of people, a prophetic function of denunciation and announcement in relation to ruling power, a function of defending the rights of all people, particularly of the poor and the oppressed, a consoling function of comforting those in fear and despair, a function of building up and sustaining human communi-ty, and a function of intercession, of offering to Christ the life and sufferings of all humankind. In pursuing these tasks, the church may again and again be tempted to exercise some direct form of social control or to impose its posi-tion on those of different convictions. Therefore it is particularly important that the ecumenical movement constantly stimulate the churches to a mutual dialogue and correction and to an open and positive relation to people of dif-ferent faiths and ideologies.

VI. Towards an ecumenical agenda

1. The role of the World Council of Churches

The WCC is a council, a "fellowship of churches", constituted to further the unity and mission, service and renewal of the churches. At the same time, it considers itself to be the "privileged instrument" of the ecumenical move-ment, which is broader than the WCC. It includes a widening network of partners within and alongside the member churches of the WCC. In par-ticular, ecumenical bodies have been formed on regional, national and local levels which share in the ecumenical task. Many of these are associated with the WCC or maintain close working relationships. The wider ecumenical movement also includes the organizations representing the major families of Christian churches.

The WCC carries out its function and tasks in cooperation with all the partners in this network. Cooperation requires acknowledgment of the specific potential as well as limitation of each of the partners involved. Being a world body, the WCC is particularly equipped and sensitive to the global implication of issues which in one way or another are present in each situation. This global perspective is all the more important in areas where piecemeal or local responses will not provide a satisfactory solution. The issues related to the search for a just, participatory and sustainable society, while being of vital concern to people in each situation, urgently require action and reflection on the global level.

In cooperation with its partners in the ecumenical movement, the WCC understands its particular role along the following lines:

a) The issues involved in the search for a just, participatory and sustainable society touch on many areas of concern, involving specialized competence. It is important, therefore, to achieve a comprehensive assessment, discovering the inter-linkages between social, economic, political, cultural and scientific-technological factors and bringing the diversified elements together into a common framework.

b) The realities of global structures of power more and more impinge on the life of people in particular situations. This inescapable inter-relatedness of local contexts poses new problems and challenges in terms of understanding as well as action. How far can local solutions affect and influence international structures? What new forms of cooperation are needed? It is to these questions that the WCC should address itself.

c) Together with the other partners in the ecumenical movement the WCC should help the churches to raise the consciousness of individual Christians and Christian communities throughout the world to the global issues involved in the search for a just, participatory and sustainable society. This can take the form of an exchange of experiences — stories of the people — from different parts of the world, which will widen the understanding of people for the realization of fuller humanity.

d) In all this the WCC must constantly seek to strengthen the inseparable relationship between spirituality and action, through worship, Bible study and training programmes for new ecumenical leadership. The search for a just, participatory and sustainable society, therefore, is intimately related to the other programme emphases of the WCC.

2. JPSS in relation to other WCC programme emphases

In 1976, the Central Committee of the WCC adopted the following four major programmes emphases for its work following the Fifth Assembly at Nairobi 1975:

— the expression and communication of our faith in the triune God;
— the search for a just, participatory and sustainable society;
— the unity of the church and its relation to the unity of humankind;
— education and renewal in search for true community.

Clearly, these four programme emphases are closely inter-related and interpret each other. Regarding the emphasis on JPSS this means:

a) Any authentic expression and communication of our faith must involve a witness to God's justice and love in the face of the contemporary structures of injustice and the threats to human survival. By the same token, doing justice is an act of witnessing to the Christian faith.

b) The unity of the church is no end in itself but a sign and an anticipation of that fuller unity of all humankind which God will bring about when he establishes his rule of justice. In the kingdom of God the unity of the church and the unity of humankind will be one.

c) The search for a just, participatory and sustainable society calls all churches to repentance and renewal. Education and renewal are basic modes of action in order to generate the necessary power and dynamics for change.

Any programme in relation to JPSS will have to be seen, therefore, in this larger context of the overall programme emphases of the WCC at the present period.

In adopting these four major emphases, however, the Central Committee not only intended to underline the inter-related character of WCC programmes. It also sought to reach a more fully integrated, more economical and more effective approach to planning and implementing the Council's activities. This is a concern not only for the WCC as such. Rather, it should be recognized that the operational structure of the WCC and the sub-units has consequences for partners on the regional and local levels, and vice versa.

At a closer look it appears that programmes directly related to the area of JPSS are spread out over five or six sub-units involving all three programme units. Could the emphasis on JPSS provide clues for a new division of labour? How can we express better the inter-related character of WCC programmes in this area, particularly in the light of the need for urgent action as well as shrinking resources?

3. Programme priorities

After this initial analysis and explanation of the issues involved in the search for a just, participatory and sustainable society, efforts should be made to arrive at a clearer concentration of WCC programmes in this area during the period following the meeting of the Central Committee in January 1979. Three points of concentration are suggested:

1. Programme of study and reflection. First priority: Focus on political ethics, i.e. an examination of structures of power, participation and political organization on local, national and international levels. This reflection should spell out the ethical insights gained in recent ecumenical programmes, giving particular attention to the relationship of church and state in various situations. It should attempt an assessment of existing socio-political frameworks in which Christians live today, i.e. societies of pluralistic, socialist, authoritarian, theocratic orientation. *Further priority:* Focus on the social and ethical implications of the technological and scientific developments, i.e. issues of food, use and waste of limited resources, energy, environmental quality, styles of technological development. There should be a strong emphasis on the interconnections between the branches of science and technology in order to provide a clearer sense of balance between them.

2. Programmes of support and promotion. The priority should be to encourage efforts of *people's participation* and to support *people's movements* in various parts of the world engaged in the struggle for a just society in local and national contexts. This includes in particular:
— fostering action/reflection processes in specific situations on crucial issues such as land rights, employment, health care, migrant labour, dialogue in community;
— strengthening international linkage between local efforts of people's participation, thus promoting worldwide solidarity and the development of networks of cooperation.

3. Programmes of education. The priority should be on programmes which help churches to raise the level of awareness in local communities for the worldwide dimension and the inter-relatedness of the issues concerning JPSS. Ways should be found as to how to render the complex debates accessible to people through processes of education and communication.

Special attention should be given to:
— curricula of theological education and the training of priests and church workers;
— liturgies, keeping together spirituality and action.

4. Next steps

The priorities for programmes in the area of JPSS are suggested for the period up to the next Assembly of the WCC. They will require further discussion and detailed elaboration. Already now, however, a number of specific steps can be indicated:

a) Every effort should be made to elaborate a *popular statement* on the JPSS emphasis for wide circulation and translation/adaptation in different idioms. This statement should include the following basic elements: biblical references, some stories of the people, simple affirmations about justice, participation, sustainability, indications of specific WCC programmes and suggestions for local and regional action. The text should be available at the time of the Central Committee in January 1979. It should be circulated in particular to theological seminaries.

b) Specific contacts should be continued with *regional ecumenical bodies* seeking their cooperation by relating their ongoing programmes to this programme emphasis. Contacts should also be established with confessional bodies and other Christian and secular world organizations, exploring possibilities of coordinating programmes, etc. Special attention should be given to already existing links with the Roman Catholic Church through SODEPAX, religious orders, and through regional or national ecumenical bodies with RCC membership.

c) The forthcoming conference on "Faith, Science and the Future provides a unique opportunity for promoting further the theological and ethical reflection on the inter-related concerns for justice, participation and sustainability, taking into account the work of this Advisory Group.

d) As a first response to the programme priorities indicated above, the appropriate sub-units of the WCC should cooperate in the preparation of a *theological study volume* developing the basic Christians presuppositions regarding *political ethics.* This effort should bring together in a synthesis the ecumenical experiences gained over the last ten years in the context of programmes on racism, development, human rights, etc. The volume could serve as a textbook for theological seminaries, adult education courses, etc.

e) Finally, the possibility should be explored of initiating a *series of study booklets* developing further specific aspects of the concern for the JPSS. The recent publications on church and state, the church and the poor, faith, science and the future, could serve as a models for items in this series. They should be distributed widely, e. g. to theological schools and seminaries. Further examples are a possible collection of relevant texts from the church fathers, a volume bringing together "stories of the people", a publication on the issue of land rights, on redistribution of work and the problem of unemployment. Existing publication patterns of WCC sub-units might be integrated into such a series.

Appendix 3
Contributors

Anwar Barkat: political scientist; Director of the Programme to Combat Racism, WCC; formerly Principal of Forman Christian College, Pakistan.

Orlando Fals Borda: sociologist, specializes in participatory and action-oriented research, especially in Latin America.

Alan Geyer: professor of political ethics, Director of the Center for Theology and Public Policy, Washington, DC.

Gabriel Habib: social scientist; General Secretary of the Middle East Council of Churches.

Wolfgang Huber: Christian ethicist; Professor of Marburg University.

Roger Hutchinson: professor of social ethics, University of Toronto, Canada.

Neville Linton: political scientist, Special Assistant to the General Secretary of the Caribbean Council of Churches.

Konrad Raiser: theologian; Deputy General Secretary, Staff Moderator of Unit on Justice and Service, WCC.

Koson Srisang: social ethicist, Executive Secretary for People's Participation, CCPD, WCC; Secretary of Staff Working Group on the Follow-up of a Just Participatory and Sustainable Society (JPSS) / Political Ethics.

Fred Timakata: pastor, politician; Deputy Prime Minister and Minister of Interior, Vanuatu.

Aaron Tolen: political scientist; Executive Director of Development Department of the Federation of Churches and Mission in Cameroon.

Gibson Winter: professor of social ethics, Princeton Theological Seminary, USA.